A LIFE-GIVING WAY

A Commentary on the
Rule of St. Benedict

Esther de Waal

A Liturgical Press Book

THE LITURGICAL PRESS
Collegeville, Minnesota

Cover design by Ann Blattner
Cover illustration by Helen Manning, London, United Kingdom

Quotations from St. Benedict's Rule are from *RB 1980: The Rule of St. Benedict,* © 1981 by The Order of St. Benedict, Inc., The Liturgical Press, Collegeville, Minnesota. All rights reserved. Reprinted with permission.

8

Library of Congress Cataloging-in-Publication Data

De Waal, Esther.
    A Life-giving way : a commentary on the rule of St. Benedict / Esther de Waal.
        p.   cm.
    Includes bibliographical references.
    ISBN 0-8146-2358-1
    1. Benedict, Saint, Abbot of Monte Cassino.   Regula.
2. Monasticism and religious orders—Rules.   3. Benedictines—Rules.
4. Spiritual life—Christianity.   I. Benedict, Saint, Abbot of
Monte Cassino.   Regula.   English.   II. Title.
BX3004.A2D4   1995
255'.106—dc20   95-8797
                                          CIP

CONTENTS

PREFACE

I have written this commentary because of the place that the Rule of Benedict has come to hold in my life. I first picked it up and read it a number of years ago, and since then this short and simple text has become a source and spring to which I return time and again. I have found that it is ancient wisdom ever new, and that as I come to it with fresh questions and demands, so it continues to yield up its riches. Through the Rule I have been helped to deepen my understanding of my Christian faith and to strengthen my experience of Christian discipleship. Benedict has been both supportive and challenging, guide and prophet. He is reassuring in the way that he accepts the frailty of our human nature and works with that, but he also believes in our human potential as sons and daughters made in the image of God. His respect for persons and for the mystery of human freedom lays on us a huge responsibility, for he is never looking for blind obedience or outward observance. Indeed one of the things that one becomes increasingly aware of is that he is never deceived by externals, but is looking all the time to the interior motive and intention, to the inner disposition of the heart. It is this, above all, that I have seen as the central thread running through the Rule, and which I hope will emerge in the commentary that follows.

When I first read the Rule, I found that it gave me much practical wisdom about how to cope with the demands of daily life and to make them a way to God. I learned about the handling of people and of material things, about how to impose some sort of rhythm and structure on my day so that there was time and space for God. All this was immensely wise and useful, and it made enormous sense in a busy life, with a large household to run, family to look after, part-time job, and all the other many multifarious demands that meant that I was continually living under considerable pressure. Since then the pattern of my life has changed radically. There are far fewer demands from outside, infinitely more on the interior life. I have had to spend much time alone, I have had to let go of people, of expectations, of much that used to fill my life. So I have come to the Rule with new questions and new demands, much more needing help and support with interiority.

This book, therefore, takes the shape of reflections, prayerful reflections, on what Benedict is telling me about my interior attitude, about the disposition of the heart. Both the external practices and the interior attitude, of course, flow from that one essential question that the novice is asked on entering the community and that is also addressed to us all: Are we truly seeking God? On that answer will depend not only the external practices that uphold that quest and are vital to it (the place of silence, the order of the day, and so on), the "simple reduction of all life to a touch of God," but more profoundly, the intention, the motive, purity of heart.

In writing this commentary I have omitted the titles generally given to each chapter, since that would predispose me as to what subject matter I was going to find. I have also disregarded all the usual neat categorizations by which succeeding sections are designated under subject headings, under themes of organization, or liturgy or discipline. Instead by simply letting each chapter build on the previous one, I found myself being led forward step by step as Benedict unfolded for me a gentle way, a way opening up new depths and new directions. I found myself gradually being led to explore Benedict's concept of living a life for God. I came to appreciate that the claim that I once heard made by Laurence Freeman that the Rule of Benedict is the decisive document for Christian living after the Bible expressed exactly what I have increasingly come to feel.

For the key to everything that I was being shown was, of course, the Bible itself. The Rule is totally scriptural. The purpose of the monastic life is to shape life according to the Scriptures. Benedict cites the Bible at every moment, and it was increasingly the many scriptural allusions and images underlying the text that came to work so forcibly on my mind. Time and time again the Scriptures are affirmed as the source of life. Right at the start in the prologue we read, "Let us get up then, at long last, for the Scriptures rouse us when they say: *It is high time for us to arise from sleep* (Rom 13:11)" (Prol., 8). In the very last chapter, Benedict calls the Bible the truest of guides for human life (73,3). This then is the whole inspiration of the Rule: "See how the Lord in his love shows us the way of life. . . . let us set out on this way, with the Gospel for our guide" (Prol., 20-21). Time and time again the Rule has been described as a masterly summary of the Gospel's teaching, and indeed in the Middle Ages it was commonly seen as a digest of the Bible. I had, of course, always realized the power of the Gospel for Benedict. It is possible to count the actual number of biblical quotations, and the biblical words and phrases in italics spring up out of the text whenever I glance at any page. For Benedict the power of the Word of God was the one reality on which his own life and belief were based, and on which he wishes me to base my own. There should never be any question that this Rule might become any sort of idol, since all the time Benedict is pointing beyond himself to the figure of Christ and to the teaching of the Gospel. One way of looking at the Rule is to see it simply as a handbook to making the very radical demands of the Gospel a practical, and therefore inescapable, reality in my daily life. Its profoundly biblical emphasis is, I believe, one of the reasons why increasing numbers of people are now turning to the monastic tradition and to the Rule of Benedict in particular.

I find it very significant that as more and more people are searching for ways in which to deepen their spiritual lives, there is a growing interest in the monastic tradition. Here is a spirituality that is grounded, coming out of the hard-won experience of men and women who have faced so many of the questions that are inescapable: How do I live with myself? How do I live with others? How do I relate to the world around me? How do I find time and space for God? There is infinite wisdom and practical insight in the writings of the monastic fathers. Thomas Merton, in writing to the Benedictine monk Ronald Roloff, says:

> It seems to me that we all need more and more to deepen the grasp we have of our rich monastic heritage, and the closer we get to the source, the more fruitful and splendid our lives will be, in all kinds of varied expressions and manifestations. . . . We have not scratched the surface of this rich land of ours that our Fathers have left us.

I feel that if Merton were writing today he would have said "Fathers and Mothers." The role of the women monastics is more and more being realized as we begin at last to recognize what we owe to Hilda of Whitby or Hildegard of Bingen or Mechthild of Magdeburg and many more like them.

As I have traveled and talked over recent years, I have had cause to reflect often on these prophetic words. I have become aware that the Rule speaks across all ecclesiastical denominations and divides. Coming from the earliest years of the Church, it takes us back to something that is basic, fundamental, universal, that we can all claim, and to which we can all turn. I much prefer to speak of this as returning to what is primal or primordial than to speak of what is early or primitive (words that may carry something of a perjorative ring), since I also have a sense that this is touching what is primal and universal in each one of us. With Benedict we are being taken back beyond the sad divides of the Reformation, beyond the schism of East and West, and not least beyond the sad splitting off of mind and heart, intellect and feelings, that came with the twelfth-century development of learning. Those Churches, which in the sixteenth century rejected the monastic tradition, are now beginning to turn to it again, finding there much that is sympathetic and unthreatening, since it is essentially based on the Scriptures. The centrality of the Word is made apparent from the moment that Benedict opens the prologue with "Listen." The way of Benedict's Rule is therefore one that can become a common ground across the denominations, and one to which people of differing persuasions can easily and naturally relate. During the "Benedictine Experience" weeks that I have organized over the past ten years, where small groups of people have gathered to live out the Benedictine rhythm of body, mind, and spirit, praying, studying, and working together, all the labels that might set us apart from one another disappear. We have found that we become a temporary community built on common ground. For, coming from the undivided Church of the past, the Rule points us all forward to the promise of the undivided Church of the future.

The fact that the Rule was written by a layman for laypeople is also significant today at a time when the role of the laity in the Church is coming to be emphasized. Many people seem surprised to learn that Benedict himself was never a priest and to discover that in its origins monasticism was essentially a lay movement. There is now a considerable amount of recent scholarship on this subject, and we are thus being reminded of the extent to which the clericalization of monasticism was the result of historical development. For those of us who are lay pepole, and who are aware of the importance of this as our vocation, the realization that this is the context of the Rule is liberating and encouraging.

When I find myself using the word "liberating," it reminds me of what a distance I have traveled since I first assumed, knowing little or nothing of its actual content, that a rule was bound to be restricting, negative, indeed life-denying. Since then I have come to feel totally differently. I have come to see it as wisdom not law, a way of life not a set of directives. The Latin word *regula,* a feminine noun, carries gentle connotations: a guidepost, a railing, something that gives me support as I move forward in my search for God. After all, Benedict does not expect the novice to enter his monastery for the Rule, but for God. The Rule is simply to point me toward God and give me something to hold on to when I might otherwise be blown off course. So also with the vows, which always sounded so threatening when I knew little of monastic life, for the suggestion they carried of being negative, restrictive chains. But living with them has shown me something quite different. I have found that they offer me modes of perception, of seeing how I can handle my life wisely and creatively. They present to people outside of a monastic community, such as myself, three promises that together form one whole process. They ask me to enter into a dynamic commitment that simultaneously holds me still (stability) and moves me forward (continual conversion) with all the time God, and not my own self, as the point of reference (obedience, listening intently). They have become tools for me, a most practical resource, which I sometimes think of as a survival kit, a lifeline that gives me practical help, not only to hold on to my relationship with God but also my relationships with others and with myself.

So the discipline of a rule and vows or promises means simply that I remain a disciple, *discipulus,* one who is a learner, a follower, all my life. The way that Benedict is showing me can never become a closed system. It is more like a series of open doors than a series of prescribed actions. Or in the words of Michael Case, it is an invitation to remain alert to the challenge of the Word of God. Benedict does not give me certainty. He does not give me easy answers. He gives me a focus, shows me the stance. He is forming me so that I can respond to each new situation, each new demand. He knows about the weakness and frailty of human nature and how we tend to cling when we are frightened and insecure. That sort of dependency is disastrous. Benedict has such a respect for each one of us that he pays us this compliment of refusing to stifle our freedom. He believes that with the help of his little Rule we will be able to respond to the challenge of the Word of God as we experience it throughout our lives. The way of Benedict is one of continuing and ongoing conversion, of growth and inner transformation, which will go on as long as I live. These are the daily questions that Benedict presents me: Am I being changed by the power of the Gospel? Am I being changed by the presence of God in my life?

For that continuous, ever-present sense of presence is something that Benedict himself experienced in those years in the cave at Subiaco when he held himself still before the gaze of God, in solitude and in silence. That laid the contemplative foundation of the rest of his life-work. As I read and reread the Rule, I realize how much this sense of awareness of presence is one of the most important of its underlying themes. There is so much about watchfulness, being alive, awake. The fullness of my humanity asks that I choose life not death. To be only half alive is death.

So I have been grateful for the way in which Benedict recognizes the whole of my person as God-given. This is utterly different from that disastrous dualism that influenced my earlier years by which the material and the spiritual were set apart and the material, including the bodily, were denigrated and treated as inferior. My upbringing told me that God was only concerned with my soul, and the spiritual side of life was of infinitely more significance than the bodily. But the Rule not only allows but actually encourages me to see my body as worthy of care and nurture, and to be honored as one element of the whole balance of body, mind, and spirit, playing its part in the daily rhythm of work, study, and prayer that Benedict establishes as the way to the fullness of our humanity.

In this holistic approach to life, Benedict is speaking a language that has resonances with much of the thought of other traditions about which there is now such widespread interest. In the Celtic tradition, for example, but also in the aboriginal or the Native American, we find a unified view of the universe in which religion permeates and informs the whole of life. The sense of the sacredness of material creation, the role of harmony and balance and interrelatedness, are all themes that are apparent the longer that one stays with the Rule. A spirituality that is essentially corporate, and addresses the totality of life, is very much in tune with the contemporary attempt to rediscover a unity of vision lost with the dualistic and mechanistic approach that has shaped thinking since the enlightenment.

On the shrine of Benedict at Fleury, St. Benoît sur Loire, France, there is a long prayer that much moved me when I saw it. The French put it delicately and it loses much in translation. It opens by saying that today we see the person *"qui est sorti de sa maison et qui a perdu la clé pour y entrer. Benoît ton message est une invitation à l'interiorité. Ton expérience est celle de l'homme regagné à lui-même. Benoît apprends nous le retour au coeur."* In putting it into English, I have made it more of a personal prayer and so avoided the gender difficulty of the original. "Today I find that I am the person who has left home and who has lost the key to get myself back there. Benedict, your message is an invitation to interiority. Your experience is that of the person who regains their sense of themselves. Benedict, teach us the return to the heart."

I find that Benedict touches us all because he shows such a deep grasp of the human psyche. He writes out of this sense of who we are and where we are on our human journey. This can only come from his own experience. He recognizes the deepest of all human needs: the need for order, inner and outer, the need to love and be loved, and above all the need to be at home in all the many levels of meaning that the word can carry.

NOTE

I have written this book for prayerful and reflective reading and so I have not wanted to interrupt the clear flow of the text with the intrusion of footnotes. But I hope that readers will turn to the back of the book if they want to find the thoughts and comments, notes and references that I have given them there in case they want to explore further.

NOTE ON THE TEXT

It would probably be very strange to Benedict himself to find how we regard his Rule today. He wrote this very short handbook as a working document to help his own family of monks in their life at Monte Cassino. He calls it a "little rule . . . for beginners" (73,8). He claims no originality for it, and in the final chapter he tells his monks to read further amongst the works of other monastic writers. For when he himself came to write, there were already a whole series of rules, and he would not want to make any claim to originality. That wisdom was common property, and Benedict would find it perfectly natural to collect and assimilate material accumulated by both his western and eastern predecessors. The most notable source was the monastic rule known as the Rule of the Master (there has been much scholarly discussion about the relationship of the two). But in Benedict's hands the tradition becomes totally his own, for this is a monasticism that he has both thought out and lived. We are not given mere eclecticism, but a process of careful selectivity and unification. Claude Pfeifer has a rather nice way of putting it: "Like the bee gathering nectar from many flowers and combining them into honey which includes all diverse fragrances but in its richness surpasses any of them."

The text of the Rule, originally written in the vernacular Latin of the sixth century and translated subsequently many times over, is little more than nine thousand words. Yet for more than fifteen hundred years this short, practical document has guided religious communities of men and women, at first in medieval Christendom and now throughout the world, and increasingly in recent years, has spoken to those outside religious communities. We should not, therefore, be misled by its simplicity and shortness. It has the moderation and the compassion of the Gospel itself, and it also has the urgency and the fire and passion of the Gospel.

Benedict wrote in an age whose precarious unity was dissolving before his eyes. In many ways, although historical parallels are dangerous, it was a world not unlike our own. Benedict was born around the year 480. Rome was sacked for the second time in 455, and in 476 the last emperor was deposed. He was watching the demise of the Roman Empire, years of social and economic insecurity. Order had broken down, the institutions that hitherto had worked were collapsing, the securities on which people believed they could count were crumbling. Markets were failing, communications becoming difficult, and there was a huge social imbalance by which the rich were getting richer and the poor were getting poorer. Above all, there was the fear that goes with the shifting of familiar landmarks.

The Church too was being torn apart by internal disputes, notably the Arian controversy that denied the divinity of Christ, and the Pelagian question and the controversy about nature and grace. In such a climate, as we well know, it becomes attractive to become inward looking, to cling to certainty, to establish barriers. But Benedict refused to do this. He remained a man whose mind was open, just as the doors of his monastery were always open, and as he wished his monks to have a heart open to all comers. His Rule is as a result a true *via media,* the middle way that holds centrifugal forces together to make them dynamic, life-giving. He holds together the emphasis on the solitary, on the withdrawal and disengagement that Cassian taught, with the emphasis from Basil on the communal or shared life. Here are the desert and the city juxtaposed. He speaks of the importance of both nature and grace. He is at once ascetic and humane. He is telling us that all these qualities are good and that we should be drawing on both. We can set up a dialectic by letting both interact with one another. This is the tension by which the one stimulates the other and produces growth.

The image of water flowing into one broad stream, or threads weaving themselves into one broad tapestry, is a good image to introduce what I am trying to do in the commentary that follows. It has been usual hitherto to present the Rule as arranged in quite clear-cut sections, the spiritual doctrine being given first in the prologue and in chapters 2–7, followed by the practical regulations in chapters 8–73. Within this second part there are also certain clear subdivisions, such as the sections dealing with the liturgical code (8–20), the penitential code (23–30), material goods (31–34), food and sleep (35–42), and so on. Instead, as I have explained above, I have tried to allow the text itself to flow without reference to any external framework. In this way I hope that it can be read as an exploration of the disposition of the heart. Of course a rule must legislate for external behavior, but Benedict knows that external conformity is not enough. He is more concerned with why things are done and how they are done, with the motivation behind the observance. His respect for persons and for the mystery of grace at work in each one means that his Rule speaks to the heart. Benedict, so generally known as a man of balance and moderation, writes with urgency and immediacy. In this, of course, he is like the Gospel itself to which he is all the time pointing us. He did not want his followers then, nor does he want any of us who are following him today, to be lukewarm, half-hearted. It is because he would wish for us all a heart overflowing with love that he first wrote his Rule and why it continues to reach out across time and space to speak anew to men and women in every generation.

NOTE

The Rule uses the psalm numbering of the Vulgate Latin Bible; in this book, when a psalm is given two numbers the first is the Vulgate number, the second the Hebrew number more usually used today.

COMMENTARY ON
THE RULE OF ST. BENEDICT

THE PROLOGUE

¹Listen carefully, my son, to the master's instructions, and attend to them with the ear of your heart. This is advice from a father who loves you; welcome it, and faithfully put it into practice. ²The labor of obedience will bring you back to him from whom you had drifted through the sloth of disobedience. ³This message of mine is for you, then, if you are ready to give up your own will, once and for all, and armed with the strong and noble weapons of obedience to do battle for the true King, Christ the Lord.

⁴First of all, every time you begin a good work, you must pray to him most earnestly to bring it to perfection. ⁵In his goodness, he has already counted us as his sons, and therefore we should never grieve him by our evil actions. ⁶With his good gifts which are in us, we must obey him at all times that he may never become the angry father who disinherits his sons, ⁷nor the dread lord, enraged by our sins, who punishes us forever as worthless servants for refusing to follow him to glory.

⁸Let us get up then, at long last, for the Scriptures rouse us when they say: *It is high time for us to arise from sleep* (Rom 13:11). ⁹Let us open our eyes to the light that comes from God, and our ears to the voice from heaven that every day calls out this charge: ¹⁰*If you hear his voice today, do not harden your hearts* (Ps 94[95]:8). ¹¹And again: *You that have ears to hear, listen to what the Spirit says to the churches* (Rev 2:7). ¹²And what does he say? *Come and listen to me, sons; I will teach you the fear of the Lord* (Ps 33[34]:12). ¹³*Run while you have the light* of life, *that the darkness* of death *may not overtake you* (John 12:35).

[14]"Seeking his workman in a multitude of people, the Lord calls out to him and lifts his voice again: [15]*Is there anyone here who yearns for life and desires to see good days?* (Ps 33[34]:13) [16]If you hear this and your answer is "I do," God then directs these words to you: [17]If you desire true and eternal life, *keep your tongue free from vicious talk and your lips from all deceit; turn away from evil and do good; let peace be your quest and aim* (Ps 33[34]:14-15). [18]Once you have done this, my *eyes will be upon* you *and* my *ears will listen* for your *prayers; and even before you ask me, I will say* to you: *Here I am* (Isa 58:9). [19]What, dear brothers, is more delightful than this voice of the Lord calling to us? [20]See how the Lord in his love shows us the way of life. [21]Clothed then with faith and the performance of good works, let us set out on this way, with the Gospel for our guide, that we may deserve to see him *who has called* us *to his kingdom* (1 Thess 2:12).

[22]If we wish to dwell in the tent of this kingdom, we will never arrive unless we run there by doing good deeds. [23]But let us ask the Lord with the Prophet: *Who will dwell in your tent, Lord; who will find rest upon your holy mountain?* (Ps 14[15]:1) [24]After this question, brothers, let us listen well to what the Lord says in reply, for he shows us the way to his tent. [25]*One who walks without blemish,* he says, *and is just in all his dealings;* [26]*who speaks the truth from his heart and has not practiced deceit with his tongue;* [27]*who has not wronged a fellowman in any way, nor listened to slanders against his neighbor* (Ps 14[15]:2-3). [28]He has *foiled* the *evil one,* the devil, at every turn, flinging both him and his promptings far *from the sight* of his heart. While these temptations were still *young, he caught hold of them and dashed them against* Christ (Ps 14[15]:4; 136[137]:9). [29]These people *fear the Lord,* and do not become elated over their good deeds; they judge it is the Lord's power, not their own, that brings about the good in them. [30]*They praise* (Ps 14[15]:4) the Lord working in them, and say with the Prophet: *Not to us, Lord, not to us give the glory, but to your name alone* (Ps 113[115:1]:9). [31]In just this way Paul the Apostle refused to take credit for the power of his preaching. He declared: *By God's grace I am what I am* (1 Cor 15:10). [32]And again he said: *He who boasts should*

make his boast in the Lord (2 Cor 10:17). [33]That is why the Lord says in the Gospel: *Whoever hears these words of mine and does them is like a wise man who built his house upon rock;* [34]*the floods came and the winds blew and beat against the house, but it did not fall: it was founded on rock* (Matt 7:24-25).

[35]With this conclusion, the Lord waits for us daily to translate into action, as we should, his holy teachings. [36]Therefore our life span has been lengthened by way of a truce, that we may amend our misdeeds. [37]As the Apostle says: *Do you not know that the patience of God is leading you to repent* (Rom 2:4)? [38]And indeed the Lord assures us in his love: *I do not wish the death of the sinner, but that he turn back to me and live* (Ezek 33:11).

[39]Brothers, now that we have asked the Lord who will dwell in his tent, we have heard the instruction for dwelling in it, but only if we fulfill the obligations of those who live there. [40]We must, then, prepare our hearts and bodies for the battle of holy obedience to his instructions. [41]What is not possible to us by nature, let us ask the Lord to supply by the help of his grace. [42]If we wish to reach eternal life, even as we avoid the torments of hell, [43]then—while there is still time, while we are in this body and have time to accomplish all these things by the light of life—[44]we must run and do now what will profit us forever.

[45]Therefore we intend to establish a school for the Lord's service. [46]In drawing up its regulations, we hope to set down nothing harsh, nothing burdensome. [47]The good of all concerned, however, may prompt us to a little strictness in order to amend faults and to safeguard love. [48]Do not be daunted immediately by fear and run away from the road that leads to salvation. It is bound to be narrow at the outset. [49]But as we progress in this way of life and in faith, we shall run on the path of God's commandments, our hearts overflowing with the inexpressible delight of love. [50]Never swerving from his instructions, then, but faithfully observing his teaching in the monastery until death, we shall through patience share in the sufferings of Christ that we may deserve also to share in his kingdom. Amen.

The prologue is a lyrical piece of writing, like an overture setting the whole tone of what is to follow. The opening words never cease to amaze me. I could never have imagined that a practical handbook and guide for community living would have this most loving, warm, accepting opening, which addresses each one of us personally. It at once promises that the individual is not going to get lost in the crowd, nor get tied up in juridical structures. "Listen" is an arresting word meant to catch my attention. It is admonition, exhortation, to arouse or awaken, to pierce the heart, to challenge. It is, in the words of Damasus Winzen, "a trumpet call."

"Listen!" I could take that as a summary of the whole of Benedict's teaching. I could spend the rest of my life pondering on the implications of that one word. It plunges me at once into a personal relationship. It takes me away from the danger of talking about God and not communing *with* him. Here is a person seeking another person in a dialogue. Right at the very beginning then, it is good to ask myself how I hear God. I must remember that it is an encounter, not a form of activity. The Pharisees, after all, studied the Scriptures and yet had not heard God's voice. God's voice is everywhere in the prologue. The whole idea of vocation, whatever form that vocation may take, implies the response to a call. If I am to live up to my vocation I must go on listening for this voice. "Today, if you hear my voice, harden not your heart." That phrase of Psalm 94 (95):7 makes a wonderful opening to daily prayer. "He speaks to me and I speak to him," as the Song of Songs says. That is why we must listen and listen intently, now, today.

It is the father who addresses us. If we then ask who this father is we may find, rather than some difficulty of interpretation, a wonderful depth of meaning. I hear the voice of Benedict himself, entering into a dialogue with me just as surely as he entered into a dialogue with all those disciples who listened to his teaching in his lifetime. He is not occupied by the questions of the philosophers. The God whom he knows and loves is the God of the Bible, both transcendent and at the same time near and close, solicitous for the welfare of his children whom he loves with a gentle and tender ache as he waits for their response in return. And yet surely the father must also be Christ, the central figure of the Rule to whom everything and everyone points, through whose saving work of salvation I am brought into the new life, which I know is what Benedict wants for us all. But Christ is the father because he is the face of the father, the first person of the Trinity. What is totally certain is that when I encounter the voice of the father, through whichever of these levels I may choose to hear it, it is the voice of love. This is the father who loves me and who speaks in my heart, that inner self where I am most truly and completely my own self. This Rule is going to be heart-to-heart talk.

Listen carefully, my son, my daughter, my child: those first words in verse 1 of the prologue address each one of us as the prodigal and at once plunge each of us immediately into that story. It is a universal story, told time and again in different generations, and each of us must have our favorite painting that expresses in images the moment of the return, the welcome, the warmth of the moment of reunion. I think of the Rembrandt in St. Petersburg, of the kneeling son whose worn and travel-damaged feet show how long is the way that he has come, whose head rests at the level of the father's heart, whose whole body is now enclosed in that strong, warm embrace of the father's loving hands on his shoulders. For that story is all our stories, lived out in each of us in our life, and probably also time and again throughout our life. It answers the deepest need in all of us, the need to come home. My most profound desire is to be at home, in all the senses that I understand it, home in my own inner self, at home in the place to which I belong, at home in the family of the Church. I long to be able to answer, from the depths of my being, *"Here I am"* (18). It is so easy to hear these words and not to let their full force be felt in me. So often that has been the reply—of Abraham, Jacob, Moses—and I take particular delight in thinking of Samuel in the middle of the night when I realize that Benedict is trying to rouse me up from sleep. But it is more than the individual response. When God calls the stars they answer, "Here we are" (Bar 3:35), or Job says, "You send forth the lightnings and they say 'Here we are' " (Job 38:35). It is the cry of the whole world in that harmony which we all so deeply long for. But it is never static, for that is not in Benedict's vocabulary. It is the cry of the one who is ready to go forth—here I am, send me. When I have this foundation, the house built on a rock (Matt 7:34), then I am able to set out on the way that will bring me home.

Benedict seems to be giving me the key to this homecoming. If I am willing to see myself as the prodigal, then I must also see that I have gone astray through the sin of pride and disobedience and that salvation lies in obedience. This process of restoration, of being rescued and restored, begins the moment that I stop and listen, listen with the ear of the heart. When I look once again at the story of the prodigal, I see that it involves certain elements: he listens, and in the light of that listening he sees the truth about his situation, and where his disobedience has led him, which is so powerfully symbolized by eating empty husks. That act of listening, responding, and taking action leads to the start of the journey, the turning and returning, that will ultimately take him back to the father. So the three moments of this process are first the listening and responding, obedience (for that is what the word means, *obaudiens,* to listen intently), the *metanoia,* or turning (which is what *conversatio morum* involves, continual conversion journeying on), and then the stability (from the Latin *stare,* to stand), being in the place of firm ground. Already Benedict has touched completely naturally on the three vows as the means of our way to God. Thus I feel he is showing us that the vows apply naturally to the human condition, to all of us, *"Whoever hears these words of mine"* (33), whoever we may be who pick up this Rule for guidance. It does indeed speak to us all, and it is interesting to learn that the prologue may well be based on a catechetical or a teaching homily given at baptism, for then in fact we see here teaching that applies to all Christians living out their faith under their baptismal vows.

One commentary, that by David Parry, says that the style of the opening suggests that we might be present at an interview between an experienced religious teacher and someone who realizes that his or her life has been dislocated in its relationship with the Creator and is therefore not oriented. I like the idea of this being a personal dialogue, and that Benedict might well be addressing any of us individually, and giving us the same message that he gave to his other followers. He has such a respect for us that he will never over-protect or collude, and so he says at once that this is going to be a hard struggle. More than that, it is going to be a battle. Military imagery is out of fashion today, and perhaps we lose something by that. Being armed with strong and noble weapons has, of course, the ring of that great passage in Ephesians (6:10-20), and Benedict as a true Roman would know only too well what this involved. This we do by ranging ourselves with Christ who has already won the victory. So this is how Christ first appears in the pages of the Rule, the true King and Lord.

It is only by a stretch of the imagination that I can fully enter into what lordship would have meant in the sixth century in the contemporary situation of slavery. The lord is the master of the house to whom all owe service. So Christ is the Lord of all. These are both vigorous metaphors, and they can leave me in no doubt of Benedict's sense of the power of this master whom we are to serve. Already the powerful presence of Christ is making itself felt in the prologue, and this figure of Christ is one whom we shall meet constantly from now on. The whole of the Rule is marked by its high Christology, partly no doubt because Arianism, which would deny the divinity of Christ, was still very much an issue when Benedict was writing. The name Jesus is never used, only Christ. For this I am personally grateful, since I have never found it easy to walk in my imagination along the lakeshore with the pale Galilean or to hold a conversation with Jesus in his earthly days, as some popular spirituality of the moment encourages me to do. But to stay with Benedict's sense of the power and the presence of the risen Christ in my life is vastly different. This, of course, makes the paschal mystery central and inescapable. It is through this dynamic Christ-centeredness that the Rule opens up the freeing journey that will take us all into our fullness of life. Perhaps it is this that brings to the prologue its distinctive note of tenderness and optimism, particularly in these opening verses (1-3), and again in the closing section (45-50), where Benedict speaks of our journey in love and of our sharing in the sufferings of Christ.

Our idea of Christ is therefore a glorious one. Benedict is instilling into us a sense of energy, of being fully alive and strong. We are following a lord and king, fighting in the army, being part of the household, of one who is God's lieutenant, restoring the order of creation. If we wear that uniform, if we are marked as a part of that household, then we too are committed, and the weapons that we use, the weapons of obedience, are glorious weapons, strong and positive, because they are a participation in the victorious fight of Christ himself over the forces of darkness.

In the following paragraph comes the service itself, and I am shown the second step that succeeds the decision to renounce my own self-will and to follow Christ as Lord. After that first step, that moment of decision, comes the determination and the perseverance, having put my hand to the plough, not to turn back but to follow this through to the end. Without constant prayer this will never be possible. Prayer will remind me all the time that whatever I do is a matter of grace. Perseverance itself is a special grace, and to receive it we have to pray constantly. Benedict is telling me now that both the beginning and the end of my way to God are in God's hands. There is always the danger that I may attribute or appropriate to myself what is really the work of God in me.

This is the new order into which I am incorporated because of my adoption as son or daughter by this loving father. It is not merely that I am legally adopted, I am also physically adopted, an adoption that is a real creation, a real transformation, so that now I may use my gifts wisely and well. God found me wandering and lost and brought me into his own family and gave me a home. But there is always the danger that I may go wandering off again, or that I may not use these gifts that God has put at my disposal. Benedict does not mince words: evil actions show the seriousness of sin. In that case I risk disinheritance or punishment. Whether I think of this in terms of the imagery of being turned out of the garden of Eden, or in the more specific terms of what it would have meant in sixth-century Italy to lose all security, to be cut loose from any sort of base in society, this is an extremely vivid warning.

Here now comes the reveille, the rousing call: Now is the hour! How well Benedict knows human nature. Even though he has so vigorously presented me with these alternatives and asked me to make choices, I could still so easily drift, put off decisions, coast along living and half living. "Let us open our eyes to the light that comes from God" (9), let us listen to the divine voice. The light that comes from God is the sacred Scriptures. Time and time again later on in the Rule the Scriptures will be affirmed as the source of life. The whole life to which it is pointing us is a search for God under the guidance of the Gospel. The Rule itself is simply gospel teaching. It is the Word itself that arouses us. The Word is a two-edged sword that will not let us sleep, that brings us to life, and it is so that we may hear the Word at work in our lives that Benedict has written the Rule. What he is asking us to do is simply to listen, listen totally, be changed by the power of the Scriptures. When Benedict makes of verses 8-21 a virtual mosaic of scriptural quotation, it is so that we may once again be reminded of this voice addressing us, calling and searching us out, trying to arouse us from sleep, trying to open our eyes and to unstop our ears. This is no once-and-for-all call, but a daily occurrence. It would be only too easy to fail to hear, to forget that each day the Word is there (10). It is up to me to listen for it, for I might well be tempted instead to harden my heart, which would mean that I cease to be vulnerable and open.

For listening to the Word is listening to the Spirit (11), and that asks a great deal of me. There are only brief references to the Holy Spirit in the Rule, and it is vital not to neglect them. We are reminded of *"the joy of the Holy Spirit"* in 49,6 in the context of the extra demands of Lent. At the end of chapter 7, we are told that the whole action of the purification of our motives and the cleansing from sins and vices has been the action of the Holy Spirit in his workman. This helps me to appreciate his thinking here. The Spirit is the one who cleanses and who leads. Above all, it is the Spirit within us who leads to growth. This growth process is therefore not separated from the cleansing process, and it is a process that will never end but go on until death. This is the initial hurdle, and we cannot achieve any further kind of perfection until we have gotten over this, the essential foundation, which is why we find it placed here.

The final quotation in this paragraph speaks of running, light, life. Benedict is offering me the chance to move from slavery to freedom, the freedom of the life of the new person in Christ. This is never going to be simple, rectilinear progress, in life or in prayer. It is a matter of many invitations of grace, some accepted, some ignored, some accepted half-heartedly, some later nullified by inconstancy. It is not easy, as Daniel Rees says, to accept the invitation to freedom in the risen Christ, to walk freely in the Spirit. This invitation opens up vistas too big for us, and we feel safer clinging to our prison bars, where at least we know where we are. "No doubt it was hard for some of the people whom Jesus set free from bondage of body or spirit to accept their freedom, to pick up their stretchers and walk, or to relinquish an accustomed way of life as a blind beggar."

Life is the ultimate goal and promise, good life, full life. This is the offer held out to us in the picture that Benedict gives in verse 15 of a crowd of people and Christ calling out to arrest their attention. *"Is there anyone here who yearns for life?"* he asks.

It is always possible to be in a hurry, or to drift, and to pay no heed to that voice. But that is the question: Do I want to live life to the fullest? It is always possible to reject that and to opt for living, or partly living, a half life. If the disciple answers yes to this invitation, then Benedict has achieved his wish for us all, which is that we should choose "true and eternal life" (17). That is his own phrase, but later on in the chapter he will quote images from the Scriptures, being called into the kingdom from Thessalonians in verse 21 or dwelling in the tent in verse 23. This is a piece of very complex narration. At first Benedict is the narrator speaking in the third person. As he narrates he personifies the Lord on the one hand and the listener on the other. He does this in such a way that both Benedict and the Lord speak to the listener who remains the passive recipient throughout. So again we are brought back to listening and hearing and responding. Then the narration changes again and Benedict is speaking as the Lord, reaching the peak in the words *"even before you ask me, I will say* to you: *Here I am"* (19). The impression that this gives is both of the present and the future; the Lord is present here now and will be present in the future. Surely the use, in verse 19, of the "we," "us" suggests that Benedict is writing out of his own personal experience. The sharing of that experience with us is, I believe, why the Rule speaks to us so immediately and directly and personally.

"Who will dwell in your tent, Lord; who will find rest on your holy mountain?" This question from verse 23 is couched in the poetic language of Psalm 14 (15). The essence of the reply comes in the phrase *"One . . . who speaks the truth from his heart"* (26). Nowhere in the prologue does Benedict actually employ Cassian's "purity of heart," yet this is in effect what he is talking about. So many of the psalms ask: Who can enter into the tabernacle? The priestly answer, of course, will be one who does this or that. The answer here is the shortest and the most succinct of the answers in the psalter. It really leads us into the heart of things. There are no external requirements, such as the washing of hands or feet. What is required is an inner washing, *"One . . . who speaks the truth from his heart."* This is that inner unity, truthfulness, and harmony that constitute the *puritas cordis* that Benedict is looking for. It is purity of heart that is the touchstone for all our thoughts and actions, and it will be there throughout the rest of the Rule as the yardstick by which Benedict will measure

progress. It is growth in purity of heart alone that is going to bring us back to the father.

The focus of this struggle of good and evil is not to be found in the outside world, but within the individual soul. The danger lies within my own self, the inner temptations, the evil thoughts that rise so easily and catch me unaware, destructive of my best intentions. This is the word of the devil, and he must be foiled. Benedict never minces words when it is a matter of the utmost seriousness, which this is. He tells me to deal with these thoughts at once, stifle them at birth as it were. The image that he uses is that of dashing them against the rock that is Christ, a vivid metaphor that again he owes to the psalms. Originally, of course, this referred to the Babylonian babies dashed on the rocks so that they might not grow up to become oppressors as their fathers had been. I think of the many times that the image of a rock comes in the psalms. In New Testament understanding that rock becomes Christ (1 Cor 10:4). I remind myself of the body of Christ laid at birth on the living rock of a trough in the stable at Bethlehem, or in his hour of death laid in the living rock of the tomb, and I know that here I have been given a powerful image of Christ as the rock whose life-giving powers I need. So as soon as wrongful thoughts come into my mind, I smash them against this Christ-rock and thus prevent them from developing and taking root.

Then there is a second danger. If things go well I may be tempted to believe that this is my own work and fail to see it as the fruit of grace and not of my own efforts. Benedict continues to quote from the psalms, for they are for him the voice of Christ himself. First, there is Christ crying out to us in the marketplace in Psalm 38 (34), inviting us to come in. Then there is the voice of Christ from inside the sanctuary in Psalm 14 (15) telling us when we enter how we should live. It follows quite easily and naturally that the paragraph ends with the voice of Christ himself in the Sermon on the Mount speaking to all who hear and who are ready as a result to build their lives on the rock.

Benedict has no time for the theoretical affirmation, by which I say that of course I give assent to all of this, with my lips, with my mind, but make no attempt to translate it into daily life. How shall I use this space of time that is a truce? It is serious for it is no less than a matter of life or death. Yet Benedict does not threaten, cajole, or bring undue pressure to bear. The repentance that he is hoping for, by which I turn back to God, comes as a response of love. I find it very moving that Benedict is always showing me the patience of God waiting and working for the return of his children. Throughout the prologue he never fails to situate our lives in the context of this patience of God, which is no less than the paschal mystery working in us through the *patientia,* the suffering of Christ.

In verses 39-44 Benedict sums up what he was saying, reiterating what we have already been told: this is a journey and a battle; we must awake from our lethargy and be ready in heart and body. We have been given a limited space of time in which to respond to the promise of heaven and escape the torments of hell. The main body of the Rule will of course be at hand to develop further all that the prologue outlines. There will be much about rousing me from sleep, encouraging me to choose light and not darkness. The ladder of chapter 7 will show me that both the heart and body are the two posts that make ascent possible. Time and again Benedict will return to the theme of obedience and show me how the weapons of obedience will give me help in purifying my soul from pride and my body from the weaknesses of the flesh. Once again (41) he wants to warn me that I can do none of this unless it is with the help of God's grace. And, above all, there is this familiar note of urgency. Benedict uses the word "run" no less than four times in the prologue. This is an allusion to John 12:35, although in the Gospel the original word used is "ambulate," walk. That he changes a gospel word in this way tells us a lot about his sense of urgency.

Throughout the prologue Benedict is continually speaking of the way, the journey, so that I see myself as the pilgrim or traveler. But equally he speaks of the rock, the tent, the firm ground, so that I see myself as the one who stands still. He is also, of course, making me aware that I must listen to the Word, the sound of God's voice. These are the threads that come together in the commitment of the vows to a life of obedience, *conversatio morum,* and stability. Benedict is giving me both the agenda and the tools that will shape the way in which he will be leading me and teaching me. It alerts me to listen attentively to what he is about to say.

"School for the Lord's service" (45). We have now reached that often quoted phrase that opens the final paragraph. To pursue this call we need help, teaching, support in order to prepare our hearts and our bodies. The word "school" as it was used in Benedict's day was simply an assembly room serving various groups, soldiers of a particular company, craftsmen of the same organization, students gathered about their teacher. The word therefore came to mean not only the room itself but also the particular group that gathered there. For me this word reminds me that I am learning not in some individual capacity, but as part of a company. I learn how to serve the Lord and actually do so. "For" is important here and "of" does not catch the fullness of the sense. Christ is the master and the teacher. The Christ who has appeared in many different roles in the prologue now asks of me that I too play differing roles: that I am pupil, *discipulus,* the one who learns, as well as son and daughter, soldier, member of the household, one who follows in the way. As the sympathetic and encouraging teacher, Benedict invites the disciple by promising that the regime of this school will be a reasonable one, and that what at first may seem difficult will, in the long run, through stability and not trying to escape, become second nature. The means and the end are the same—love. If Benedict is strict at the start, the purpose is to safeguard love. But then as we progress in the way, we shall find "our hearts overflowing with the inexpressible delight of love" (49), surely one of the most incomparable phrases of all time. The way of the heart is now seen for what it is.

In that final sentence Benedict brings us once again to the paschal mystery, just as the whole of his teaching and his way of life can only be understood if this is central. For the early community in Acts, which Benedict so frequently takes as his point of reference (the allusion comes again in that phrase "faithfully observing his teaching" [50], which is an echo of Acts 2:24), the resurrected Christ was not an abstract idea but experiential fact. And for these first six centuries in the Church, it might be no exaggeration to say that Christianity equalled Easter. There is the figure of *Christus Victor,* the Christ who triumphed over the forces of death and opened up for men and women the possibilities of light and life and energy and a new kind of spiritual power, which represents the defeat of death in all its many aspects. Is this promise of life one that I want to grasp? Christ has reached down into the depths and has grasped Adam's hand and hauled him out of the pit. "Awake, O sleeper, and arise from the dead, and Christ shall give you light." To those in prison he says, "come forth" and to those in darkness, "have light." The images are ones that are universal and they touch my own inner experience.

The readings for Holy Saturday could hardly be more immediate, more vivid. "Arise, O human, work of my hands, arise, you were fashioned in my image. Rise, let us go hence: for you in me and I in you, together we are one undivided person." For those of us who are truly seeking God and who have entered into the journey through the waters of baptism, Benedict points the way forward into light and life and love.

*

And so the prologue teaches us Christ. This is the paschal Christ, the Christ risen in fullness from the grave, the risen Christ who has come through death-embracing love into his fullness that is our liberation from the dark powers within and without. In Benedict's school we shall learn Christ, not in any intellectual or cerebral way but in heart and mind and feeling. If Christ is my true self, living out of whom I discover my fullest humanity, then the Rule is there to lead me into the growth of the Christ-self. It is its Christ-centeredness that will make what the Rule has to say about the lived-out love between brothers and sisters a real and practical possibility. It is this dynamic centering on Christ triumphant over darkness and sin that offers hope to me as I walk into that freedom of son or daughter of the loving father that is the promise that the Rule holds out to us all.

CHAPTER ONE

¹There are clearly four kinds of monks. ²First, there are the cenobites, that is to say, those who belong to a monastery, where they serve under a rule and an abbot.

³Second, there are the anchorites or hermits, who have come through the test of living in a monastery for a long time, and have passed beyond the first fervor of monastic life. ⁴Thanks to the help and guidance of many, they are now trained to fight against the devil. ⁵They have built up their strength and go from the battle line in the ranks of their brothers to the single combat of the desert. Self-reliant now, without the support of another, they are ready with God's help to grapple single-handed with the vices of body and mind.

⁶Third, there are the sarabaites, the most detestable kind of monks, who with no experience to guide them, no rule to try them *as gold is tried in a furnace* (Prov 27:21), have a character as soft as lead. ⁷Still loyal to the world by their actions, they clearly lie to God by their tonsure. ⁸Two or three together, or even alone, without a shepherd, they pen themselves up in their own sheepfolds, not the Lord's. Their law is what they like to do, whatever strikes their fancy. ⁹Anything they believe in and choose, they call holy; anything they dislike, they consider forbidden.

¹⁰Fourth and finally, there are the monks called gyrovagues, who spend their entire lives drifting from region to region, staying as guests for three or four days in different monasteries. ¹¹Always on the move, they never settle down, and are slaves to their own wills and gross appetites. In every way they are worse than sarabaites.

¹²It is better to keep silent than to speak of all these and their disgraceful way of life. ¹³Let us pass them by, then,

and with the help of the Lord, proceed to draw up a plan for the strong kind, the cenobites.

Benedict begins the text of the main body of the Rule by describing four different kinds of monks. It seems clear that he is writing out of his own personal experience. It is therefore possible to read this chapter as giving us a picture of the strengths and weaknesses that he found in contemporary monasticism. But I can also approach it at another level and see in it differing attitudes and approaches to Christian discipleship. In that case I find a yardstick, as it were, to consider differing approaches to my own discipleship, perhaps at successive times in my life, which will help me to become aware of them so that I can either embrace or reject them.

He starts with what he most approves, the cenobites, those living in community, even though he deals with them only briefly since it is for them that he is writing all that is to follow. The Rule is about living with others and its demands. There is no escaping this. We are all social beings and we are all part of this inter-connectedness. But he also knows that for some there may come a time when they leave this shared life and go out to live alone, the life of the hermit, the solitary. In those years in the cave at Subiaco, he had lived alone, a time of solitude and silence. Benedict always writes out of his own experience, never in the abstract. That is one of the reasons why we can hear what he is saying to us today.

Nor does he ever romanticize or pretend that things are going to be easy. In speaking of the solitary life, he calls it a battle and he uses military terms, as he has done already in the prologue (3,40) and as the New Testament does so frequently. It is no bad thing to be reminded of the idea of spiritual warfare, which is something not much written or talked about today, for it will prevent any illusions about just how tough the fight against evil is bound to be. The battle goes on both with the body and the mind. Here it is useful, as throughout the Rule, to put this into its biblical context and to recognize that Benedict is not speaking of a dualistic division of body and soul as the Greeks might. Throughout the Rule, in fact, Benedict is always taking us away from the dualism that would juxtapose the material and the spiritual. He is using these words in the sense in which they would be used in the New Testament so that if we think of flesh as it is used in

Galatians 5:19, or thoughts as it is used in Mark 7:21, we shall come closer to what Benedict is intending.

"They have built up their strength. . . . Self-reliant now . . . single-handed . . ." (5). When Benedict here speaks of self-reliance, he will probably touch many people who find themselves living the solitary life, and not necessarily by choice. Because of old age and the greater length of life, or because of divorce, marriage break-up, exile, financial failure, economic dislocation, more and more people are alone today. It is then, above all, that we need to hear this assurance that we can stand on our own feet, yet also simultaneously be reminded that we can do nothing without God's help.

When he comes to his third category, Benedict becomes extremely fierce and uses very strong language. He is describing the sort of monks who lie to God with their tonsure, that is, the outward claim belies the disposition of the heart, and as we shall see Benedict is always more concerned with motive, disposition, and attitude than with such externals as dress or behavior. His concern here is with exposing what is false. He has no time for pretence. He challenges any self-deception. It is all too easy to claim that a way of life is the Lord's when in fact it is for one's own interest or convenience. If I put my own self-interest first and make that my point of reference, then I am living a life entirely in relation to self. That means that I have neither rule nor teacher as a touchstone and therefore that I lack the humility to turn to the handed-down tradition of lived-out experience of others.

Benedict uses the two images of lead (6) and of the sheepfold (8), which help me to reflect on what this can mean in my own life. First, he makes a contrast between lead and gold. Lead that looks so strong is in fact soft and pliable and therefore not to be relied upon when demands are made on it, whereas gold tried in the furnace is strong and pure. He is in effect asking me of which I am made. Then there are two sheepfolds, my own and God's. We are all encouraged to become more and more inward-looking; narcissism is rife and the tools for self-analysis and self-help are so readily available that I can only too easily enclose myself in a sheepfold of my own making. A sheepfold, if I build it for myself, suggests a safe haven into which I can settle comfortably, penned up in my own self-chosen world, finding a moral reason for doing whatever strikes my fancy. If, however, I choose to be in the Lord's sheepfold, then I must listen to the voice of the shepherd rather than my own voice. So Benedict presents me with this choice, and it is only too clear what his message is.

Finally, he looks at the life of the gyrovagues and paints a vivid picture of people who drift aimlessly, never settle down, live off others. Ultimately this is running away from commitment. One of the foundations of the Benedictine life is stability, which involves not simply remaining in one place but a deeper stability, the stability of a mind that stays still and does not endlessly search, constantly switching from one thing to another, hoping for something new or better somewhere else. Benedict has no illusions about the damage that this can do. Today when there is so much on offer, so much to read, so many alternative spiritualities, therapies, self-help manuals, we could all very easily spend our time drifting from one to the other, picking and choosing what appeals and whenever anything becomes too demanding moving on to something new. Benedict uses the word *miserrima,* which can be translated as wretched (Fr. Luke Dysinger) or lamentable (Sr. Catherine Wybourne). Indeed I appreciate this vivid word, for I know only too well from my own experience that a life without boundaries can never become a life that is constructive, creative, or life-giving.

But Benedict does not want to spend any more time on such people. Instead he is anxious to set out on his task of drawing up a plan, with the help of the Lord, to explore this Rule that is written ''for the strong kind'' (13).

CHAPTER TWO

¹To be worthy of the task of governing a monastery, the abbot must always remember what his title signifies and act as a superior should. ²He is believed to hold the place of Christ in the monastery, since he is addressed by a title of Christ, ³as the Apostle indicates: *You have received the spirit of adoption of sons by which we exclaim, abba, father* (Rom 8:15). ⁴Therefore, the abbot must never teach or decree or command anything that would deviate from the Lord's instructions. ⁵On the contrary, everything he teaches and commands should, like the leaven of divine justice, permeate the minds of his disciples. ⁶Let the abbot always remember that at the fearful judgment of God, not only his teaching but also his disciples' obedience will come under scrutiny. ⁷The abbot must, therefore, be aware that the shepherd will bear the blame wherever the father of the household finds that the sheep have yielded no profit. ⁸Still, if he has faithfully shepherded a restive and disobedient flock, always striving to cure their unhealthy ways, it will be otherwise: ⁹the shepherd will be acquitted at the Lord's judgment. Then, like the Prophet, he may say to the Lord: *I have not hidden your justice in my heart; I have proclaimed your truth and your salvation* (Ps 39[40]:11), *but they spurned and rejected me* (Isa 1:2; Ezek 20:27). ¹⁰Then at last the sheep that have rebelled against his care will be punished by the overwhelming power of death.

¹¹Furthermore, anyone who receives the name of abbot is to lead his disciples by a twofold teaching: ¹²he must point out to them all that is good and holy more by example than by words, proposing the commandments of the Lord to receptive disciples with words, but demonstrating God's in-

structions to the stubborn and the dull by a living example.
¹³Again, if he teaches his disciples that something is not to
be done, then neither must he do it, *lest after preaching to
others, he himself be found reprobate* (1 Cor 9:27) ¹⁴and
God some day call to him in his sin: *How is it that you repeat my just commands and mouth my covenant when you
hate discipline and toss my words behind you* (Ps 49[50]:16-
17)? ¹⁵And also this: *How is it that you can see a splinter
in your brother's eye, and never notice the plank in your
own* (Matt 7:3)?

¹⁶The abbot should avoid all favoritism in the monastery. ¹⁷He is not to love one more than another unless he
finds someone better in good actions and obedience. ¹⁸A
man born free is not to be given higher rank than a slave
who becomes a monk, except for some other good reason.
¹⁹But the abbot is free, if he sees fit, to change anyone's
rank as justice demands. Ordinarily, everyone is to keep to
his regular place, ²⁰because *whether slave or free, we are all
one in Christ* (Gal 3:28; Eph 6:8) and share alike in bearing
arms in the service of the one Lord, for *God shows no par-
tiality among persons* (Rom 2:11). ²¹Only in this are we
distinguished in his sight: if we are found better than others
in good works and in humility. ²²Therefore, the abbot is to
show equal love to everyone and apply the same discipline
to all according to their merits.

²³In his teaching, the abbot should always observe the
Apostle's recommendation, in which he says: *Use argument,
appeal, reproof* (2 Tim 4:2). ²⁴This means that he must vary
with circumstances, threatening and coaxing by turns, stern
as a taskmaster, devoted and tender as only a father can
be. ²⁵With the undisciplined and restless, he will use firm
argument; with the obedient and docile and patient, he will
appeal for greater virtue; but as for the negligent and dis-
dainful, we charge him to use a reproof and rebuke. ²⁶He
should not gloss over the sins of those who err, but cut them
out while he can, as soon as they begin to sprout, remem-
bering the fate of Eli, priest of Shiloh (1 Sam 2:11–4:18).
²⁷For upright and perceptive men, his first and second warnings should be verbal; ²⁸but those who are evil or stubborn,
arrogant or disobedient, he can curb only by blows or some
other physical punishment at the first offense. It is written,

The fool cannot be corrected with words (Prov 29:19); [29]and again, *Strike your son with a rod and you will free his soul from death* (Prov 23:14).

[30]The abbot must always remember what he is and remember what he is called, aware that more will be expected of a man to whom more has been entrusted. [31]He must know what a difficult and demanding burden he has undertaken: directing souls and serving a variety of temperaments, coaxing, reproving and encouraging them as appropriate. [32]He must so accommodate and adapt himself to each one's character and intelligence that he will not only keep the flock entrusted to his care from dwindling, but will rejoice in the increase of a good flock. [33]Above all, he must not show too great concern for the fleeting and temporal things of this world, neglecting or treating lightly the welfare of those entrusted to him. [34]Rather, he should keep in mind that he has undertaken the care of souls for whom he must give an account. [35]That he may not plead lack of resources as an excuse, he is to remember what is written: *Seek first the kingdom of God and his justice, and all these things will be given you as well* (Matt 6:33), [36]and again, *Those who fear him lack nothing* (Ps 33[34]:10).

[37]The abbot must know that anyone undertaking the charge of souls must be ready to account for them. [38]Whatever the number of brothers he has in his care, let him realize that on judgment day he will surely have to submit a reckoning to the Lord for all their souls—and indeed for his own as well. [39]In this way, while always fearful of the future examination of the shepherd about the sheep entrusted to him and careful about the state of others' accounts, he becomes concerned also about his own, [40]and while helping others to amend by his warnings, he achieves the amendment of his own faults.

If we have listened seriously to this opening chapter, we shall now be ready to face the issue that Benedict raises in the chapter that follows: our need for guidance of someone or something outside ourselves. He wrote only briefly about the cenobites, but he praised them because they waged their spiritual warfare "under a rule and an abbot" (1,2). So now he looks at this question of authority, both how we are going to live under authority and also how we ourselves are going to exercise it. This is one of the most carefully devised chapters in the Rule (supplemented by chapter 64), and it gives a wonderful portrait of the abbot, the man who is the model and example, both in his attitudes and in his actions, of how any of us should handle authority.

"He is believed to hold the place of Christ in the monastery" (2). That small phrase sets the tone. Christ is the ultimate source of authority, both for the abbot and for the Rule, for the Rule itself is simply a practical guide to living out the teachings of the Gospel, which are the teachings of Christ himself. There are these two channels of authority that subtly interact so that neither becomes an end in itself but the one acts as check to the other, and both point all the time to the figure of Christ. Since the abbot is believed to act as Christ's representative, it is clear that it is his task to discover God's will and to communicate it. He must ensure that whatever he does will mediate the will of God, which means a total dedication to seeking out and implementing that will, not to propounding any personal agenda that he might have.

In the prologue Benedict shows me the many roles that Christ plays: king, teacher, guide. Now Christ is designated as the father of the monks, and the role of the abbot is that of derivative or surrogate father, the one who holds the place of Christ. The word "abbot" itself, of course, comes from the Aramaic *abba,* "father." Here we see that not only is he father to the community, but that there is this idea, which seems at first rather alien to us now but that was common in the monasticism of the time, of the fatherhood of Christ. When Benedict calls Christ *Abba,* father, it signifies that there is a filial relationship between the monks and Christ. This opening establishes at once the keynote of loving gentleness and takes me back to the very first words of the prologue that addressed us as sons and daughters. This will be a discussion of leadership that carries no sense of hierarchy or episcopacy.

The image that Benedict uses for the abbot is that of the shepherd, a term that perhaps has become too familiar through over use in sentimental hymns and pictures (1,7-10). I can only fully appreciate what he has in mind if I think of its biblical resonances or the meaning that it held in the early Church. We have lost some of the immediacy of the early Church when, since the gallows were something too shocking to be portrayed, the catacombs were full of paintings and sculptures of the good shepherd. The passage in Ezekiel that describes the shepherd who calls each sheep by name presents us with the good shepherd who knows all of his sheep and they know him. He stands in the middle and keeps them in view, ready when and where help and healing are needed. The strays are brought back, the wounded bandaged, the weak strengthened. He keeps them and he guards them, but he does not own them. This Christ-figure is the image of the abbot, but it also gives an exemplar of how anyone should treat others. It applies not least to me.

The abbot leads by a two-fold teaching (1,13), for it is as much by his example as by his words that his monks will learn. When Benedict comes to write of the "equal love" due to each in any community, I feel that he is speaking out of his personal knowledge of the community life at Monte Cassino. As Jean Le Clerq reminds us, the Italy of his time was a class-ridden and hierarchical society with "categories of people more or less distinct from one another." The only thing that they shared was the economic deprivation of a post-war period. Everyone's place was determined at birth and delineated for life by external marks, and this was as true of the invading Goths with their own nobility and their inferior classes as it was of the Italians.

This is the context in which we should read the descriptions of life at Monte Cassino in the *Dialogues of St. Gregory*. We can see from some of the episodes that he recounts just what a motley crowd these first monks were, drawn from differing social backgrounds and racial origins. A wall fell down one day and crushed a young man whose father was a member of the Senate. Another monk who had an accident with a sickle was a simple Goth. One monk was a Roman slave called Exhilaratus whose master used to send Benedict wine. (Was it these occasions of bringing it that led him into the monastery? We shall, of course, never know.) Maurus and Placid on the other hand were the sons of Roman noblemen. Benedict himself was of comparatively low social origins amongst his monks, coming from a minor noble family.

It needs little imagination to picture how, in a small group of men like this, tensions might erupt. One such moment is caught for us in the *Dialogues*. It took place during an evening meal when a young monk from a higher class happened to be holding the lamp for Benedict. While standing at the table, the spirit of pride began to stir in his heart. " 'Who is this' he thought to himself, 'that I should have to stand here holding the lamp for him while he is eating? Who am I to be serving him?' " Benedict read the thoughts of the young man and to him they were one of the clearest indications during his abbacy of the work of the devil. We are also told of the day on which the Goth dropped his bill-hook into the lake and could not help trembling when he owned up to Maurus, who, though young, was of noble birth. When Benedict, alerted by Maurus, returned the bill-hook that he had recovered from the water, he said with Roman exactitude but also with affection, "Here you are, carry on working and do not be sad any longer."

People come from all quarters and he turns no one away. The nobleman arrives with his large endowment and stands next to the penniless son of a peasant. There are freeborn patricians and there are serfs; there are illiterates and academics, clerical and lay, all ages. There is room for all on one condition: that they forget their old connections. When they cross the threshold of the monastery, they break with that old hierarchical society. They even leave behind their name, that civil name that can betray their origins. Since some rank and regular place is necessary for the smooth working of community life, they are given a new name and a new rank, determined by the date on which they enter. They address one another with respect and tenderness, "all the courtesy of love," that lovely small phrase that Benedict uses in 53,3. Slave or free, we are all one body in Christ. This is the end of all those labels that differentiate a person on account of birth, background, or education. Benedict not only quotes St. Paul, *"whether slave or free, we are all one in Christ* (Gal 3:28; Eph 6:8)" (20), he actually makes it the cornerstone of his community. Seeing each single person as the unique son or daughter of a loving father is a sentiment to which I can easily pay lip service and let it stop there. Yet recognizing the worth of each and every individual is fundamental to Benedict's way of life. If I am to take the Rule seriously, then I am forced to ask myself some honest questions about my attitude toward other people that I would probably prefer to evade.

"Discretion" is a gentle word that describes how the abbot handles the members of his family, which is the subject of verses 22-29. It is the art of being able to distinguish, to choose what is appropriate. The abbot does not over-protect or prolong a state of immaturity. He handles each one according to his true self.

He recognizes in each person, in any particular situation, that there is a level at which they will work best. So one is to be humored, another restrained; one to be treated tenderly, another sternly. There comes a time when it is right to reprove and rebuke. The art of loving someone as they need to be loved does not ask us to turn a blind eye. But when and why? Benedict is showing me here the need for discernment in choosing the point at which I should intervene, and I think that once again it is the disposition of the heart, the true motives, that must dictate that. If my real purpose, even if it is a hidden agenda (even if I scarcely like to admit it to myself), is to improve or to control for my own ends, then that is wrong. What assurance there is in the way in which the abbot handles people, showing his concern to empower and to enhance them, to nurture them in a way that will promote growth. This is a journey that all must make on their own two feet. It is learning of discipline and inner asceticism under a master that has much in common with the Zen master. Here is a guide who has traveled the road on which the disciple embarks and is now available to point that way to each member in his own. For this to be possible, as Kardong reminds us, "The leader must be secure in his own self-image, knowing that he is dear to God and to others." We are brought back all the time to the figure of Christ. We are to see the abbot (but this is equally true of each of us in any role of authority) at work as a true Christ-agent who works tirelessly to promote the Christ-life of his sons and daughters.

The real point in the growth that the abbot encourages is growth in the love of Christ. If there is anything characteristic of the Rule, it is the way in which Benedict constantly stresses the love of Christ as the focal point. It is always the love of Christ that is the center of our growth process . . . everything must lead to this. . . . The role of authority is to help the individual to develop that personal relationship, to foster growth in the love of Christ. Rembert Weakland, whom I am quoting here, adds, "and I would like to repeat that a hundred times." There is never anything static about Benedict or the Rule. This dynamic element, with the sense of growth, progress, opening out, is vital. As I come to the end of this chapter, I appreciate the image that Benedict uses in verse 5 when he likens the abbot's teaching to leaven that would permeate the minds of his disciples. These are words that suggest a process that is slow and thorough, working so that change will take place at its own pace. This is a leadership that understands about growth, spiritual and psychological, and will help to promote it. It is God at work, which will lead to the rising like yeast in each individual.

Yet even while he is being reminded of how he is to act gently, the abbot is also being reminded that at the day of judgment both his teaching and the obedience of his disciples will be examined (38). Benedict again adheres to gospel teaching. Christ more than once affirmed the fearful possibility of falling short of his love. Benedict does not let us forget the sobering thought that God will one day judge our actions. So the abbot is to bear this in mind, to anticipate God's judgment on his actions, to make the same judgment that God would make, and so not to act without regard to the consequences. Yet Benedict also puts limits to what might sound a huge responsibility, for he never says that the salvation of each soul depends on the abbot. If the monks spurn and reject the abbot in spite of all that he has tried to do to cure their unhealthy ways, then their final punishment lies with themselves and not with him. There is never any idea that the sheep belong to him; they belong to "the father of the household, the *paterfamilias*" and that is God himself. So I too must impose the same limitations on those for whom I feel responsible, in family, marriage, or work, for I must never forget that ultimately they belong to God. Somewhere I remember Thomas Merton telling me that I can be brother or sister to another but I must never try to play the role of keeper, for to do that is to abrogate to myself a role that belongs to God alone. In *No Man Is an Island,* Merton reminds us, "A person is a person insofar as he has a secret and is a solitude of his own that cannot be communicated to anyone else . . . which God alone can penetrate and understand." This standing back is a recognition that everyone of us is unique and that uniqueness must be respected.

While each one may be equal in love, differences in personality and temperament, or of a physical and a psychological kind, must not be overlooked. "Everyone has his own gift from God, one this and another that." Later in chapter 40 Benedict will quote from 1 Corinthians. He is here emphasizing the flexibility of approach that the abbot will need. The respect and reverence is due to each as a unique creature of a loving father (echoes once again of the opening words of the prologue). Being ready to adapt appropriately to each requires the gift of discernment, and Benedict shows the skills of a spiritual director as he tells the abbot to use encouragement and persuasion or reproof as the spiritual needs of those in his care require. He is also responsible for the material welfare of his monks and while he does not want to deny the earthly and perishable things, Benedict is saying that we are to seek the things of the kingdom *first* and God's justice. The quotation from Matthew 6 in verse 35 brings me back to the thread of "divine justice" that runs throughout this chapter. God's justice is not justice in terms of just rewards for desserts as the world would understand it. The secrets of each heart, the intentions, the struggles, are known to God alone, and it is on this that each will be judged at the end. The reference in verse 5 to the leaven of "divine justice" carries an implication whose significance I should not miss, for it clearly refers to Matthew 20:1-16, the parable of the workers in the vineyard. The behavior of the owner turns the accepted order of things on its head. Am I really expected to reward someone as much for one hour's work as for ten? This is not a description of just desserts as today's world understands it. It is rather a description of the overflowing of a generous love that does not count the cost, or reward by achievement, or weigh up time and labor and results. If I am going to take this seriously, then Benedict is challenging me to make the radical demands of the Gospel real and practical in my daily relationships.

The abbot is not only responsible for others; he is also responsible for himself. The position of leadership does not put the leader apart from the rest in the responsibility that he is also to exercise toward himself. Here is a caution that is only too wise for anyone involved in caring for others: they too will be held responsible on the day of judgment for the way in which they have handled their own gifts and talents, dealt with their own faults. It is something that I need to hear myself, to take seriously.

CHAPTER THREE

¹As often as anything important is to be done in the monastery, the abbot shall call the whole community together and himself explain what the business is; ²and after hearing the advice of the brothers, let him ponder it and follow what he judges the wiser course. ³The reason why we have said all should be called for counsel is that the Lord often reveals what is better to the younger. ⁴The brothers, for their part, are to express their opinions with all humility, and not presume to defend their own views obstinately. ⁵The decision is rather the abbot's to make, so that when he has determined what is more prudent, all may obey. ⁶Nevertheless, just as it is proper for disciples to obey their master, so it is becoming for the master on his part to settle everything with foresight and fairness.

⁷Accordingly in every instance, all are to follow the teaching of the rule, and no one shall rashly deviate from it. ⁸In the monastery no one is to follow his own heart's desire, ⁹nor shall anyone presume to contend with his abbot defiantly, or outside the monastery. ¹⁰Should anyone presume to do so, let him be subjected to the discipline of the rule. ¹¹Moreover, the abbot himself must fear God and keep the rule in everything he does; he can be sure beyond any doubt that he will have to give an account of all his judgments to God, the most just of judges.

¹²If less important business of the monastery is to be transacted, he shall take counsel with the seniors only, ¹³as it is written: *Do everything with counsel and you will not be sorry afterward* (Sir 32:24).

Benedict was at pains in chapter 2 to show that there must be a balance between the abbot and the Rule. Here he is continuing that theme and showing that it must also take into account the living community that he has just been describing. The abbot is shaping that community so that it too becomes a bearer of the spirit to which the abbot must listen. Now there must be a very delicate balancing between the superior and his personal gifts, the insights of the living community and the Rule that is the bearer of the accumulated wisdom of tradition. It is as if on the institutional level Benedict is already showing me what is so central to his whole way of life, and that is the vital necessity of holding differing things in balance. Later on the importance of that balance will emerge with reference to the role of body, mind, and spirit, or in the three-fold Benedictine promises. It is a warning against going to extremes or allowing polarization in any shape or form. Any balancing act must be a delicate operation, and I enjoy seeing the delicacy with which Benedict handles it in this chapter.

Already Benedict has given us a description of how the abbot is to exercise discernment in his handling of those in his pastoral care. Discernment is much talked about today, particularly in Jesuit circles. In fact, it goes back well beyond Benedict to the Desert Fathers. It was a key qualification for the *abba,* father. We do not see here a discernment process such as the Jesuits have devised, but we are given something that will help us with the underlying attitudes and approach that we might need. In this chapter discernment is being exercised in a corporate situation, in the context of community. The purpose of consultation and consensus is to open the heart and mind so that the Holy Spirit may reach us in whatever way it may come. This is an exercise in listening. For Benedict that means listening with a total openness. God is no respecter of persons. He may choose to reveal truth to the youngest.

If we have really taken seriously the expectation to respect the value of each individual member of the community, as chapter 2 has been encouraging us to do, it is now being put to the test. It is only too easy when policy is being made, when a vision is being created, for the articulate and the astute to dominate, and for the weak, the shy, the marginal to be forgotten or put to one side. But if there is to be a communal vision that is truly a shared vision, then it is up to the abbot to make that accessible to all by finding a way to broaden the participation of all. I like to think of it in these terms as a reminder that mere intellectual understanding is not the point; rather, it is the focus of the ideal, the goal of the shared journey.

"The Lord reveals" is the key phrase here. Openness to the working of the Spirit in both individual and in community is vital, life-giving. Without it there will be a closed-up person, a closed-up community, lacking the growth that Benedict holds out so urgently in the prologue. God chooses many different ways to reveal himself—in a blinding flash on the road; in a still, small voice; in human form; through another. There is nothing neat or predictable in any of this. It is a reminder that without attentiveness at that moment or on that occasion, the gift of God will pass by me ignored. Benedict wants all of us to be open, alert, attentive. The daily saying of "Today if you will hear my voice . . ." is a constant, daily reminder of this responsibility that I must learn to listen to the will of God. If I live daily, hourly in this way it will predispose me to be ready for those times when it becomes particularly urgent to discover what God's will means for me, and for others.

The worth of each, the need for authority, the overriding necessity to find the will of God—how are all these strands to be woven together in day-to-day community life, particularly when it comes to decision making? Benedict shows himself to be a shrewd realist, for without abandoning any of his ideals, he manages to present a workable system—and indeed one which any community today (family, parish, school, etc.) could do well to learn from. The essential process is that of consultation, listening. Benedict shows that he knows human nature sufficiently well to insert a note of caution. Those who are *speaking* should exercise restraint and present their opinions with humility (4). Then having listened the abbot must take time, ponder, weigh it within himself (an important concept here, which perhaps recalls what *lectio* is doing, chewing over slowly and meditatively), until he decides the wiser course. He is to do this with prudence, with foresight, and with fairness. He, just as much as the other monks, is under the Rule. Nor is he to forget that at the day of judgment he will have to answer for his actions. These are considerable restraints that leave little room for arbitrary behavior.

The actual moment of consultation is not isolated and apart from the rest of the ongoing life of the community; rather it grows out of the openness and growth that should be there all the time. In the more day-to-day decision making, the abbot is to rely on the *pars sanior* (12), the wiser and more experienced. Recognizing what shall be deemed "less important" will therefore depend on his own sensitivity to others and to being in touch with what is going on in the community.

> I feel this can be done only with an enormous amount of suffering. I see no other way out of it. You know it is trial and error and if anybody thinks the superior plays God in this, he is utterly wrong. The superior goes through enormous turmoil trying to analyze and find out what the Spirit wants at any given moment.

The words of a contemporary abbot may strengthen me when I find myself with this responsibility on my own shoulders.

CHAPTER FOUR

[1]First of all, *love the Lord God with your whole heart, your whole soul and all your strength,* [2]*and love your neighbor as yourself* (Matt 22:37-39; Mark 12:30-31; Luke 10:27). [3]Then the following: *You are not to kill,* [4]*not to commit adultery;* [5]*you are not to steal* [6]*nor to covet* (Rom 13:9); [7]*you are not to bear false witness* (Matt 19:18; Mark 10:19; Luke 18:20). [8]*You must honor everyone* (1 Pet 2:17), [9]and *never do to another what you do not want done to yourself* (Tob 4:16; Matt 7:12; Luke 6:31).

[10]*Renounce yourself in order to follow Christ* (Matt 16:24; Luke 9:23); [11]*discipline your body* (1 Cor 9:27); [12]do not pamper yourself, [13]but love fasting. [14]You must relieve the lot of the poor, [15]*clothe the naked,* [16]*visit the sick* (Matt 25:36), [17]and bury the dead. [18]Go to help the troubled [19]and console the sorrowing.

[20]Your way of acting should be different from the world's way; [21]the love of Christ must come before all else. [22]You are not to act in anger [23]or nurse a grudge. [24]Rid your heart of all deceit. [25]Never give a hollow greeting of peace [26]or turn away when someone needs your love. [27]Bind yourself to no oath lest it prove false, [28]but speak the truth with heart and tongue.

[29]*Do not repay one bad turn with another* (1 Thess 5:15; 1 Pet 3:9). [30]Do not injure anyone, but bear injuries patiently. [31]*Love your enemies* (Matt 5:44; Luke 6:27). [32]If people curse you, do not curse them back but bless them instead. [33]*Endure persecution for the sake of justice* (Matt 5:10).

[34]You must *not* be *proud,* [35]*nor be given to wine* (Titus 1:7; 1 Tim 3:3). [36]Refrain from too much eating [37]or sleep-

34

ing, ³⁸and *from laziness* (Rom 12:11). ³⁹Do not grumble ⁴⁰or speak ill of others.

⁴¹Place your hope in God alone. ⁴²If you notice something good in yourself, give credit to God, not to yourself, ⁴³but be certain that the evil you commit is always your own and yours to acknowledge.

⁴⁴Live in fear of judgment day ⁴⁵and have a great horror of hell. ⁴⁶Yearn for everlasting life with holy desire. ⁴⁷Day by day remind yourself that you are going to die. ⁴⁸Hour by hour keep careful watch over all you do, ⁴⁹aware that God's gaze is upon you, wherever you may be. ⁵⁰As soon as wrongful thoughts come into your heart, dash them against Christ and disclose them to your spiritual father. ⁵¹Guard your lips from harmful or deceptive speech. ⁵²Prefer moderation in speech ⁵³and speak no foolish chatter, nothing just to provoke laughter; ⁵⁴do not love immoderate or boisterous laughter.

⁵⁵Listen readily to holy reading, ⁵⁶and devote yourself often to prayer. ⁵⁷Every day with tears and sighs confess your past sins to God in prayer ⁵⁸and change from these evil ways in the future.

⁵⁹*Do not gratify the promptings of the flesh* (Gal 5:16); ⁶⁰hate the urgings of self-will. ⁶¹Obey the orders of the abbot unreservedly, even if his own conduct—which God forbid—be at odds with what he says. Remember the teaching of the Lord: *Do what they say, not what they do* (Matt 23:3).

⁶²Do not aspire to be called holy before you really are, but first be holy that you may more truly be called so. ⁶³Live by God's commandments every day; ⁶⁴treasure chastity, ⁶⁵harbor neither hatred ⁶⁶nor jealousy of anyone, ⁶⁷and do nothing out of envy. ⁶⁸Do not love quarreling; ⁶⁹shun arrogance. ⁷⁰Respect the elders ⁷¹and love the young. ⁷²Pray for your enemies out of love for Christ. ⁷³If you have a dispute with someone, make peace with him before the sun goes down.

⁷⁴And finally, never lose hope in God's mercy.

⁷⁵These, then, are the tools of the spiritual craft. ⁷⁶When we have used them without ceasing day and night and have returned them on judgment day, our wages will be the reward the Lord has promised: ⁷⁷*What the eye has not seen nor the ear heard, God has prepared for those who love him* (1 Cor 2:9).

[78]The workshop where we are to toil faithfully at all these tasks is the enclosure of the monastery and stability in the community.

My immediate reaction on reaching this chapter is one of bewilderment. I have been following Benedict as he writes of the role of the abbot and the community, at once sensitive and practical, and now I am faced with what appears to be a random catalog of maxims of an ethical and moralizing nature. They seem to be basic elements in any Christian life, and it is difficult to see why they should appear here. I am reminded of those pious expectations with which I was presented in my childhood and which I have been trying to escape from in adult life. In the face of an apparent hodge-podge, it is tempting either to decide that they represent a completely random listing or else to try to impose some sort of convincing pattern that would organize them into bundles or clusters and so make the chapter more mangeable. Instead of either of these alternatives, I like what Michael Casey has to say. He argues for the value of paying attention to the literary structures of the text and shows that the structural analysis of the chapter produces significant coincidences, with a number of minor groupings within the whole:

> These minor groupings may not represent an explicit, reasoned progression, but they can be the result of an intuitive association of ideas, which causes one bloc to be laid beside another and perhaps a number of blocs put in orbit around a central item. It is an unconscious process, and perhaps all the more valuable for being so since it enables us to see the whole person at work, rather than merely his head and pen.

I like this suggestion of an intuitive association of ideas that allows us to see something of Benedict's mind at work. This is not a list of virtues to be nourished and vices to be eradicated, a simple ethical code to be followed, but rather a challenge to the process of discernment as the prerequisite of the life that he is encouraging me to follow. Once again his concern is not with externals, but with interiority. In the preceding two chapters he has been concerned to remind the abbot, and also each one of us, not to forget the day of judgment. He has been helping us to try to discern whether or not we are trying to find and follow God's will in all that we think and do. If not, then we shall have to answer for that on the day of judgment when the secrets of all hearts will be revealed. His concern is with the inner disposition and attitude, with the disposition of the heart, and in this chapter we are being given a practical yardstick that we can apply in our daily lives. He puts this here, at this juncture in the Rule, since he knows that unless we get this right at this point, all that follows, whether on prayer or obedience or humility or day-to-day routine, will lack its essential and necessary foundation.

So I am here being equipped, in the most basic and practical way possible, with the tools essential for my spiritual life. When Bishop Fox of Winchester was writing on the Rule for the nuns of his diocese in the sixteenth century, he prefaced this chapter by reminding them that just as "worldely artificers have materyuall instrumentes apte for the accomplysshement of their worldely werkes" so we too must have instruments ready for the "crafte of religiose living." The concept of handling tools is totally down to earth and practical. Since Benedict sees me as a workman in a workshop (78), I must collect a supply of tools ready at hand to use when and how they are needed in my spiritual life. At the end of the chapter, the use of the tools will be explained. They are the thoughts and actions with which to fill my days in God's service. They cannot be imposed by any external authority, for they concern interior understanding. Again there is this insistence that it is by willingness or unwillingness, humility or pride, loving zeal or the spirit of competition, that actions are to be judged. Only on the day of judgment will the workman's task be over and the tool-box handed back to God.

Discernment therefore remains the underlying concern. How am I to distinguish between good and evil at every step of my life, and at every moment of my day? How can I be totally clear-sighted so that I avoid illusion and am free of inner deception? Benedict sees through any dissimulation. Verse 24 puts it bluntly, not in any biblical quotation but in his own voice, "Rid your heart of all deceit." The externals in my life, my outward behavior, reflect my inner disposition. Benedict knows a great deal about the innermost self, that world of my deepest thoughts and intentions, where much lies buried that I would not like to see the light of day. If I am to grow into a whole and free person then there must be a harmonious relationship between the inner and the outer. Without it there comes that crippling disunity within myself that will lead to ill-health, whether physical, psychological, or spiritual. External conformity is not good enough. The outwardly good behavior that is without interior motivation becomes automatic, deadening. It is therefore with questions of my own interior attitude in mind that I must read this chapter.

The opening verse presents me with the essential law of the Gospel. I am forced to ask: Do I love God with my whole heart and my neighbor as myself? If I am going to look on each of these successive verses as an aid to discernment, then Benedict is facing me here with the foundational questions on which the whole of the rest will be built. These two precepts sum up the whole purpose of the Benedictine life, as of any Christian life, and I feel that Benedict is placing them here so that they are the keystone of the chapter. They present me with the yardstick to judge every thought, word, and action: Is what I am thinking or doing contributing to the fulfilment of this commandment? Verses 3-8 give six articles of the Decalogue in the words of the New Testament. Verse 9 is the golden rule; it is a call to love. We are to see the other as Christ, treat the other as Christ.

The call is to follow Christ, which is simply the scriptural invitation that had been so vivid in the prologue. Now Benedict is reminding us that this asks for restraint, abnegation, discipline. He is showing us the renunciation that is necessary if we are to be free to love. Verses 10-13 spell this out. It will never be possible to follow Christ while I put myself and my own pleasures first. The contemporary interest in dieting and weight-watching, and the popular search for a more disciplined way of life as a reaction from the tyranny of the pleasure principle, once again demonstrate the wisdom of the Rule. To *love* fasting suggests a good, positive attitude. Philip Jebb writes of how fasting has become part of his life. "You are given a new freedom." He tells how much he learned from it; the cutting down of one's sense of independence, pride, and self-sufficiency; the clarity of perception it brought; and the discovery of the interdependence of the body and the material universe.

The "you did it to me" passage in chapter 25 of Matthew's Gospel is the inspiration for verses 14-19, which list what are familiarly known as the corporal works of mercy, or what might be rendered in more modern language service to the needy. "Here we have a principle which is as destructive of selfishness as the practice of renunciation and mortification. By offering ourselves in service, by putting ourselves out for others, we are freed from the domination of our own immature need for comfort.'' It is not enough to be a successful ascetic if it means that I neglect the needs of my brothers and sisters. The familiarity of these maxims must not be allowed to blunt their message. I have an obligation to those in need, and I cannot pretend that I do not know how much suffering there is in today's world. Even if it is perhaps further away, or more hidden than the encounter with the poor or naked or sick would have been in the past, that is no excuse.

Verses 20-21 bring a restatement of what holds this chapter together: the absolute priority of our love of Christ. This, and the seven verses that follow, are no longer that mosaic of biblical quotation. Here we have Benedict's own voice. Verse 20 is totally a reflection of the man himself, in the world and yet not of the world, accepting the material and yet not bound by it. Again Michael Casey summarizes the significance of what is being said here.

> Separation from the world is not primarily an act of distancing or detachment, but an act of joining oneself to Christ and to the holy community: an act of attachment. . . . No Christian can scorn the world for which Christ died; he can however refuse to accept its unevangelical standards of behavior.

If I were looking for one single, simple phrase to sum up Benedict's whole way of life, I would find it in verse 21: ''The love of Christ must come before all else.'' It will be said again in 72,11, the chapter that is a great lyrical outpouring about love and to which Benedict returns at the end of the Rule when he has shown us how his way of living will enable us to incarnate that love. This Christ-love is the center of the whole Rule and the center of our lives. If there is any one thing that is characteristic of Benedict, it is that he makes the love of Christ the focal point to which everything must lead. One should really not talk about a verse like this, but just stop and meditate on it.

In verses 22-28 Benedict is looking at personal wholeness, showing me how I can so easily fail through anger, carrying grudges, nursing resentments, and being deceitful. We are not given a quotation, but short comments from Benedict himself, the fruit perhaps of his own experience of community at Cassino. ''Rid your heart of all deceit . . . . Speak the truth with heart and tongue." Again we are brought back to the dangers of being untruthful, whether inwardly or outwardly.

Then follows a section on peaceful living and the making of peace. Nonviolence means that I do not repay injuries or return curses, that I absorb the hurt in a Ghandian fashion. These are verses on the subject of forgiveness to which Benedict will return later.

Verses 34-40 run through a list of fairly obvious failings: too much drink, too much sleep, grumbling, laziness. But nonetheless we should not despise this and think that we have grown far beyond it. In verses 41-43 there comes another of these breathing spaces that gives Benedict the opportunity for the wider perspective. Any of this will be impossible if I am going to be self-reliant. I am being asked to put my trust in God and admit my total dependence on him. The decision is mine whether to accept or to reject the graces that are offered to me. An ascetical life will be unprofitable unless my gaze is fixed all the time on God, just as surely as Benedict's own life of denial in the cave at Subiaco was totally God-ward oriented. Without that point of reference, without that love, these will become negative practices.

I must take responsibility for myself since, at the end of my life, I will be called to account. Benedict will not let us forget the last things, the day of judgment, and he returns to it again in verses 44-47. He helps me to live responsibly by telling me to think daily of my own death. If read in isolation, "Day by day remind yourself that you are going to die" (47), it could appear that death is to be dreaded. But the sequence here is important. Benedict does not separate death and eternal life (46). Death is the passage to eternal life, the beginning of the everlasting encounter with Christ. In *The Dialogues* St. Gregory tells us that Benedict said: "Death which nearly everyone regards as punishment, I cherish as the entry to life and the reward for labor." The holding together of dying and new life, the paschal mystery, runs throughout the Rule. In chapter 49 we are told that while our life should be a perpetual Lent, we should also daily look forward to Easter with "joy and spiritual longing" (49,7).

This makes me ask myself if I think sufficiently about preparation for death during life. I cannot escape awareness of death, for I am surrounded daily by the most horrific reminders of killings and disasters brought to my attention by the media. But to think of my own death is a very different thing. Yet Benedict reminded me in the prologue that to follow his way means perseverance until the day of my death, a journey to the very end. In that moment, although my family and friends may be present, I shall ultimately be utterly alone with Christ, and in death I shall really reach him, see him, return to him. I can bury the thought of this moment or deny it or run away from it, but I shall not in the end escape it. To think of my life objectively in the light of death will bring a very different perspective to the way in which I live now. If death is the gateway to life with Christ, then daily I want to rejoice in that prospect. "Yearn" and "desire" in verse 46 are strong, passionate words, as are "joy and spiritual longing" (49,7); words of love and rejoicing, not fear and dread. We are not prepared to die unless we are first prepared to live.

Once again I feel that Benedict is reminding me of ultimate values, and these reflections on the last things are to help me to see my life in perspective. So the verses on mindfulness and awareness (48-49) follow naturally here. I am not going to drift through life half awake, unaware. The prologue had attempted to instil the sense of urgency that life is not to be wasted through being half-alive, half-awake. God's gaze upon me all the time is the gaze of a compassionate love searching out the corners of my heart, knowing all my secret thoughts and intentions. When the wrongful thoughts come creeping in, as they inevitably are going to do, he tells me to dash them against the rock that is Christ, picking up something that had come in the prologue: "While these temptations were still *young, he caught hold of them and dashed them against* Christ" (Prol., 28). The idea of God as rock runs throughout the psalms, and a rock is a wonderful image for what is strong, irremovable, dependable. It feels quite natural to find that Benedict applies the term to Christ. The specific reference is to that phrase in Psalm 136 (137) about smashing the Babylonian babies against the rocks. While that appalls me, it is nonetheless salutary to visualize that scene in order to grasp what is being asked of me: that these wrongful thoughts are dashed against Christ while they are still in their infancy, before they have time to grow any further. There is the danger that I might harbor malicious or destructive thoughts that might escape and do damage. It is to prevent this that Benedict speaks in the following four verses about the need to keep guard over my tongue. It is here that those remarks about laughter come, remarks that have so often been held against him. I do not believe that he has no sense of humor, or that he disapproved of laughter as such, but laughter can sometimes be cruel, and it can be used in a negative way to cut a person down.

The purpose of controlling mindless chatter and incessant noise, whether it is external or internal, is to make room for an inner silence and space to be filled with God. Silence is a working tool for Benedict since the love of silence opens up the capacity to hear. In verse 55 Benedict again uses the word "listen" and reminds me that the whole purpose of my life is to listen to God. One of the tools for that is the reading, or *lectio*, that turns the Scriptures into prayer. Verses 57-58 deal with penitence and penance as part of that prayer, and as looking toward the future. This is not guilt or remorse, which far too often leave me caught in the coils of the past, but that true sorrow and contrition which leads me on to a desire for change. A twelfth-century Irish poem asks for the gift of tears, "a well of tears": "Grant me, O great God . . . fierce floods of tears." It is also a good prayer for me. I pray for a softening of the heart that brings me to tears, or close to tears, for then I am not hard-hearted or half-hearted, but have a heart open to the workings of God. The change or conversion of verse 58 is a demand that I live in accordance not with my own will, but with the will of God, which is simply another way of describing obedience. Since obedience is ultimately listening to the Word and responding to it, the natural conclusion of this particular cluster of verses is to emphasize again the role of obedience in my life.

In verse 62 Benedict returns to the importance of the inner reality rather than the external appearance. He is never deceived by appearances, and he is only too aware of the self-deception that he warned against earlier on and what it can do. Just in case I might begin to feel rather good about myself and my progress, at this stage in this chapter he is careful to take me down a peg or two by putting his finger once more on this point. We are to live the truth. It is a matter of discernment again: What are my real motives here? That I gain the applause of the world because I appear to be so deeply spiritual, living such a committed Christian life?

A miscellaneous collection of texts follows in verses 63-73, and at first it is difficult to see any underlying coherence. They are pretty basic virtues and vices: chastity is good, hatred and jealousy, quarrelling and arrogance, are not. Reverence for both old and young, praying for our enemies, trying to keep the peace— these are all instruments for survival in community life. But as I read them time and again, I find that "treasure chastity" in 64 sets the key note. It is asking me to respect and revere the other, for a sense of restraint by which I hold myself back from intruding on them, for so often what lies behind my quarrelling and contentiousness is this desire to impose myself, my ideas, my demands upon the other.

In verse 74, at the end of this long list, Benedict hands me his final tool. I am never to lose hope in God's mercy. I cannot do any of this on my own. I know that in this life I will never arrive. I am sure that in this life I will continue to struggle. My one certainty is that I do not have to go it alone.

The coda is Benedict at his most practical and down to earth. These tools for my spiritual life are not so very different from the tools for my day-to-day life at work in the garden or kitchen. They have been issued to me. I am responsible for using them properly, and on the day of judgment I will return them and render account. It is good to read verse 76 and then look at 35,10 where the same verb is used, and so find a parallel: that tools are handed out and should be returned washed, which I take to mean in good order. Then comes the moment when the good workman claims his wages. But they are not wages that the world might chalk up, based on any outward achievement. What the eye hath not seen nor the ear heard surely brings me back to the disposition of the heart, to the secret intention of the heart known to God alone. And as to the workshop—in this case it is the place in which I find myself, and the people who surround me. I do not run away or try to escape from the reality of this, for this is where I shall find God and find my true self.

CHAPTER FIVE

¹The first step of humility is unhesitating obedience, ²which comes naturally to those who cherish Christ above all. ³Because of the holy service they have professed, or because of dread of hell and for the glory of everlasting life, ⁴they carry out the superior's order as promptly as if the command came from God himself. ⁵The Lord says of men like this: *No sooner did he hear than he obeyed me* (Ps 17[18]: 45); ⁶again, he tells teachers: *Whoever listens to you, listens to me* (Luke 10:16). ⁷Such people as these immediately put aside their own concerns, abandon their own will, ⁸and lay down whatever they have in hand, leaving it unfinished. With the ready step of obedience, they follow the voice of authority in their actions. ⁹Almost at the same moment, then, as the master gives the instruction the disciple quickly puts it into practice in the fear of God; and both actions together are swiftly completed as one.

¹⁰It is love that impels them to pursue everlasting life; ¹¹therefore, they are eager to take the narrow road of which the Lord says: *Narrow is the road that leads to life* (Matt 7:14). ¹²They no longer live by their own judgment, giving in to their whims and appetites; rather they walk according to another's decisions and directions, choosing to live in monasteries and to have an abbot over them. ¹³Men of this resolve unquestionably conform to the saying of the Lord: *I have come not to do my own will, but the will of him who sent me* (John 6:38).

¹⁴This very obedience, however, will be acceptable to God and agreeable to men only if compliance with what is commanded is not cringing or sluggish or half-hearted, but free from any grumbling or any reaction of unwillingness.

¹⁵For the obedience shown to superiors is given to God, as he himself said: *Whoever listens to you, listens to me* (Luke 10:16). ¹⁶Furthermore, the disciples' obedience must be given gladly, for *God loves a cheerful giver* (2 Cor 9:7). ¹⁷If a disciple obeys grudgingly and grumbles, not only aloud but also in his heart, ¹⁸then, even though he carries out the order, his action will not be accepted with favor by God, who sees that he is grumbling in his heart. ¹⁹He will have no reward for service of this kind; on the contrary, he will incur punishment for grumbling, unless he changes for the better and makes amends.

I am to handle all these tools with the help of constant vigilance, by being alert to the presence of God in the workshop of my life at every moment of my day, with the help of obedience (4,59-61), of silence (4,51-54), and humility (4,48-50). Chapter 4 has therefore introduced me to the importance of what Benedict is to make the subject of the following chapters. He starts by looking at obedience, but all three are closely linked, for humility is essentially the emptying of my own self-love and self-will, and obedience is the listening to God that will never be possible without interior silence. We are not to approach these in negative terms as difficult or restrictive demands, for they will all come "naturally to those who cherish Christ above all" (2), one of Benedict's marvelous short sayings. Time and again the Rule gives me little phrases, aphorisms, which I hold in my hand like some precious gem or small stone, weighing it, turning it over and over again in my mind, savoring it. So here it is: "cherish Christ above all" (2). Again, my eyes are drawn to the figure of Christ himself, central to the pages of the Rule just as Christ must have been the ever-present reality in Benedict's own life, which is what he would wish for all of us.

We are told in the first verse that this is to be unhesitating obedience. The Latin word is *statim,* at once, without delay, just abandoning everything, dropping whatever you might be doing— as the disciples put down their nets to follow Christ when he called them. This sense of urgency comes again at intervals throughout the chapter: in verse 4 we are told to act *promptly,* in verse 7 to put aside our concerns *immediately,* and in verse 9 to act so *quickly* that command and action become virtually one. This is a radical demand and it asks for a radical response, as Henri Nouwen was to discover during his seven months at the abbey of the

Genesee: "We are called to a radical break away from our selves and a total surrender to God. St. Benedict, who is often praised for his moderation and has even been called a humanist, is no less radical when he speaks about humility and obedience. . . ."

It is important to read these early verses (1-9) in junction with the third section of this chapter (14-19), otherwise it might suggest a promptness and alacrity to do what one is told to do that would be supine, subservient. Those final verses show us that obedience comes from the heart, that it is a joyful, generous response, a joyful running, whole-hearted and not half-hearted. The original meaning of the word "obedience" is to listen intently, and to respond, and when I see it in these terms it opens up for me the idea of becoming receptive. Fr. Leonard Vickers thinks that we can be clearer about the nature of obedience if we think of it as "acceptance." When we put ourselves first, when we insist on our own way, we know that we are not accepting our lives as God's gift. So in giving us a list of what he has learned to accept at many different stages in his life, he starts with: "I must accept my being and life from my Creator as a gift and a task," and concludes: "Finally, I must accept my own weakness and limitations." Obedience calls for the determination to go on, to say yes, to refuse nothing. Obedience is therefore a matter of growth. That very first word of the Rule, "Listen," is one that I must return to time and time again, for only a listening with total openness can bring me spiritual growth.

Benedict's understanding of obedience is essentially scriptural, and it is necessary to keep this in mind if we are to put it into the right perspective. He is basing this teaching on two texts, one from Luke (10 and 15) and the other from John (13). Both involve Christ, but from differing perspectives. Luke 10:16 is about Christian authority: "He who hears you hears me," words spoken by Christ to the seventy-two disciples as he sends them out on their preaching missions to the Palestinian towns. If the abbot is believed to hold the place of Christ in the community (2,2), then the monk can presume that the superior is a reliable mediator of God's will. But John 6:38 is about Christ's own obedience: "I have come not to do my own will, but the will of him who sent me." In verse 13 Benedict tells us that we must join Christ in that obedience, that sharing in the passion, and so here our understanding of obedience must take us into the paschal mystery. The loneliness in the garden, the anguish, and the cost of saying "not as I will but as you will" show me the lengths to which that obedience goes.

But when Benedict reminds me that it is love that underlies obedience, the love of Christ, it becomes easier to make the connection between obedience and freedom. It is the voice of Christ that is heard in the abbot, in superiors, in one another. How do I experience this in my own life? I come to discover the will of God through people, teachings, institutions, traditions. Benedict's spirituality is all about listening and about the totality of listening. It begins with listening to the Word itself, for it is the Word that shapes and judges us. Just as Benedict himself is totally fed, directed, energized by the Scriptures, he expects the same for us. We are to listen to the Rule since it is through the Rule that the voice of the Gospel is made practical and immediate in daily life.

Next there comes the voice of the community, the father and the brothers, the mother and the sisters. For those of us outside the monastery or the convent, there are equally the demands and insights of those with whom we live, beginning with parents, and then teachers and tutors, employers and managers, spiritual directors and gurus. It is here that we learn mutual listening, mutual giving and receiving. Finally, we are to listen to the world around since we are placed in this world as part of it, and the material is not separated from the spiritual. Can we learn to handle this material world so that God may reach us in it and through it?

It is listening to the voice of God wherever that may be found. What a total demand this is, how fundamental, how far reaching. If I could be selective, I might do quite well. But Benedict has no time for the easy option. If he is leading me to wholeness, it is impossible unless there is a complete opening up of myself to the voice of God in the many and varied ways in which he is reaching out to me. Every time that I face a choice or make a decision, I find myself in particular circumstances to which I must be obedient. As a writer I can only be creative if I impose on myself certain disciplines and limitations so that ideas are translated into words. Just as being responsive to these demands will shape what I finally produce, my obedience to God's will rather than my own will shape me into what I am created to be.

It is reassuring that Benedict knows that this is not easy. I am grateful that in the prologue he spoke of the labor of obedience and told me that the way will be narrow at the start: "Do not be daunted immediately by fear and run away from the road that leads to salvation. It is bound to be narrow at the outset" (Prol., 48). Verse 11 and the quotation from St. Matthew's Gospel bring that back to mind. But it remains the cornerstone on which the whole way of life of the Rule is built. At the heart of my original sin lies my propensity to do my own will rather than the will of God, to judge as good whatever attracts me, and to follow my own desires of the moment, giving in to my own whims and appetites (12). Now I am being told to turn away, just as Christ himself turned away, to follow instead the will of God (13). Again we are brought back to the figure of Christ.

This labor is a very real labor of the heart. It is possible only when I listen with the ear of the heart. So obedience, as Benedict is showing me, lies in listening to the voice of God rather than my own voice, laboring, struggling to know what is required of me. This is, as Augustine Roberts tells me, a very delicate operation. It is one that respects my freedom. The one thing that obedience is not is dependence, for dependence is the way in which I avoid responsibility, it is static, it is an obstacle to psychological growth.

In this final section (from verse 14) Benedict tells me once again that mere outward conformity, appearing to be willing and docile, is simply not good enough. Grumbling is mentioned four times in this chapter. I enjoy the Latin word *murmurare* or *murmuratio* because of the way in which its sound demonstrates what that incessant noise is like. When Thomas Merton was teaching his novices about *murmuratio,* he gave them the Old English translation, "grouching, griping," and told them it was like cramps in the stomach. This is a vivid etymology and describes something that most of us will recognize: that sort of inner cramp, constant complaining, that seizes us and holds us in its grip and will not let us go. Merton went on to liken it to a vice that gets a grip on the soul or to a disease that can cause serious damage. He said that it was vital and essential to root it out. It remains hidden, it goes on in the heart, for it lacks the courage to show itself outwardly for what it is, a lack of love. Benedict writes about it vigorously and at length, for he knows just how serious a matter it is and how destructive it can be. Interior griping of this sort ruins otherwise valid obedience. God is displeased with it (18) and, knowing the secrets of the heart, looks on it with disfavor. Mere outward compliance will not do. Obedience should come cheerfully, freely, and gladly. It is only when I remind myself that obedience is *ob-audiens,* listening intently to God rather than listening to my own self, that what Benedict is telling me—even though it may still seem difficult—is not impossible, for it is a response of love to love.

CHAPTER SIX

¹Let us follow the Prophet's counsel: *I said, I have resolved to keep watch over my ways that I may never sin with my tongue. I have put a guard on my mouth. I was silent and was humbled, and I refrained even from good words* (Ps 38[39]:2-3). ²Here the Prophet indicates that there are times when good words are to be left unsaid out of esteem for silence. For all the more reason, then, should evil speech be curbed so that punishment for sin may be avoided. ³Indeed, so important is silence that permission to speak should seldom be granted even to mature disciples, no matter how good or holy or constructive their talk, ⁴because it is written: *In a flood of words you will not avoid sin* (Prov 10:19); ⁵and elsewhere, *The tongue holds the key to life and death* (Prov 18:21). ⁶Speaking and teaching are the master's task; the disciple is to be silent and listen.

⁷Therefore, any requests to a superior should be made with all humility and respectful submission. ⁸We absolutely condemn in all places any vulgarity and gossip and talk leading to laughter, and we do not permit a disciple to engage in words of that kind.

When there is so much writing and talking today about silence—such idealization of solitude and romantic talk of the desert—I have to confess that to read what Benedict has to say about keeping silent seems at first a grave disappointment. But if I am to fully appreciate what Benedict expects of silence, and understand why he sees it as so formative, I need to keep in mind what he is saying about it elsewhere in the Rule. In chapter 38 (5-9) he speaks of silence in relationship to the Word, and in chapter 52, in relationship to prayer, the keeping of silence after the divine office so that those who remain can pray over the Word. There is thus a connection between silence and God's revelation in the Word. As Dietrich Bonhoeffer wrote, "We keep silence solely for the sake of the Word, and therefore not in order to show disregard for the Word but rather to honour and receive it."

This chapter might seem to open with entirely negative reasons for silence unless I keep in mind the important distinction between *taciturnitas* (used in verses 2 and 3), which simply means not speaking, and *silentium,* which is the wider understanding of being still and silent. The first quotation, from Psalm 38 (39), gives the motivation for guarding one's tongue as the avoidance of sin through evil speech (2), and again in verses 4 and 5 the emphasis is on restraint of speech in order to avoid sin. So I am brought back once again to the fear of the Lord always present in judgment, an idea that has come up earlier in the prologue in verses 17 and 25-26 where Benedict has given the desire for eternal life as the motivation for the guarding of the tongue.

In verse 5 he does not mince his own words when quoting from Proverbs: *"The tongue holds the key to life and death."* The passage from which this phrase is taken suggests that anyone who loves words will tend to let themselves be satisfied by them, and as a result stop short of true satisfaction. For true satisfaction— and here at last in the following verse comes the moment that I have been waiting for—comes when I am silent and listen. Finally, we are told why silence is so important. As soon as I read this it takes me at once back to the opening words of the Rule and to the need to listen. Benedict's spirituality, if I were to reduce it to one single concept, is that of listening to the voice of God in my life. When God's voice is drowned out by incessant clamor, whether inner or outer, in whatever shape or form, then continuous dialogue with God becomes impossible. An inner monologue with myself, constant chatter with others, the invasion of the spoken word through the press and television are all the ever-present realities in my daily life over which I need to exercise some sort of discipline if I am to keep any quiet inner space in which to listen to the Word. This is the stillness of heart, the guarding of the heart, which touches the very deepest levels of my consciousness.

Benedict does not so often use the word *discipulus* as *frater* (thirteen times compared with 102), for he prefers to address us as sons or daughters rather than as pupils or students. It is, therefore, more significant that it should come in this chapter, and I take it to mean that he is treating me as someone who needs to learn. Silence is a working tool that I need if I am to listen and to learn. So if I am being addressed as disciple, I must examine very seriously the issues that Benedict is raising in this chapter. Benedict gives me not so much speculation or theological discussion about the role of silence, rather he is insisting that to hear the Word, which is both the means and the end of the Christian life, we must be able to hold on to silence in the face of both the internal and the external threats.

The title usually given to this chapter is "restraint of speech," and restraint must be one of the most neglected virtues at the moment. To be asked to take it seriously will therefore be something of a challenge. Benedict has no illusions about the harm that I can do with my tongue, whether it is grumbling, gossip, the wrong sort of laughter, the easy dismissing of another. Spoken words are a reflection of what is going on in my heart, and an uncleansed heart can be a dangerous and destructive thing. In the final verse of the chapter, he totally and absolutely condemns loose talk and idle words. The English translation does not bring out the force of the Latin, for *aeterna clausura* carries the image of enclosure, so that the mouth is like the door of an inner cloister and Benedict wants that door shut, closed to certain kinds of speaking. It is quite clear that silence was not total in Benedict's monastery. It is clear that there was normal social conversation between the brethren (see 26,1-2 for example). In 67,5-6 it is taken for granted that a brother who has been out has occasion to recount his experiences. In chapter 68 we see the proper place for discussion between a monk and the superior, and this discussion is very carefully described: patiently, at the right moment, without pride or obstinacy. It is clear that Benedict is trying to help us with the discipline of how to handle speech and is looking at the right, gentle, positive way of breaking silence. Speaking is something that must be undertaken reverently and responsibly. If I reflect on what he is saying, I find guidelines for my own situation. This is not a call for absolute silence (silence can after all become an instrument of the passive aggressive, and it can be isolating, hurtful), but for a restrained, disciplined, and thoughtful approach to speech.

CHAPTER SEVEN

¹Brothers, divine Scripture calls to us saying: *Whoever exalts himself shall be humbled, and whoever humbles himself shall be exalted* (Luke 14:11; 18:14). ²In saying this, therefore, it shows us that every exaltation is a kind of pride, ³which the Prophet indicates he has shunned, saying: *Lord, my heart is not exalted; my eyes are not lifted up and I have not walked in the ways of the great nor gone after marvels beyond me* (Ps 130[131]:1). ⁴And why? *If I had not a humble spirit, but were exalted instead, then you would treat me like a weaned child on its mother's lap* (Ps 130[131]:2).

⁵Accordingly, brothers, if we want to reach the highest summit of humility, if we desire to attain speedily that exaltation in heaven to which we climb by the humility of this present life, ⁶then by our ascending actions we must set up that ladder on which Jacob in a dream saw *angels descending and ascending* (Gen 28:12). ⁷Without doubt, this descent and ascent can signify only that we descend by exaltation and ascend by humility. ⁸Now the ladder erected is our life on earth, and if we humble our hearts the Lord will raise it to heaven. ⁹We may call our body and soul the sides of this ladder, into which our divine vocation has fitted the various steps of humility and discipline as we ascend.

¹⁰The first step of humility, then, is that a man keeps the *fear of God always before his eyes* (Ps 35[36]:2) and never forgets it. ¹¹He must constantly remember everything God has commanded, keeping in mind that all who despise God will burn in hell for their sins, and all who fear God have everlasting life awaiting them. ¹²While he guards himself at every moment from sins and vices of thought or tongue, of hand or foot, of self-will or bodily desire, ¹³let

53

him recall that he is always seen by God in heaven, that his actions everywhere are in God's sight and are reported by angels at every hour.

¹⁴The Prophet indicates this to us when he shows that our thoughts are always present to God, saying: *God searches hearts and minds* (Ps 7:10); ¹⁵again he says: *The Lord knows the thoughts of men* (Ps 93[94]:11); ¹⁶likewise, *From afar you know my thoughts* (Ps 138[139]:3); ¹⁷and, *The thought of man shall give you praise* (Ps 75[76]:11). ¹⁸That he may take care to avoid sinful thoughts, the virtuous brother must always say to himself: *I shall be blameless in his sight* if *I guard myself from my own wickedness* (Ps 17[18]:24).

¹⁹Truly, we are forbidden to do our own will, for Scripture tells us: *Turn away from your desires* (Sir 18:30). ²⁰And in the Prayer too we ask God that his *will be done* in us (Matt 6:10). ²¹We are rightly taught not to do our own will, since we dread what Scripture says: *There are ways which men call right that in the end plunge into the depths of hell* (Prov 16:25). ²²Moreover, we fear what is said of those who ignore this: *They are corrupt and have become depraved in their desires* (Ps 13[14]:1).

²³As for the desires of the body, we must believe that God is always with us, for *All my desires are known to you* (Ps 37[38]:10), as the Prophet tells the Lord. ²⁴We must then be on guard against any base desire, because death is stationed near the gateway of pleasure. ²⁵For this reason Scripture warns us, *Pursue not your lusts* (Sir 18:30).

²⁶Accordingly, if *the eyes of the Lord are watching the good and the wicked* (Prov 15:3), ²⁷if at all times *the Lord looks down from heaven on the sons of men to see whether any understand and seek God* (Ps 13[14]:2); ²⁸and if every day the angels assigned to us report our deeds to the Lord day and night, ²⁹then, brothers, we must be vigilant every hour or, as the Prophet says in the psalm, God may observe us *falling* at some time into evil and *so made worthless* (Ps 13[14]:3). ³⁰After sparing us for a while because he is a loving father who waits for us to improve, he may tell us later, *This you did, and I said nothing* (Ps 49[50]:21).

³¹The second step of humility is that a man loves not his own will nor takes pleasure in the satisfaction of his desires;

[32]rather he shall imitate by his actions that saying of the Lord: *I have come not to do my own will, but the will of him who sent me* (John 6:38). [33]Similarly we read, "Consent merits punishment; constraint wins a crown."

[34]The third step of humility is that a man submits to his superior in all obedience for the love of God, imitating the Lord of whom the Apostle says: *He became obedient even to death* (Phil 2:8).

[35]The fourth step of humility is that in this obedience under difficult, unfavorable, or even unjust conditions, his heart quietly embraces suffering [36]and endures it without weakening or seeking escape. For Scripture has it: *Anyone who perseveres to the end will be saved* (Matt 10:22), [37]and again, *Be brave of heart and rely on the Lord* (Ps 26[27]:14). [38]Another passage shows how the faithful must endure everything, even contradiction, for the Lord's sake, saying in the person of those who suffer, *For your sake we are put to death continually; we are regarded as sheep marked for slaughter* (Rom 8:36; Ps 43[44]:22). [39]They are so confident in their expectation of reward from God that they continue joyfully and say, *But in all this we overcome because of him who so greatly loved us* (Rom 8:37). [40]Elsewhere Scripture says: *O God, you have tested us, you have tried us as silver is tried by fire; you have led us into a snare, you have placed afflictions on our backs* (Ps 65[66]:10-11). [41]Then, to show that we ought to be under a superior, it adds: *You have placed men over our heads* (Ps 65[66]:12).

[42]In truth, those who are patient amid hardships and unjust treatment are fulfilling the Lord's command: *When struck on one cheek, they turn the other; when deprived of their coat, they offer their cloak also; when pressed into service for one mile, they go two* (Matt 5:39-41). [43]With the Apostle Paul, they bear with *false brothers, endure persecution,* and *bless those who curse them* (2 Cor 11:26; 1 Cor 4:12).

[44]The fifth step of humility is that a man does not conceal from his abbot any sinful thoughts entering his heart, or any wrongs committed in secret, but rather confesses them humbly. [45]Concerning this, Scripture exhorts us: *Make known your way to the Lord and hope in him* (Ps 36[37]:5). [46]And again, *Confess to the Lord, for he is good; his mercy*

is forever (Ps 105[106]:1; Ps 117[118]:1). ⁴⁷So too the Prophet: *To you I have acknowledged my offense; my faults I have not concealed.* ⁴⁸*I have said: Against myself I will report my faults to the Lord, and you have forgiven the wickedness of my heart* (Ps 31[32]:5).

⁴⁹The sixth step of humility is that a monk is content with the lowest and most menial treatment, and regards himself as a poor and worthless workman in whatever task he is given, ⁵⁰saying to himself with the Prophet: *I am insignificant and ignorant, no better than a beast before you, yet I am with you always* (Ps 72[73]:22-23).

⁵¹The seventh step of humility is that a man not only admits with his tongue but is also convinced in his heart that he is inferior to all and of less value, ⁵²humbling himself and saying with the Prophet: *I am truly a worm, not a man, scorned by men and despised by the people* (Ps 21[22]:7). ⁵³*I was exalted, then I was humbled and overwhelmed with confusion* (Ps 87[88]:16). ⁵⁴And again, *It is a blessing that you have humbled me so that I can learn your commandments* (Ps 118[119]:71, 73).

⁵⁵The eighth step of humility is that a monk does only what is endorsed by the common rule of the monastery and the example set by his superiors.

⁵⁶The ninth step of humility is that a monk controls his tongue and remains silent, not speaking unless asked a question, ⁵⁷for Scripture warns, *In a flood of words you will not avoid sinning* (Prov 10:19), ⁵⁸and, *A talkative man goes about aimlessly on earth* (Ps 139[140]:12).

⁵⁹The tenth step of humility is that he is not given to ready laughter, for it is written: *Only a fool raises his voice in laughter* (Sir 21:23).

⁶⁰The eleventh step of humility is that a monk speaks gently and without laughter, seriously and with becoming modesty, briefly and reasonably, but without raising his voice, ⁶¹as it is written: "A wise man is known by his few words."

⁶²The twelfth step of humility is that a monk always manifests humility in his bearing no less than in his heart, so that it is evident ⁶³at the Work of God, in the oratory, the monastery or the garden, on a journey or in the field, or anywhere else. Whether he sits, walks or stands, his head

must be bowed and his eyes cast down. ⁶⁴Judging himself always guilty on account of his sins, he should consider that he is already at the fearful judgment, ⁶⁵and constantly say in his heart what the publican in the Gospel said with downcast eyes: *Lord, I am a sinner, not worthy to look up to heaven* (Luke 18:13). ⁶⁶And with the Prophet: *I am bowed down and humbled in every way* (Ps 37[38]:7-9; Ps 118[119]:107).

⁶⁷Now, therefore, after ascending all these steps of humility, the monk will quickly arrive at that *perfect love* of God which *casts out fear* (1 John 4:18). ⁶⁸Through this love, all that he once performed with dread, he will now begin to observe without effort, as though naturally, from habit, ⁶⁹no longer out of fear of hell, but out of love fcr Christ, good habit and delight in virtue. ⁷⁰All this the Lord will by the Holy Spirit graciously manifest in his workman now cleansed of vices and sins.

What has gone before in the earlier chapters has predisposed me to listen, and I have found a master who is at once gentle and understanding, tough and demanding. Benedict now gives me one of the longest, perhaps the most crucial, of the chapters in the Rule. It is the final part of this opening section of the Rule that deals with underlying, spiritual questions. I am therefore now ready to undertake this exploration into *humility,* which is better translated as exploration into reality, into the reality of being earthed in myself and God. The derivation of the word from *humus,* "earth," is enormously reassuring. For so often the idea of humility that springs to mind is servile and unattractive, while to be earthed, centered, with my feet on the ground immediately appeals to me. Here we are given one of the most profound explorations into self-knowledge, that true self-knowledge that is not in the least narcissistic but leads me on to the true self and so to God.

Benedict opens this chapter with a quotation from the Gospel of Luke and, in the context of everything that has preceded it, this is just what I should expect, that what I am about to hear should be based on the Word. He takes it from that episode in Luke where Christ is speaking to the Pharisees, those people who were comfortably and complacently self-righteous. But the externals of self-righteousness will not stand up to the judgment of the Word that cuts like a two-edged sword. The Word reverses everything: high becomes low, rich becomes poor, the empty are filled so that, as the Sermon on the Mount shows, the value system of the world is totally upset.

Ever since I can remember I have grown up in a world that is highly competitive, that likes success, that encourages me to play roles. I like to be busy, appreciated, applauded. It is important to me that I am seen to be a success at school and college, in my work, my career, my salary, in the sort of household I run, in the social life I lead. I am looking for applause and self-validation. Yet Benedict is asking of me the honesty that means that I cease to play games, whether with myself, with others, with God. Unless I desire this with the whole of my being, to the extent that I am willing to undergo a holocaust to achieve it, as one Cistercian abbot puts it so dramatically, then it is hardly worth beginning. For it will mean embarking on a ruthless campaign against all forms of illusion, and this is a thoroughly alarming undertaking. It is also a lengthy undertaking, in which there are no shortcuts. "Our rebirth in integrity takes time and many repentances."

But the quotation from the psalms in verse 4 shows me that this is a gentle exercise. The psalmist is saying that he eschews whatever might be pretentious, presumptuous, arrogant, and instead his soul rests tranquilly, trusting in God just as a small child will lie trustfully on its mother's breast. The reference to weaning is confusing if it suggests any form of dependency. Christ, always Benedict's model, demanded that we become as little children (he himself totally trusted the Father), but with that maturity which he hopes for from all of us. When so often my own life seems to be dominated by struggle, expectation, external demands, I want now to stay with this image of the gentle, tender, and trusting relationship of mother and child, and to tell myself that this same absolute, unconditional trust in God is the prerequisite for embarking on Benedict's ladder.

Once again what Benedict is looking for from me has nothing to do with external behavioral patterns, but with the disposition of my heart. Humility makes no sense if it is regarded as an end in itself; it is the way of the disciple, part of the learning process of anyone who is following the master who says, "Learn of me, for I am meek and humble of heart." Here, if I am willing to listen and to follow, is a "return to truth." When there are so many alternative therapies and techniques that promise self-knowledge and self-awareness, what is it that Benedict is offering me? There are three aspects of his approach that I greatly like and find reassuring. First, it is strictly scriptural, and that brings me firmly back to base all the time. Second, he is presenting me with an interior journey, a process that will never end, yet one that does not necessarily involve the familiar pattern of movement toward some successful and predetermined goal. I see the steps as indicators carrying me forward, yet as I come to each I never leave any behind, for I simultaneously need all of them all the time. Perhaps I should think more of a spiraling and never-ending inward process, a process that will go on until death. Third, it is an undertaking that involves the whole of myself, body as well as mind and spirit. If I look at Psalm 130 (131), which is quoted in verse 2, I can see what a total commitment this is, for the heart in its ancient usage was the center of the personality, and I take eyes to indicate the way in which I see the world and relate to others, and walk to include all my physical activity. The two sides of the ladder, which is essentially what this chapter is all about, are the body and the soul. Both are needed, neither must be pulling against the other, for both have a vital role to play and are equally important.

In verse 6 Benedict brings us to the image of the ladder, that ancient classical symbol of unity and integration. It reaches from earth to heaven, and for Benedict, of course, the ground on which it was placed was the monastic enclosure, but for those of us outside any religious community, it can just be taken to mean the place of our ordinary life and work, wherever we may find ourselves. It was St. Augustine who gave us those marvellous words, "Do you seek God? Seek within yourself and ascend through yourself." Like the child now weaned I have to take on the responsibility of growing into my own maturity. There can be no escape and no postponement. It lies with me.

Having presented me with this ladder, Benedict again reverses everything, and I find that up is down and ascending is descending. This is the self-emptying of Christ himself, which Paul celebrated in his wonderful hymn in Philippians and which Benedict will be quoting in the third step. While it must ultimately remain a mystery, it is yet also something whose truth I experience in my own life when loss, displacement, and letting go become a place of new truth, a step forward into a deeper understanding of God and of myself. Of course, this need not necessarily be so, and this can also be a negative process, destructive, full of recrimination, resentment, and confusion. I know how much I need help in this painful exodus toward total freedom, and it is in order to find it that I turn to these twelve steps to initiate, for me, "a process of deliverance."

That small phrase gives me a keynote with which to encounter this chapter. To work through Benedict's ladder is therefore going to be a journey into freedom. I have to realize at the outset that this is not some once and for all exercise, but something that I shall continue to do time and time again throughout my life. Although the steps are presented sequentially, they are also integral one with the other, so I shall be moving on all of them together, both simultaneously and consecutively.

Step 1, verses 10-30

What is the spring of my thinking and acting? Benedict at once asks whether I keep a fear of God, a sense of his presence always, always uppermost in my mind. Without this, all that will follow will be utterly useless, hollow. I may deceive others, and I may deceive myself, but God knows my innermost thoughts, *"From afar you know my thoughts"* (16). This is the God who sees me and knows me at every moment of my life.

In the prologue Benedict had established that he wanted us all to awake from sleep and be alive, alert, aware. The opposite of this is forgetfulness, *oblivio,* which is a comfortable almost complacent way of drifting along. *Memoria,* mindfulness, on the other hand is going to wake me and help me to live fully attuned to the presence of God in my life and what that is asking of me.

As I read this I am struck by the force with which Benedict addresses me. He strikes home again and again, repeating himself, hammering it in—always, always he says at intervals in verses 13-18. In the Latin the word *semper* sounds almost like the blows of a hammer. Am I always, always aware of the presence of God? Benedict is shaped by the psalms, steeped in them, so it is hardly surprising that verses 14-18 are a mosaic of quotations from the psalms insistent on the God who searches me, probes my innermost depths, knows all my thoughts. The implications of what this means are quite terrifying. All my subterfuges are unmasked. All the ways in which I delude myself are revealed for what they are—escapes from making real that phrase of the Lord's Prayer that I pray daily that it may be God's will and not my own that I follow. So the next group of verses (19-22) takes on this theme of my own self-will and the will of God for me. If I consciously ask whether what I am doing is part of the working out of the will of God in my life or not, then I have a rigorous guideline to apply. Verses 23-25 remind me once again that it is the whole of myself with which Benedict is concerned, total, all the senses.

The final verses of this first step return again to Benedict's insistence on mindfulness of God's presence in my life. This is the God who is always looking down on me, watching me. If my response is one of vigilance it is because this is a presence of love, that of a father who so believes in his child that he puts on us the expectation that we will respond to that love. He waits patiently believing in me. How can I then fail to respond to a loving father who knows me through and through, watches and waits?

Step 2, verses 31-33

It might be all very well to think about this, to recognize it all in theory, but Benedict is looking for good thoughts to be translated into good actions. Therefore, if I am not to live a life that is a sham, I must take this second step, submission to God's will. But I must do this for the most fundamental reason of all, the reason without which nothing in the Rule can ever make sense, and that is that in all these things I am following Christ. I model myself on him, the Christ who says, "I came not to do my own will. . . ." This means that I am being asked to give up my self-will. This is not my free will which is one of God's greatest gifts to me.

The question is that of responsibility: How am I going to use it? I have the choice to use it to serve my own drives and impulses and assert my independence (which in the end means my self-centeredness), or to use it to return to Christ. If I have a firm grasp on this second rung, I find myself pointed toward God rather than my own self; I open myself up to letting my life be guided by the law and governance of God rather than my own wants and concerns. I am being asked to make my life an earnest search for the will of God. That would never be possible if I did not have the pattern of Christ himself and his own relationship with the Father. But how deeply attached am I to my own ambitions and desires? Until I can be honest about this I am not ready to go any further.

Step 3, verse 34

How do I know what is God's will? Where do I begin to find it, search it out? Benedict continues to develop this point: it lies in the imitation of Christ's own obedience. When I turn to look at Christ, I see that in his life the motive force is love, which is, of course, the point that Benedict is making. But the working out of this obedience in my own life is something that needs the support of human guidance and direction. This does not have so much to do with the acceptance of authority as with the renunciation of power. I do not necessarily have the final answer, the clearest understanding. I have to be ready to listen to the words, directions, insights of the one who is the voice of Christ for me. To resist those who can bring that help and guidance in my life (parents, teachers, Church) is, in Joan Chittister's words, "a dangerous excursion into arrogance and a denial of the very relationships that are the stuff of which our sanctity is made."

Christ's obedience was obedience unto death. This gives me the perspective. I am being asked to let go of something in me that must die before the new can be born. Two things help to make this possible: that the motive force is love; that I do it in imitation of Christ. At this point in the commentary, it becomes impossible to deal in words. I find that I simply need to stand in silence at the foot of the cross, the place where words cease. I ask myself whether I am ready, for the love of God, to face up to whatever may be asked of me in following Christ in this obedience.

Step 4, verses 35-43

Benedict, being a realist, knows that life is unfair—perhaps the most important lesson that all parents should teach their children at an early age. But how am I going to handle this? I know only too well how destructive it is to my own inner peace of mind when I fall into a self-justifying, inner conversation full of recrimination and resentment in which I tell God (and probably any other audience that I can find) that life is unjust, that I have done nothing to deserve such treatment. It is destructive of my sense of my own self-worth, for I know that I deserve better than this. While I am deafening myself with all this turmoil, I fail to hear Benedict when he is telling me to *"be brave of heart and rely on the Lord"* (37). Only dependence on God can see me through this. He even goes so far as to speak in verse 39 not simply of courage but of holding on *joyfully.* That is possible "because of him who so greatly loved us" (Rom 8:37).

I can hear what Benedict is saying because I feel that he knows the degree and the complexity of suffering, and he is not patronizing me, as so many well-meaning friends seem to do in times of trouble, by saying that they understand what I am going through or that the whole thing is somehow enobling. The biblical quotations that he uses bring vivid images of every conceivable sort of pain: being put to death; being led into a snare; being tried as silver is tried by fire; having affliction placed on our backs; being struck on the cheek; being deprived of a cloak. Each of these presents itself to me as an image of the different ways in which I have experienced injustice at various times in my life.

But Benedict, in verses 42-43, puts everything into perspective by asking if that is not something that I should expect if I am following Christ. It is the knowledge of Christ crucified, the example of Christ on the cross, that is at the heart of Benedict's ascesis here. It is the daily perseverance in all the trials and difficulties of my life that conforms me to the example of Christ as he suffers on the cross. Perseverance, patience, stability, holding on, not seeking to escape—the virtues of patience in the fullest meaning of that word and its derivation from the Latin *patientia,* suffering, deepens the way in which I understand it.

But it is the quiet heart of the opening verse to which I return as I try to make this fourth step into a prayer that I may have the strength and the courage to hold on quietly and in patience. For if I am patient under these circumstances, I am fulfilling the new law, the law of the Gospel, the law of the Sermon on the Mount. Benedict sets it out, quoting from St. Matthew's Gospel, to show me that we must bear injuries with patience, love, and forgiveness so that we may overcome evil with good. Listening to the voice of Christ, I realize that what I am being asked to do here is simply to fulfill the law of love, which is where in the end everything in Benedict's rule of life is leading me.

Step 5, verses 44-48

Here comes a pivotal step. Hitherto Benedict has been concerned with my inner world of motive, disposition, and intention.

Now he is asking me to tear down the walls of my private inner sanctuary and to become open and vulnerable to others. I must not expect to be able to manage on my own; that would indeed be an example of self-sufficiency and a lack of dependency. If I am to grow, I must be ready and open for self-disclosure and interaction with others. I have to be ready to admit my own weaknesses and limitations and not be either too proud or too self-sufficient not to lean on others and to ask them to support me. The struggles we hide, psychologists tell us, are the struggles that consume us.

Self-revelation is necessary to growth. There is nothing more debilitating than going over and over again in my own mind my secret sins and failings. But onto whom shall I unload it all? When Benedict suggests the abbot, I interpret that in my own circumstances. This means someone who is wise, standing in a position of authority, and, most important of all, taking the place of Christ. Then I can confess my weakness, both in thought and in action, receive forgiveness, and, with that help, trust in the mercy of God to transform my weakness into strength.

Step 6, verses 49-50

I am gradually being stripped of all those pretentions and games that allow me to say that I am better, superior, more interesting, and more worthwhile than other people. It is all part of the process of removing the mask. God does not want an ambitious and competitive person, but one who is content even in the lowliest of occupations. Contentment is the key word. (Later on Benedict uses it in a very nice way to describe visiting monks who are to be encouraged to stay in the monastery if they are *content* with what they find there.) Lack of inner contentment means that I am reliant on externals, of whatever sort, for satisfaction. Lack of contentment lets me become trapped in the coils of the competitive society, competing for material goods, social status, the sort of car I drive, the place in which I live. I must not forget that these steps are steps into freedom, and their purpose is to help me to disentangle myself from all that would prevent inner freedom.

The short quotation from Psalm 72 (73) in verse 50 shows me where to find the heart of this step, the small phrase that sums it all up: *"I am with you always."* In the words of the Grail translation it becomes a prayer:

I was always in your presence
You were holding me by your right hand
You will guide me with your counsel
And you will lead me to glory. . . .

Step 7, verses 51-54

On a first and superficial reading, the vocabulary that Benedict is using makes for difficulties. It is when I put it into the context of sixth-century Italy that I can better appreciate it. Here was
a society of conflicting cultures in which tribal, social, and economic divisions marked status and place in society, the result being that individual worth was apparently determined by external
marks. Now Benedict is telling us that in the eyes of the heavenly
father all of this is totally irrelevant. Instead, we should take as
our example the one who was content to make of himself a servant. Christ as the suffering servant of Isaiah is an image that
will come again in the Rule. It is part of the riches of that portrait of Christ which Benedict is giving me as a model to follow.

This step has nothing to do with doubts about my self-worth.
It has to do with accepting my own fragility and smallness (and
how much we all owe to Jean Vanier, who has helped us to see
that our woundedness and weakness are blessings). What is essential is that I do not lie to myself about this, that I deal gently
with myself, and that, of course, I deal gently with others who
are just like me. For the older I grow the more I realize that behind the facades that people present to the world there is fear and
insecurity and perhaps emptiness. When I am so vulnerable there
is a temptation to develop a hard shell, to grow a thick skin—the
metaphor is an apt one! But if I accept myself as ordinary, weak,
frail, in other words, totally human and totally dependent upon
God, then I am stripped of any sense of being in some way set
apart, different, superior. It is then that the genuine, real self may
begin to emerge.

I am also open to learn. I should not miss the significance of
Benedict's use of Psalm 118 (119) here. This is above all the psalm
of learning the way of God's statutes, being open and ready to
hear, standing like the publican with open hands ready to receive.
He also quotes from Psalm 21 (22), the Psalm of Christ on the
cross. As always, Benedict draws us back to the paschal mystery.

Step 8, verse 55

Just in case I am becoming complacent as a result of these earlier steps, Benedict floors me with a thoroughly down-to-earth demand in this step. He tells me to stay in line, keep a low profile, not draw attention to myself. This must mean in my situation, outside a community, that I should be willing to be guided by others, to remain in the main-stream, and not become a law to myself. In a world of alternative therapies and spiritualities, it is humbling to be told to stay with the tradition; in an individualistic world to be reminded of corporate wisdom. I am brought back to one of the most vital of all the threads that run through the Rule: the tension of the individual and the community, the separate and together, solitary and shared. I am inserted into a set of concentric circles—marriage, family, work, parish, wider interests—and I have a responsibility to play my part in all of these. Much of this may involve dull and mundane demands when I would prefer things to be more exciting or rewarding. But to walk in step with others inserts me into a common humanity and earths me into the reality of ordinary life from which Benedict never wants us to escape.

Steps 9–11, verses 56–61

I like the way in which each successive step of the spiral leads me on to the next. If I had been given these three steps, which are about silence, stillness, gentleness, at the beginning, I would have come to them in a very different frame of mind. Treatises on attentiveness and mindfulness, inner stillness (particularly drawing on the understanding of the East) are immensely attractive, often beguiling, but they can also encourage introspection. I wonder if Benedict is not extremely shrewd in asking me to face the question of silence in the context of the world outside of myself. I have an enormous amount to learn along the way in my journey of discipleship, and I need to learn it from others. If I talk too much, then I cannot hear. If I laugh too readily, make the clever and witty comment to turn something into a joke, then I can dismiss what I may not want to hear, or fail to take it seriously.

These three steps are about my right relationships with others. Speech can lead to openness, to learning, and to growth, or it can become a trap into which I plunge, and endless talk can become an excuse for putting off action, for achieving nothing. The words that Benedict chooses in verse 60, gently—seriously, briefly, reasonably—are all immensely wise. The psalm from which the quotation in verse 58 comes is one in which verbal violence is explored, a prayer asking to be rescued

> from those who plan evil in their hearts
> and stir up strife every day;
> who sharpen their tongue like an adder's
> with the poison of viper on their lips.

Instead Benedict speaks to us of gentleness, respect for the other, willingness to listen rather than dominate, receive rather than control. If I take his advice, I shall recognize them as sensitive and wise words that I should listen to.

Step 12, verses 62-66

The steps have led from the inward outward, but the two must be united. Here again is a good grasp of the human psyche: it is vital that the inner landscape corresponds with the outer. What Benedict is looking for is the whole of myself, the total person in which the material and the spiritual are held together (like the sides of his ladder) without that disjunction and pulling apart that brings loss of energy or depression. This is a unity and integration that will be reflected in the way I behave not only at prayer, but at work. So this final step of the ladder applies to me wherever I am. It has not brought me to some glorious spiritual high. There is something iconoclastic here that reminds me of the Zen saying, "Before enlightenment hewing wood and drawing water; after enlightenment, hewing wood and drawing water."

And now at the end, in verse 65, Benedict presents me with the figure of the publican, with eyes cast down and head bowed. As I read that story in St. Luke's Gospel and see the contrast between the Pharisee and the publican, it seems to me that the Pharisee represents everything that this chapter is helping me to free myself from. If I am always concerned with the image that I present to the world, then I live nervously behind a mask, conscious of the opinion of others. If I think that God is pleased by a meticulous keeping of the law, then I anxiously try to fulfill every jot and tittle. But if I know, with the publican, that there is only one reality, and that is the mercy and love of God, then I stand there with open hands in total honesty confessing my need of that mercy and love.

Coda, verses 67-70

The chapter suddenly bursts out into a song of love, and we are given another of those lyrical pieces of writing in which Benedict reminds us yet again that this Rule is pointing us toward Christ and the gospel of love. The movement of my life is away from the negative motivation of fear toward the positive motivation of love. In verse 67 Benedict quotes from that most marvellous exposition of love in 1 John: "He that dwelleth in love dwelleth in God. . . . Herein is our love made perfect. . . . There is no fear in love but perfect love casts out fear. . . . We love him because he first loved us." Here is the summary of what the ladder of humility is all about: it is not any progression into human perfection; it is growth into a relationship of love.

As I read these two passages, St. John's and Benedict's, everything that has gone before now falls more fully into perspective. The key to my growth in humility is that it brings me closer to God as it subjects me more and more to the pull of the gravitational force of God's love. What I have been seeing in this chapter is that, as I progress in humility, so that love gains more and more complete possession of my soul. It is the work of God, but one with which I cooperate. It is a love that must grow, but no growth process comes automatically. Thus, it is only honest of Benedict to address me as worker in verse 70. That final verse also contains one of the rare mentions of the Holy Spirit. It is through the cleansing and the leading of the Spirit that I shall stay open to growth: growth into freedom, growth into love.

CHAPTER EIGHT

¹During the winter season, that is, from the first of November until Easter, it seems reasonable to arise at the eighth hour of the night. ²By sleeping until a little past the middle of the night, the brothers can arise with their food fully digested. ³In the time remaining after Vigils, those who need to learn some of the psalter or readings should study them.

⁴Between Easter and the first of November mentioned above, the time for Vigils should be adjusted so that a very short interval after Vigils will give the monks opportunity to care for nature's needs. Then, at daybreak, Lauds should follow immediately.

If I am to be the publican rather than the Pharisee, then the reality of my prayer will lie in the inner disposition and not the outward show. Benedict has predisposed me to understand the subject of prayer in all that he has been telling me in chapter 7 and so now, if in this chapter he turns naturally to the subject in an entirely practical way, this should not really surprise me. I can also now see that the three preceding chapters have been trying to help form in me the attitude that is to underlie the art of praying: the fear of the Lord, the total dependence on God, the constant awareness of God's presence, the demand of continual perseverance and patience, and, above all, the motivation of love. The whole end of life is to hear the Word and respond to it. The whole of my life is to become prayer.

But mindfulness and awareness, though the essential foundation of a life of prayer, are not in themselves sufficient. There must be some structure and framework, regular times for prayer, particularly shared prayer, and it is these that Benedict is establishing here. Prayer is never taken out of the natural flow of life itself. It is firmly inserted within the rhythm of the changing seasons, of winter and summer, of day and night, and not least of the rhythm of my own body. In a world in which the techniques of prayer are widely discussed and so many varying techniques seem to be offered, it is rather startling to have the subjects of sleep, digestion, and making time to go to the lavatory introduced into this short chapter. This, however, at once makes it clear that the daily office is tailored to suit the needs of the monks, rather than according to some idealized blueprint or an abstract principle. Benedict respects our total humanity—body, mind, and spirit—and recognizes that balance here: praying is disassociated neither from a gentle handling of bodily needs, nor from intellectual demand. The gap between the first two offices of the day is to be used for reading and for study, for memorizing the psalms in order to make them one's own, "to possess the psalms and be possessed by them."

In the world of his day, Benedict's monks would go to bed at 6:00 p.m., so that after eight full hours of sleep they would awaken at 2:00 a.m. They would thus start the day in the dark, and the slow coming of the dawn would be a symbolic daily reminder of the movement from dark to light, from sleep and death to new life. Anyone who has read what Thomas Merton has told us of his life in his hermitage at Gethsemani will know, even if they have not experienced it for themselves, that those hours before dawn are perhaps the best time of all for prayer. Merton himself would rise at 2:15 a.m., when the night was at its darkest and most silent.

> It is necessary for me to see the first point of light which begins to dawn. It is necessary to be present alone at the resurrection of Day, in blank silence when the sun appears. In this completely neutral instant I receive from the eastern woods, the tall oaks, the one word "Day" which is never the same. It is never spoken in any known language.

CHAPTER NINE

[1]During the winter season, Vigils begin with the verse: *Lord, open my lips and my mouth shall proclaim your praise* (Ps 50[51]:17). After this has been said three times, [2]the following order is observed: Psalm 3 with "Glory be to the Father"; [3]Psalm 94 with a refrain, or at least chanted; [4]an Ambrosian hymn; then six psalms with refrain.

[5]After the psalmody, a versicle is said and the abbot gives a blessing. When all are seated on the benches, the brothers in turn read three selections from the book on the lectern. After each reading a responsory is sung. [6]"Glory be to the Father" is not sung after the first two responsories, but only after the third reading. [7]As soon as the cantor begins to sing "Glory be to the Father," let all the monks rise from their seats in honor and reverence for the Holy Trinity. [8]Besides the inspired books of the Old and New Testaments, the works read at Vigils should include explanations of Scripture by reputable and orthodox catholic Fathers.

[9]When these three readings and their responsories have been finished, the remaining six psalms are sung with an "alleluia" refrain. [10]This ended, there follow a reading from the Apostle recited by heart, a versicle and the litany, that is, "Lord, have mercy." [11]And so Vigils are concluded.

The bloc of chapters 8–20 are commonly called the liturgical code, and academic discussion on the subject continues to fascinate scholars. By now there is considerable literature about it and it would not be difficult to engage with it. But I am simply content to know that Benedict gathered elements from various liturgies foreign to one another—Rome, Milan, the East—and combined and brought them together into a harmonious whole.

71

These opening chapters look at the Office of Vigils, the subject not only of chapters 8 and 9, but also 10, 11, and 14, which tells us something about the importance that Benedict gave to it. It was the Office that would end shortly before sunrise when Lauds would be said. It was unlikely to be done by candlelight, and so, except for the cantors and readers, it would mean mostly listening to the Word of God and responding with texts known by heart. It is essentially about waiting.

Lauds is the hour that symbolizes the Easter light of Christ when this spiritual longing reaches its fulfillment. Starting prayer by saying three times, "Lord, open my lips," at once proclaims that this is the work of God, that prayer is God at work in our mouth, our heart, our life. I pray not only because I am seeking God, but because God is also seeking me.

This is followed by Psalm 3, a morning prayer with the words

I lie down to rest and I sleep
I wake for the Lord upholds me.

This is followed by Psalm 94 (95) with its invitation to come in, joyfully (1), reverently (6), and penitently (8). It also has in verse 7 that wonderful line that brings us back yet again to the opening word of the Rule and to the underlying theme, "O that today you would listen to his voice." Praying should be a dialogue of listening with "the ear of your heart" (Prol., 1), and I am given this daily reminder so that I must never let my ears be closed or my heart be hardened.

This is the first time that Benedict mentions the *Gloria,* which he recommends to be used at the end of the psalms or a group of psalms. It was a way of "Christianizing" the psalms—appropriating their meaning in the light of the New Testament so that they become the words of Christ and speak of his message and his mission. It also had a particular significance at the time when the Rule was being written in the context of the current Arian heresy that emphasized the humanity of Christ to the exclusion of his divine nature. To rise therefore in public and stand and say, "Glory be to the Father, to the Son, and to the Holy Spirit" was to make a public proclamation of faith and commitment to the Trinity.

This chapter also contains the first reference to the Ambrosian hymn (4). There are many hymns attributed to St. Ambrose, composed for every day of the week for the Divine Office. Ambrose had a great reputation for hymn writing, but many hymns attributed to him cannot be authentic, and so it is difficult to know what exactly Benedict had in mind here. They change with the season, time of the day, and the day of the week.

The reading of the Word is an essential element of the night Office. But Benedict is not content with merely listening to Scripture. He also wants a deepening of our understanding of it. How can we be fed if we do not stretch our minds? It is only too easy to let familiar passages from the Bible drift over me. Benedict wants me to make use of my intellect in my prayer. This means I should study them, use my mind critically, see what others have to say about them, and let myself be humble enough to learn from their interpretations.

The Office centers upon the psalms (as it has always done from the earliest times in monasticism). The psalter was regarded as a prophetic book (which explains why Benedict, when quoting from the psalms, will often say "the Prophet says") and was read through from beginning to end. There were various ways in which the psalms might be said in choir, but then, as the monks knew them by heart, they would also rise naturally from their lips while they were at work so that "pray always," which is the essence of monastic prayer, was a reality. As Henri Nouwen became more at home with the life of the abbey of the Genesee he grew to love the psalms, and he found that they began to weave themselves into his life. I like what Nouwen says, for it is something that I too have often felt: "How happy are those who no longer need books but carry the psalms in their heart wherever they are and wherever they go. Maybe I should start learning the psalms by heart so that nobody can take them away from me." He goes on to say, "Many time I have thought: If I am ever sent to prison, if I am ever subjected to hunger, pain, torture, or humiliation, I hope and pray that they let me keep the psalms. The psalms will keep my spirit alive. . . ." That was, of course, exactly what Brian Keenan found when he spent those years imprisoned, and he discovered the great solace in the psalms.

The psalms are the songs of a journeying people, and I can identify in them many of my feelings on my own journey to God. They express hope, fear, anger, delight. They are wonderfully honest. Sometimes they seem like incantations lulling me into the certainty of the goodness of God. Sometimes they are battle hymns that will not let me forget the tremendous battle against the forces of evil that surround me. Sometimes God is close, sometimes God is distant. Sometimes they speak of fullness and riches, at other times they come out of poverty and emptiness.

"When you take the psalms seriously and receive their spirit as your own, you soon come into contact with some basic realities about human nature," says Matthew Kelty. "What are you going to do when it dawns on you that the words of David are true not only of David, but of you?" He goes on to say that the answer lies in Christ, to pray the psalter with Christ who shares our humanity and who will help us to cope with the forces of darkness that we recognize in our own depths. Whatever the mood of the psalms, or whatever my own mood, saying the psalms day in and day out, for year after year after year, no matter how I feel, unites me with thousands of men and women across all divides of time and place who have shared them with me.

CHAPTER TEN

¹From Easter until the first of November, the winter arrangement for the number of psalms is followed. ²But because summer nights are shorter, the readings from the book are omitted. In place of the three readings, one from the Old Testament is substituted. This is to be recited by heart, followed by a short responsory. ³In everything else, the winter arrangement for Vigils is kept. Thus, winter and summer, there are never fewer than twelve psalms at Vigils, not counting Psalms 3 and 94.

As the seasons change and the nights grow shorter, Benedict chooses to shorten the time of prayer rather than the time of sleep. The old and unhealthy practices of an asceticism that seemed to delight in the punishment of the body found no place in Benedict's scheme of things. The body needs its full complement of rest, and Benedict wants us to respect that. We have already seen that body, mind, and spirit each have their part to play in worship, and here once again we are shown how that balance is to be kept.

The essence of the night office—of "nightly praise"—lies here in the psalms, in the full complement of twelve. So during these summer nights the readings may be reduced, but never the psalms. The primacy of psalmody is once more emphasized.

CHAPTER ELEVEN

¹On Sunday the monks should arise earlier for Vigils. ²In these Vigils, too, there must be moderation in quantity: first, as we have already indicated, six psalms are said, followed by a versicle. Then the monks, seated on the benches and arranged in their proper order, listen to four readings from the book. After each reading a responsory is sung, ³but "Glory be to the Father" is added only to the fourth. When the cantor begins it, all immediately rise in reverence.

⁴After these readings the same order is repeated: six more psalms with refrain as before, a versicle, ⁵then four more readings and their responsories, as above. ⁶Next, three canticles from the Prophets, chosen by the abbot, are said with an "alleluia" refrain. ⁷After a versicle and the abbot's blessing, four New Testament readings follow with their responsories, as above. ⁸After the fourth responsory, the abbot begins the hymn "We praise you, God." ⁹When that is finished, he reads from the Gospels while all the monks stand with respect and awe. ¹⁰At the conclusion of the Gospel reading, all reply "Amen," and immediately the abbot intones the hymn "To you be praise." After a final blessing, Lauds begin.

¹¹This arrangement for Sunday Vigils should be followed at all times, summer and winter, ¹²unless—God forbid—the monks happen to arise too late. In that case, the readings or responsories will have to be shortened. ¹³Let special care be taken that this not happen, but if it does, the monk at fault is to make due satisfaction to God in the oratory.

In this chapter Benedict looks at the ordering of Vigils on Sunday, for it was common in monastic tradition to keep watch on

Saturday night in order to greet the coming of Sunday morning, the first day of the week, the day that celebrates both creation and resurrection. As a result the Office is longer and more solemn. It centers on the reading of the Gospel by the abbot while all the monks stand in reverence and awe. The response, "We praise you, God" precedes the Gospel, and "To you be praise" follows it (8-10). The first day of the week is one on which to remember the gift of life through our creation and the promise of new life through the resurrection.

As I read through this detailed and rather complicated chapter, I appreciate the intention that underlies it, and that is the need to impose structure and framework. Benedict is willing to make allowance for human weakness in accepting that if monks oversleep certain things will have to be shortened. He does not mind going into detail where this will result in something more humanly convenient and stimulating. A judicious concern for detail is not the same thing as fussiness (it can make the difference between banality and beauty). But he has no room in his scheme of things for chance or carelessness.

So I find that if I read through this chapter very openly and honestly, it presents me with a number of questions on which I could do well to reflect. Am I sufficiently grateful for the gift of life? Is praise as central as it should be in my prayer? Do I try to hold onto some sort of framework and structure in the pattern of my prayer? Do I keep Sunday as a day apart, a day of celebration and thanksgiving that reminds me of the place of God in my life?

CHAPTER TWELVE

¹Sunday Lauds begin with Psalm 66, said straight through
without a refrain. ²Then Psalm 50 follows with an "alleluia"
refrain. ³Lauds continue with Psalms 117 and 62, ⁴the Canticle of the Three Young Men, Psalms 148 through 150, a
reading from the Apocalypse recited by heart and followed
by a responsory, an Ambrosian hymn, a versicle, the Gospel
Canticle, the litany and the conclusion.

We know from chapter 8, verse 4 that Lauds was always
celebrated at daybreak. To welcome the dawn, greet the rising
sun, and rejoice in the coming of the light of the new day touches
a universal instinct. A Native American describes how his people,
at the turn of this century, began their day:

> In the life of the Indian, there was only one inevitable duty—the
> duty of prayer—the daily recognition of the Unseen and Eternal.
> His daily devotions were more necessary to him than daily food.
> He wakes at daybreak . . . he stands erect before the advancing
> dawn, facing the sun as it dances upon the horizon, and offers
> his unspoken orison.

It needs a leap of the imagination for those of us who live in an
artificial or an urban environment today, who have lost any close
touch with nature, to appreciate what power the sun would hold
for people in a world totally dependent on natural forces for light,
warmth, life itself.

If we look carefully at the very detailed account of the structure of Lauds on solemn feasts that Benedict gives in this chapter, we are able to appreciate the way in which it flows in a
succession of carefully thought-out steps. It opens with the in-
troductory Psalm 66 (67), which includes the verse "Let your face
shed its light upon us." In chapter 7 Benedict had reminded me

that the gaze of God is always upon us, and now I feel that this idea is carried on in the reference to the light reflected from the face of God. The psalm that follows is a penitential psalm. In the light of God's goodness I become aware of my own darkness and sin, and my cry is: "Have mercy on me, cleanse me from my sin, purify me, wash me." This act of acknowledging my weakness and failure is not a morbid dwelling on sin but a turning in confidence to the God who sees a humble and contrite heart and is there to rescue me just as he rescued his people in the past. Psalm 117 (118) is a psalm that is traditionally used to celebrate Christ's resurrection: "This is the day the Lord has made." It is a psalm of confidence that springs out of the certainty of God's care and love in the past and his continuing help today. Our God is a God who is good, his love is a love that has no end. This is the God for whom I long and Psalm 62 (63):2, 9 expresses that longing:

> My body pines for you
> like a dry, weary land without water.
> My soul clings to you;
> your right hand holds me fast.

Benedict then inserts the canticle of the three young men in the fiery furnace, the *Benedicite* from the third chapter of the Book of Daniel, which has formed part of the Christian liturgy from earliest times. In it the totality of the universe, from the furthest spheres and elements to all living things on earth, is called on to give glory to God. It always reminds me of St. Patrick's breastplate, that wonderful song of creation that also has this sense, which I find unparalleled anywhere else, of the unity of the world, of the whole created order, although in this case it starts with the Trinity, the heavens and angelic beings, and then moves through fire, water, sun, and moon to birds and beasts and man and woman. Daybreak on the first day of the week is the time above all other for thanksgiving for the wonders of the whole created world.

> Bless the Lord all created things:
> sing his praise and exalt him for ever.

The final psalms, as was common usage in both East and West, were psalms 148–150 joined together and known as the Praises (Lauds). They open:

Alleluia!
Praise the Lord from the heavens,
praise him in the heights.
Praise him, all his angels,
praise him all his host.

And they close:

Let everything that lives and that breathes
give praise to the Lord. Alleluia!

The short reading from the Book of Revelation is chosen because it carries the theme of the victory of the lamb, which is particularly appropriate for a Sunday morning. The Office then
returns to what will be said daily at Lauds throughout the coming week: the Song of Zechariah. In Jewish tradition the morning is the hour of deliverance from the darkness of night, and
here again we touch on the powerful symbolism of the movement
from dark to light and sleep to life, which has come so strongly
throughout this whole discussion of Lauds. "The dawn from on
high shall break upon us, to shine on those who dwell in darkness and the shadow of death. . . ." How easily this leads on
into the litany so that the last prayer of Sunday Lauds is outward
looking, a petition for deliverance for the Church and the world,
the sick and the suffering, those in need, in fear, in darkness.

CHAPTER THIRTEEN

¹On ordinary weekdays, Lauds are celebrated as follows: ²First, Psalm 66 is said without a refrain and slightly protracted as on Sunday so that everyone can be present for Psalm 50, which has a refrain. ³Next, according to custom, two more psalms are said in the following order: ⁴on Monday, Psalms 5 and 35; ⁵on Tuesday, Psalms 42 and 56; ⁶on Wednesday, Psalms 63 and 64; ⁷on Thursday, Psalms 87 and 89; ⁸on Friday, Psalms 75 and 91; ⁹on Saturday, Psalm 142 and the Canticle from Deuteronomy, divided into two sections, with "Glory be to the Father" after each section. ¹⁰On other days, however, a Canticle from the Prophets is said, according to the practice of the Roman Church. ¹¹Next follow Psalms 148 through 150, a reading from the Apostle recited by heart, a responsory, an Ambrosian hymn, a versicle, the Gospel Canticle, the litany and the conclusion.

¹²Assuredly, the celebration of Lauds and Vespers must never pass by without the superior's reciting the entire Lord's Prayer at the end for all to hear, because thorns of contention are likely to spring up. ¹³Thus warned by the pledge they make to one another in the very words of this prayer: *Forgive us as we forgive* (Matt 6:12), they may cleanse themselves of this kind of vice. ¹⁴At other celebrations, only the final part of the Lord's Prayer is said aloud, that all may reply: *But deliver us from evil* (Matt 6:13).

Lauds on a weekday opens with Psalm 66 (67) and Psalm 50 (51) as in the Office of Sunday. These are permanent features of this morning Office because they express two things that Benedict wants us always to keep together in tension. In the first psalm comes a plea for continued grace, which asks, "May God still

81

give us his blessing," and in the second a recognition of our need for continual forgiveness:

> Have mercy on me, God, in your kindness
> In your compassion blot out my offense.
> O wash me more and more from my guilt
> and cleanse me from my sin (50 [51]:3-4).
>
> A pure heart create for me, O God
> put a steadfast spirit within me.
> Do not cast me away from your presence,
> nor deprive me of your holy spirit (50 [51]:12-13).

If I make this psalm my daily prayer, it will not allow me to forget "a sense of God's goodness and our brokenness, a sense of God's greatness and our dependence, a sense of God's grandeur and our fragility."

Then, combining the regular and the familiar with the changing and the new, Benedict chooses differing psalms for each succeeding day of the week. The very first words of Psalm 5 for Monday morning are:

> To my words give ear, O Lord. . . .
> It is you whom I invoke O Lord.
> In the morning you hear me
> in the morning I offer my prayer,
> watching and waiting.

What could be a better start to the week? On Friday Psalm 75 (76) and Psalm 90 (91) speak of the protection that comes with the victory of the Cross. Saturday brings a sense of passing time as the week draws to its close: "I remember the days that are past" (Psalm 142 [143]). Then comes the sense of looking forward: "Make me know the way I should walk."

In the final paragraph of this chapter, Benedict says that the Lord's Prayer is to be recited aloud daily. This, he explains, is so that each day we admit our constant and continuing need for forgiveness. He knows all about community life (and what is true for community is as true in marriage, family, school, parish, or whatever the set of relationships in which I find myself), about the hurts that we do to one another and the damage they can do if they are allowed to go unhealed. In making the Lord's Prayer primarily a prayer for forgiveness, he is, of course, in the spirit of its setting in Matthew 6:9-15, where it comes after Christ has been teaching about forgiveness. Once again we see how totally the Rule is shaped by the Gospel. When in verse 13 Benedict uses the word "covenant" (a better translation than "pledge"), it is to show that the commitment to continual forgiveness is to become a constitutive part of life. Daily reading of Scripture is a reminder of the faithfulness of God in his covenant relationship with his chosen people, and that is not less true of his people today.

That short phrase "thorns of contention" (12), which in Latin runs *propter scandalorum spinas,* presents me with two vivid images. First, I have a picture of thorns springing up and choking the green shoots of new growth. "Contention" brings to mind the idea of a snare, since it comes from *skandalon,* a Hellenistic Greek word used for a stick in a trap on which a bait is placed and when touched by the animal springs up and shuts the trap. The failure to forgive prevents new life springing up and traps me in the coils of a snare from which I cannot escape. To fail to forgive is to be trapped in the past, caught up in resentment and bitterness, staying with wounds that remain open and raw— everything that will prevent new life and new growth. It is not only damaging to the individual, but destructive of community life as well.

When I choose not to forgive, I am choosing death rather than life, and Benedict, who is trying to lead us all the time forward into freedom and fullness of life, wants to rescue me. Since he knows only too well that forgiveness is neither easy nor finished, he sees that we remember this twice each day. "We need to forgive and be forgiven every day, every hour—unceasingly. That is the great work of love among the fellowship of the weak that is the human family," as Henri Nouwen says.

To forgive and to be willing to receive forgiveness means admitting that things have gone wrong and that I am involved in all that muddle and mess, for the situation is never likely to be clear-cut or simple. I must take responsibility for my part in it all, just as much as Benedict will later tell me that I must take responsibility for any damage or loss to material things (46:1-4). In the end what makes it possible to forgive is the knowledge that I myself am already forgiven. If I am truly the prodigal, and if the way of Benedict is that of the return to a loving father from whom I have strayed, then I also know that the father awaits me with unconditional love and unconditional forgiveness. Forgiving myself means accepting this forgiveness, not being too proud to receive it. If I am not able to accept this gift of loving forgiveness held out to me, how can I hope in turn to be able to forgive?

CHAPTER FOURTEEN

[1]On the feasts of saints, and indeed on all solemn festivals, the Sunday order of celebration is followed, [2]although the psalms, refrains and readings proper to the day itself are said. The procedure, however, remains the same as indicated above.

How glad I am to find this short chapter on the celebration of Vigils or Matins on the anniversaries of saints. It adds another dimension to the sense of time and order that Benedict is giving us. Once again I find it brings me something that I find so strongly in the Celtic tradition: the sense of an almost physical presence of the saints around me so that it is quite natural to feel oneself "keeping house amid a cloud of witnesses." I am reminded of how I am linked to the communion of saints. If at intervals during the year I am recalled to their life on earth and their presence in eternity, this helps me to become aware of my part as a member of the body of Christ. Here is one more element in that corporate sense that Benedict is building up. I am inserted into a community here on earth; I am also part of a community in the wider context of the Church beyond time and space. It makes me think in gratitude of what I owe to the saints, living and dead, known and unknown.

CHAPTER FIFTEEN

¹From the holy feast of Easter until Pentecost, "alleluia" is always said with both the psalms and the responsories. ²Every night from Pentecost until the beginning of Lent, it is said only with the last six psalms of Vigils. ³Vigils, Lauds, Prime, Terce, Sext and None are said with "alleluia" every Sunday except in Lent: at Vespers, however, a refrain is used. ⁴"Alleluia" is never said with responsories except from Easter to Pentecost.

Alleluia is a Hebrew phrase meaning "Praise Yahweh!" It passed into Christian usage without translation, and in the Book of Revelation the chants of triumph of the blessed begin *"Alleluia, victory and glory and power to our God."* Here we see how Benedict links it as an exclamation of joy in relation to Easter. It is to be said abundantly during the paschal season, the time above all of rejoicing in the victory of Easter. In Lent, it is a mark of the fasting and repentance of the forty days waiting for the coming of Easter that it will not be used. So once again Benedict is showing us a pattern to be observed in the year that centers us on Easter, the paschal mystery at the heart of the Gospel becomes the central pivot of the Rule. As we saw already in the prologue, Benedict's implicit theology is wholly paschal, and all the time we are being pointed forward to new life in the risen Christ. This short chapter encourages me to ask myself what role the reality of death and new life, of dying and rebirth, plays in my life. Do I say *Alleluia* sufficiently often in recognition of the victory of the Cross?

CHAPTER SIXTEEN

¹The Prophet says: *Seven times a day have I praised you* (Ps 118[119]:164). ²We will fulfill this sacred number of seven if we satisfy our obligations of service at Lauds, Prime, Terce, Sext, None, Vespers and Compline, ³for it was of these hours during the day that he said: *Seven times a day have I praised you* (Ps 118[119]:164). ⁴Concerning Vigils, the same Prophet says: *At midnight I arose to give you praise* (Ps 118[119]:62). ⁵Therefore, we should *praise* our Creator *for his just judgments* at these times: Lauds, Prime, Terce, Sext, None, Vespers and Compline; and *let us arise at night to give* him *praise* (Ps 118[119]:164, 62).

Twice in this short chapter that looks at the celebration of the Divine Office during the day Benedict repeats the line from the psalmist that says "seven times." The number seven has always carried an almost mystical sense of completion, perfection. But the reality, of course, was that in his monastery his monks were praying eight times a day, so he finds a nice quotation to explain why they get up at midnight for Vigils (Matins), which allows him to give scriptural justification for the pattern of the monastic Office.

Each of the five quotations from the psalms includes the word "praise." This is what this chapter, and the whole of the liturgical code, is ultimately all about. There are so many ways of praying, so many ways of addressing God, in repentance, in petition, in intercession. But in the end we were made "to praise our Creator." Gratitude puts everything into a different perspective. It prevents me from taking anything for granted. It helps me to live my life awake, alert to those good gifts that I am given, in a state of mindfulness or awareness. Then, when I look at the world with

87

eyes of wonder, I discover, rather to my chagrin, that it is often only too easy to drift and become neglectful, lazy, forgetful of gratefulness. I enjoy that line of W. H. Auden, "Practice the scales of rejoicing," because of its suggestion that it really is hard work and needs discipline. I might rewrite those familiar words "pray without ceasing" so that they become "praise without ceasing," giving thanks to my Creator for all the good gifts in my life.

CHAPTER SEVENTEEN

¹We have already established the order for psalmody at Vigils and Lauds. Now let us arrange the remaining hours.

²Three psalms are to be said at Prime, each followed by "Glory be to the Father." ³The hymn for this hour is sung after the opening versicle, *God, come to my assistance* (Ps 69[70]:2), before the psalmody begins. ⁴One reading follows the three psalms, and the hour is concluded with a versicle, "Lord, have mercy" and the dismissal.

⁵Prayer is celebrated in the same way at Terce, Sext and None; that is, the opening verse, the hymn appropriate to each hour, three psalms, a reading with a versicle, "Lord, have mercy" and the dismissal. ⁶If the community is rather large, refrains are used with the psalms; if it is smaller, the psalms are said without refrain.

⁷At Vespers the number of psalms should be limited to four, with refrain. ⁸After these psalms there follow: a reading and responsory, an Ambrosian hymn, a versicle, the Gospel Canticle, the litany, and, immediately before the dismissal, the Lord's Prayer.

⁹Compline is limited to three psalms without refrain. ¹⁰After the psalmody comes the hymn for this hour, followed by a reading, a versicle, "Lord, have mercy," a blessing and the dismissal.

As Benedict's careful explanations continue, I am being drawn deeper and deeper into the sense of time being punctuated by prayer, that praying is inseparable from life itself. For here, having dealt with Vigils and Lauds, he looks at the remaining hours. The opening versicle, *"God, come to my assistance"* (3), is a small phrase commonly used by monastics as a means of recalling oneself to the presence of God in one's mind and heart. It prompted Cassian to write some of his most inspiring teaching in which he said that if those words were repeated throughout the day—at work, in reading, in physical weakness, in moments of temptation —they would lead to a continuous state of prayer and so to contemplation:

> This thought in your heart may be to you a saving formula and not only keep you unharmed by all attacks of devils, but also purify you from all faults and earthly stains, and lead you to that invisible and celestial contemplation. . . .

"Lord, have mercy" is equally a phrase that can become like some continuous underground stream that flows on quietly in my heart whatever I may be doing externally. Some sorts of physical work lead nicely into prayer, some sorts of travel are wonderful settings for praying. But much of the time what I really need help with is to control the constant prattling of the mind. As an Eastern tradition describes it: "The mind is like a thousand chattering monkeys." Cassian's insight, which passed into the monastic tradition of the West, that the repetition of a short phrase is the best aid in the stilling of the mind, gives me a tool to help me live from a contemplative center even when I seem almost devoured by the demands of a seemingly impossibly busy life.

The last Office of the day is Compline for which the three psalms set never change but are repeated nightly. It was usual simply to say Compline wherever the monks might be gathered together, and since these psalms were known by heart, no light was needed. For all of us too they bring the day to an end on this note of certainty: that we can rely on the knowledge of the protecting power of God through the hours of night as we have during the day. After he had spent two months at the Trappist monastery of the Genesee, Henri Nouwen wrote in his diary:

> I start realizing that the psalms of Compline slowly become flesh in me; they become part of my night and lead me to a peaceful sleep. Trust is written through the evening prayer:
>
>> He who dwells in the shelter of the Most High
>> and abides in the shade of the Almighty
>> says to the Lord: "My refuge,
>> my stronghold, my God in whom I trust!"

Slowly these words enter into the center of my heart. They are more than ideas, images, comparisons: they become a real presence. After a day with much work or with many tensions, you feel that you can let go in safety and realize how good it is to dwell in the shelter of the Most High.

CHAPTER EIGHTEEN

¹Each of the day hours begins with the verse, *God, come to my assistance; Lord, make haste to help me* (Ps 69[70]:2), followed by "Glory be to the Father" and the appropriate hymn.

²Then, on Sunday at Prime, four sections of Psalm 118 are said. ³At the other hours, that is, at Terce, Sext and None, three sections of this psalm are said. ⁴On Monday three psalms are said at Prime: Psalms 1, 2 and 6. ⁵At Prime each day thereafter until Sunday, three psalms are said in consecutive order as far as Psalm 19. Psalms 9 and 17 are each divided into two sections. ⁶In this way, Sunday Vigils can always begin with Psalm 20.

⁷On Monday at Terce, Sext and None, the remaining nine sections of Psalm 118 are said, three sections at each hour. ⁸Psalm 118 is thus completed in two days, Sunday and Monday. ⁹On Tuesday, three psalms are said at each of the hours of Terce, Sext and None. These are the nine psalms, 119 through 127. ¹⁰The same psalms are repeated at these hours daily up to Sunday. Likewise, the arrangement of hymns, readings and versicles for these days remains the same. ¹¹In this way, Psalm 118 will always begin on Sunday.

¹²Four psalms are sung each day at Vespers, ¹³starting with Psalm 109 and ending with Psalm 147, ¹⁴omitting the psalms in this series already assigned to other hours, namely, Psalms 117 through 127, Psalm 133 and Psalm 142. ¹⁵All the remaining psalms are said at Vespers. ¹⁶Since this leaves three psalms too few, the longer ones in the series should be divided: that is, Psalms 138, 143 and 144. ¹⁷And because Psalm 116 is short, it can be joined to Psalm 115. ¹⁸This is the order of psalms for Vespers; the rest is as arranged above: the reading, responsory, hymn, versicle and canticle.

[19]The same psalms—4, 90 and 133—are said each day at Compline.

[20]The remaining psalms not accounted for in this arrangement for the day hours are distributed evenly at Vigils over the seven nights of the week. [21]Longer psalms are to be divided so that twelve psalms are said each night.

[22]Above all else we urge that if anyone finds this distribution of the psalms unsatisfactory, he should arrange whatever he judges better, [23]provided that the full complement of one hundred and fifty psalms is by all means carefully maintained every week, and that the series begins anew each Sunday at Vigils. [24]For monks who in a week's time say less than the full psalter with the customary canticles betray extreme indolence and lack of devotion in their service. [25]We read, after all, that our holy Fathers, energetic as they were, did all this in a single day. Let us hope that we, lukewarm as we are, can achieve it in a whole week.

In this chapter, Benedict is giving us his detailed organization of the psalter so that it can be said in its entirety during one week. He tells us that the ancients had been used to saying the entire psalter during a day, but he is concerned to model it in rather more humane terms. In doing this he is following the advice he gives to the abbot: the Rule has to be made livable, and then there is no reason not to keep it. He is ready to be firm and flexible, rather than absolute or extreme. If we can improve on his scheme, then he is humble enough (or sufficiently relaxed about himself!) to say that that is fine provided the commitment is there, that the obligation is taken seriously. What he abhors is that we should be lazy or lukewarm.

For the most part the psalms are to be recited numerically, which suggests that he saw them primarily as material for meditation, a means of lifting the mind to God. But for the three short day of Offices of Terce, Sext, and None at the start of the week he chooses Psalm 118 (119), the wisdom psalm, with its theme of following God's law, doing God's will, learning God's commandments, pondering God's precepts:

Teach me the demands of your statutes
And I shall keep them to the end (v. 33).

93

I ask God to open my eyes, bless my lips, to guide my footsteps, as I seek God's Word with my whole heart:

> Your word is a lamp for my eyes
> and a light for my path (v. 105).

If I do not find myself with time to recite an Office during working hours, almost any verse from this psalm can recall me to base and bring my heart back to a sense of the presence of the Word. The longer that I stay with the psalms, the more I come to realize my debt to them. As Henri Nouwen said: "Slowly these words enter into the center of my heart."

CHAPTER NINETEEN

¹We believe that the divine presence is everywhere and *that in every place the eyes of the Lord are watching the good and the wicked* (Prov 15:3). ²But beyond the least doubt we should believe this to be especially true when we celebrate the divine office.

³We must always remember, therefore, what the Prophet says: *Serve the Lord with fear* (Ps 2:11), ⁴and again, *Sing praise wisely* (Ps 46[47]:8); ⁵and, *In the presence of the angels I will sing to you* (Ps 137[138]:1). ⁶Let us consider, then, how we ought to behave in the presence of God and his angels, ⁷and let us stand to sing the psalms in such a way that our minds are in harmony with our voices.

The inner and the outer must correspond, my heart must be in tune with the words that I speak—this is something that Benedict has said before, and he comes back to it at the end of this long discussion of the Office. He challenges any behavior that depends on the outward observance and lacks the inner attention. The words of Psalm 46 (47) quoted in verse 4 can be translated "Sing with wisdom," showing that they mean that the words framed by the lips are echoed by the heart and mind. As Michael Casey says, commenting on this chapter:

> In this way the monk is shaped, in his whole inner being, according to the inspired words of the text he is saying. He is possessed by God's Word; it enters into composition with his own subjectivity and acts as a leaven in the process of his transformation.

In verse 3 Benedict returns to the theme of the fear of the Lord, for that is foundational, as he has shown me in the first step of the ladder of humility in chapter 7. His concern is always with attitude, with the disposition of the heart, awareness of the presence of God, response to that presence, habitual attention. This simple chapter is one of the most important in the Rule.

CHAPTER TWENTY

¹Whenever we want to ask some favor of a powerful man, we do it humbly and respectfully, for fear of presumption. ²How much more important, then, to lay our petitions before the Lord God of all things with the utmost humility and sincere devotion. ³We must know that God regards our purity of heart and tears of compunction, not our many words. ⁴Prayer should therefore be short and pure, unless perhaps it is prolonged under the inspiration of divine grace. ⁵In community, however, prayer should always be brief; and when the superior gives the signal, all should rise together.

The theme of reverence in prayer follows on from the previous chapter, and together these two bring to a close this section on the *opus Dei* by looking at the relationship of its two main elements, psalm and prayer. The psalms were an invitation to prayer, the silent prayer of the heart. In the older monastic practice the psalm was not regarded as human homage rendered to God but rather as God's message to humanity, awakening the response of prayer. So the reading of the psalm, like any other part of Scripture, was a reading that invited and encouraged the interior prayer of the heart.

The usual practice was that, following each psalm, every member of the community would silently prostrate themselves to allow time to appropriate its deeper meaning. This private response might then be gathered up into the words of a public prayer or prayer collect in order to have a three-stage movement—reading, personal interior prayer, and public shared prayer.

As always Benedict does not give us any direct methodology for prayer. Instead he expects us to find our own way with his guidelines. He reminds us of humility and reverence and attention and fear—all the attitudes that will predispose our prayer to be sincere and simple, which will encourage purity in prayer. With this chapter he ends all that he has to say on the liturgical code.

I notice that, just as in chapter 8, which opened this section, there is no scriptural quotation, which is extremely unusual for Benedict. I get the feeling that this is a simple summary of his own experience, so that if what he has written here has any resonance in my own life and in my own heart, it is because he has himself lived and prayed in this way. Like the abbot himself, he would never teach anything that he did not himself practice.

CHAPTER TWENTY-ONE

¹If the community is rather large, some brothers chosen for their good repute and holy life should be made deans. ²They will take care of their groups of ten, managing all affairs according to the commandments of God and the orders of their abbot. ³The deans selected should be the kind of men with whom the abbot can confidently share the burdens of his office. ⁴They are to be chosen for virtuous living and wise teaching, not for their rank.

⁵If perhaps one of these deans is found to be puffed up with any pride, and so deserving of censure, he is to be reproved once, twice and even a third time. Should he refuse to amend, he must be removed from office ⁶and replaced by another who is worthy. ⁷We prescribe the same course of action in regard to the prior.

"The sharing of burdens," the small phrase that we find in the third verse of this chapter, gives us the keynote of what follows now. We have seen the strength of shared prayer; here we are to look at the strength that comes from what we might rather more self-consciously today call collegiality or the "ministry of the laity." The concern of the next two chapters is with the quality of community, with shared life. The abbot is to appoint deans, men to be in charge of groups of ten, who will look after things both material and spiritual, just like the abbot himself. In Benedict's holistic spirituality, there is no separation of the material and the spiritual. The men who are in charge of sleeping arrangements in the dormitories must also be ready to console and comfort those who need help.

Here we see something about the exercise of power. This is delegation but still under the authority of the abbot, and more fundamentally, under God, for it is to God that all are to look in the handling of affairs of the monastery. Rank and position are not determinants of office. Benedict lists the virtues that he is looking for: virtuous living, wise teaching, confidentiality. In all of the office-holders that he describes in the Rule (and later we shall be given a vivid portrait of the cellarer to add to the list), Benedict is seeking men who will model the Christian life to the brothers. It is clear that he is looking for truly spiritual people to hold office. In chapter 64 the abbot is to be chosen for "goodness of life and wisdom in teaching" (2). In chapter 31 the cellarer is to be wise and mature (1). Here the deans are described in terms that are found in Acts: "men of good repute." This is close to the Old Testament experience in which Moses' father-in-law Jethro advises him to choose elders who are "wise and experienced" to help with his leadership burdens (Deut 1:13-15). It is, therefore, their holy way of life rather than any technical efficiency or specialized expertise that commends them for office or rank, and their appointment is not for reasons of administrative convenience but to encourage spiritual growth.

This, says Adelbert van der Wielen commenting on this chapter, is not possible without an intense effort of love and prayer, "The double-carrying power by which we can help others."

> You will be able to bear responsibility in so far as you bear others by your virtue and your contemplation, by your charity and your prayer. If I want to know whether I am able to bear this responsibility I must check on how I meet my brothers and sisters in daily life: whether I love them prayerfully and pray with them lovingly. Such an attitude is restful and disarming for the other. So they will be free and will be themselves with me.

It feels as though something changes at verse 5, perhaps, it has been suggested, in the light of some negative experiences of Benedict himself. There is a hint here of tension, and the positive note at the start of the chapter seems to have turned sour. Yet when he puts an attitude of pride or becoming puffed-up with one's own self as the root causes of things going wrong, he is only returning to a favorite theme. This is something that I know myself, that what most militates against the shared life, the common good, is when individualism pulls away and self-interest is placed before the good of the whole. So once again we are being shown a model that has much wisdom to offer to anyone living and working in today's world. Here is order with flexibility, authority being used to weld the larger group, not to fracture it, but above all the attitude of loving wisdom that in the end makes it all possible.

CHAPTER TWENTY-TWO

¹The monks are to sleep in separate beds. ²They receive bedding as provided by the abbot, suitable to monastic life.
³If possible, all are to sleep in one place, but should the size of the community preclude this, they will sleep in groups of ten or twenty under the watchful care of seniors. ⁴A lamp must be kept burning in the room until morning.
⁵They sleep clothed, and girded with belts or cords; but they should remove their knives, lest they accidentally cut themselves in their sleep. ⁶Thus the monks will always be ready to arise without delay when the signal is given; each will hasten to arrive at the Work of God before the others, yet with all dignity and decorum. ⁷The younger brothers should not have their beds next to each other, but interspersed among those of the seniors. ⁸On arising for the Work of God, they will quietly encourage each other, for the sleepy like to make excuses.

Here we are given a chapter that is typical of the way in which Benedict handles some of the most mundane and down-to-earth aspects in the organization of daily life. It is important not to let ourselves be distracted by some of the details that can easily strike a jarring note and appear quaint or amusing. So often in Benedict's hands, the daily and the material are made to yield up spiritual insights. He followed the common monastic dormitory arrangement of his day, which became the norm in the sixth century after the Emperor Justinian decreed that monastics of the Empire must sleep in common dormitories to protect against sexual immorality. It would be quite easy to read this chapter simply in these terms, for there are many details that could be interpreted as guards against immorality. But I think that Benedict's main and over-riding interest is in so planning the dormitory that the monks may rise with the utmost speed and ease.

In the prologue he wanted to rouse us all from sleep, and his concern is always that we should live life fully, alert, alive, not half asleep and half awake. So much of the Rule, and also the Gospel, is about life—coming to life, fullness of life. There is a connection between light and life. To stay with the dark is the denial, the opposite of life. The cornerstone of St. John's Abbey, Collegeville, Minnesota, bears an inscription in Greek letters that translates into English: "LIGHT—LIFE." Those two words sum up the Christian life. Here I find, as so often, that Benedict refreshes my awareness of them as he puts them into the context of the most mundane and daily of situations.

The whole thrust of this chapter is toward what Benedict is saying in verse 6: that the monks will be always ready to rise without delay, for the *opus Dei,* the work of God, is the whole purpose of their life. So they sleep in a state of availability. It makes us think of the many parables of Christ's return, so it would not seem unlikely that Benedict wanted his monks to resemble the servants in the gospel who await their master's return in the dead of night. The sense of urgency, therefore, explains why they sleep clothed (later, chapter 55 will mention change of clothes, so we should be wrong to assume anything unhygienic here). They sleep with a light burning, and they have put aside the knives that might harm them as they make quick movements, all in order that they can hasten when the signal is given. Here for once there is an uncharacteristically competitive note: that they might arrive at the place of prayer before their fellows.

It is entirely typical of this way of life to find a combination of real tenderness and concern for the welfare of each, in the matter of separate beds and adequate bedding, with an overriding concern for good order and community living, so that all are placed under the watchful eye of the seniors. Benedict's humanity is most clearly seen in that final verse. Silence is to be discreetly broken in the interests of encouraging one another. In Benedict's way the spirit is always of more consequence than the law.

CHAPTER TWENTY-THREE

¹If a brother is found to be stubborn or disobedient or proud, if he grumbles or in any way despises the holy rule and defies the orders of his seniors, ²he should be warned twice privately by the seniors in accord with our Lord's injunction (Matt 18:15-16). ³If he does not amend, he must be rebuked publicly in the presence of everyone. ⁴But if even then he does not reform, let him be excommunicated, provided that he understands the nature of this punishment. ⁵If however he lacks understanding, let him undergo corporal punishment.

There is a very real danger that we might either be tempted to look on chapters 23-30, generally known as "the penal code" or "a code of discipline," as some new departure, different in emphasis from what has gone before, or that we might dismiss them as outdated and irrelevant. No less a scholar than de Vogüé has said that "of all the parts of the Rule, this one that we are about to consider is without doubt the most outmoded." The attitude toward corporal punishment and excommunication is totally alien to present-day thinking, and it might seem very doubtful that there could be much spiritual profit in spending time considering these chapters. Yet if we are to add on to this section chapters 43-46, which are also concerned with the correction of faults, we shall find that the subject of sin and of discipline occupies no less than ten percent of the entire text.

What are we to make of this? If we do not pay it full attention we shall fail to do justice to a central tension in the Rule. While Benedict points us toward life, fullness of life, the risen self, and Easter, he also tells us that our life should be thoroughly penitential, a perpetual Lent. The sorrow of the prodigal, repentance, and *metanoia* are an essential part of our Christian discipleship. Daily we should internalize both Lent and Easter, for they belong together. Again my discovery of the Celtic tradition has deepened my appreciation of what Benedict is saying, for there is never any doubt that we can have the light without the dark, creation without redemption. The tradition that has given us creation celebrations of unparalleled beauty has also given us penitential literature.

When he used military imagery in the prologue, Benedict was introducing an important theme that runs through the Rule. The struggle against evil, above all in our hearts, underlies the spiritual section of chapters 1–7, and the theme of purification from vices and sins is constantly recalled, as in 7,70. The previous chapter has looked at community at the point where the flesh is weakest and in most need of support, and Benedict has been showing the vital role of the building up of trusting and supporting relationships as the very fibre of community life and of the communal way to God. Anything therefore that might threaten this or do damage to the welfare of others is seen as extremely serious.

In a time of individualism this rings strangely in our ears, for we are encouraged to think of our sins either individually (between ourselves and God) or against another individual, rather than seeing what effect they have upon the community or the society as a whole. Perhaps it would be no bad thing if I were now to spend time reflecting on the common, shared nature of sin. Benedict wants the monk to realize the communal dimension of his fault so that what is at issue is a question of social responsibility as well as individual responsibility. He sees sin as deep, structural, and pervasive, tying the individual and the corporate together. It must not be buried and denied, but exposed and lived with in terms of repentance and new life.

The point of departure of the Rule is that we are all responsible beings who have "departed" through a sinful act of self-will, through disobedience (Prol., 1-2). This is recalled in the words "stubborn or disobedient or proud" with which this chapter opens, and it reminds us again of Benedict's determination not to allow vices to grow unchecked (2,26-29; 64,16). When the good of the whole is at stake Benedict is prepared to take a firm line. David Parry suggests that this chapter can jolt us into thinking about sinful states of mind and the damage that they can do. If I turn what Benedict is saying to his monks into a questioning of my own conscience, I am forced to ask myself if I am proud or arrogant. Am I contemptuous of the ruling of those in charge? Do I grumble and protest? Am I discontented and frequently telling just how unfair life is? For it is the interior attitude that more than anything else can create or disrupt the common well-being and peace of the shared life.

Eradication of these faults is, however, not for the sake of good discipline. It is essentially pastoral concern for healing, not punishment of the wayward but the "loving correction" of the Gospel. Once again Benedict is pointing us to the teachings of Christ. The movement of amendment proceeds by successive steps, following the outline given in Matthew 18:15-18. The correction begins gradually with private warning before further action is taken, but if there is no amendment, there must be public correction, and finally excommunication. The corporal punishment that he suggests was probably quite mild according to the standards of his day. But the point that he is making remains valid whatever the circumstances of the times. He is speaking of growth and of responsibility. If things go wrong he expects reform, atonement. Later on he will be clear about this in the handling of material things: if anything gets lost or broken, then one must own up at once. When things are wrong, they must be put right. Ultimately the message is as simple and clear as that.

CHAPTER TWENTY-FOUR

[1]There ought to be due proportion between the seriousness of a fault and the measure of excommunication or discipline. [2]The abbot determines the gravity of faults.

[3]If a brother is found guilty of less serious faults, he will not be allowed to share the common table. [4]Anyone excluded from the common table will conduct himself as follows: in the oratory he will not lead a psalm or a refrain nor will he recite a reading until he has made satisfaction, [5]and he will take his meals alone, after the brothers have eaten. [6]For instance, if the brothers eat at noon, he will eat in midafternoon; if the brothers eat in midafternoon, he will eat in the evening, [7]until by proper satisfaction he gains pardon.

The greater the fault, the greater the exclusion from the community. Failure and punishment are in step: there are corresponding degrees of severity, so that there is no arbitrary exercise of power. Here, for lighter offenses, a person is separated from the shared meal and from the right to lead prayer. In effect this is what had been happening. By his behavior and, above all, by his attitude, the individual has already made that break by behaving like an outsider, separating him or herself from the whole body. This punishment is a recognition of that fact.

CHAPTER TWENTY-FIVE

¹A brother guilty of a serious fault is to be excluded from both the table and the oratory. ²No other brother should associate or converse with him at all. ³He will work alone at the tasks assigned to him, living continually in sorrow and penance, pondering that fearful judgment of the Apostle: ⁴*Such a man is handed over for the destruction of his flesh that his spirit may be saved on the day of the Lord* (1 Cor 5:5). ⁵Let him take his food alone in an amount and at a time the abbot considers appropriate for him. ⁶He should not be blessed by anyone passing by, nor should the food that is given him be blessed.

This isolation from the community is not only to move the sinner to repentance (2-3), but to serve as a reminder that continuing and further hardening of faults could eventually exclude a person from salvation, that full and permanent exclusion of which St. Paul wrote so severely in the passage that Benedict quotes from 1 Corinthians. It is significant, however, that he omits from this quotation the mention of being handed over to Satan, for that would mean expulsion not only from the monastery but from the Church. The withholding of a blessing or greeting in verse 6 has to be seen in the context of the early Church's understanding of the "communion of saints," which was not that of communication of earth and heaven but of the sacramental sharing of "holy things to holy people" of Christians of the time.

The separation that we are shown here is something of a vacuum into which the individual enters, distanced from the community and from what has been going wrong there, since if anyone really wants to be a part of the family they will feel this solitude as a privation. Yet in this isolation there may well be a chance to stand back and to see with greater clarity where the origin of the sin lies. Here is the opportunity to find a space of time for the making of right choices.

CHAPTER TWENTY-SIX

¹If a brother, acting without an order from the abbot, presumes to associate in any way with an excommunicated brother, to converse with him or to send him a message, ²he should receive a like punishment of excommunication.

In this chapter Benedict continues to handle the situation with tough love. He wants to make sure that the patient is given time to cure his wounds without undue meddling or interference, for he knows that what is apparently loving and supporting may do greater good to the giver than to the recipient. It is tempting to the one who is standing and watching to intrude, and Benedict is quite clear that this must be resisted, unless, of course, it comes from the one who is in charge and who may be assumed to be handling the case sufficiently well on their own. Again he is telling us about responsible behavior on all sides.

CHAPTER TWENTY-SEVEN

¹The abbot must exercise the utmost care and concern for wayward brothers, because *it is not the healthy who need a physician, but the sick* (Matt 9:12). ²Therefore, he ought to use every skill of a wise physician and send in *senpectae,* that is, mature and wise brothers ³who, under the cloak of secrecy, may support the wavering brother, urge him to be humble as a way of making satisfaction, and *console* him *lest he be overwhelmed by excessive sorrow* (2 Cor 2:7). ⁴Rather, as the Apostle also says: *Let love for him be reaffirmed* (2 Cor 2:8), and let all pray for him.

⁵It is the abbot's responsibility to have great concern and to act with all speed, discernment and diligence in order not to lose any of the sheep entrusted to him. ⁶He should realize that he has undertaken care of the sick, not tyranny over the healthy. ⁷Let him also fear the threat of the Prophet in which God says: *What you saw to be fat you claimed for yourselves, and what was weak you cast aside* (Ezek 34:3-4). ⁸He is to imitate the loving example of the Good Shepherd who left the ninety-nine sheep in the mountains and went in search of the one sheep that had strayed. ⁹So great was his compassion for its weakness that *he* mercifully *placed it on his* sacred *shoulders* and so carried it back to the flock (Luke 15:5).

Here comes a most loving and gentle portrait of the healer exercising "the utmost care and concern" (1). One way of reading the Rule is to see Benedict's whole purpose as remedial and the monk's life-work as a healing process of the wounds of sin. The purpose of all these recent chapters is never with discipline per se, but with healing, with *metanoia,* with ongoing conversion

111

and opening up into freedom from all those forces that would threaten or destroy that.

In his wisdom the abbot recognizes that he needs to turn to those with particular wisdom and skill in discerning needs. He is still in charge, and this chapter does not, therefore, contradict anything that has gone before, but he also knows that those who are hurt and wounded need especially loving and wise guidance. The exercise of total confidentiality is also a vital safeguard, and here again Benedict shows a grasp of the best counseling practice. I love the use of such gentle words and counsel, so that the sufferer does not feel overwhelmed. I love the emphasis on affirming love and on prayer. Anyone who has known tiredness to the point of exhaustion or depression that suffering so often carries with it will appreciate Benedict's wisdom in providing for skilled support when it might be all too easy to sink into apathy and negativity.

How significant it is that in the middle of what is usually called the penal code, we should be given this passage, one of the most lyrical in the whole Rule, on compassion! There are two models for the abbot, the skillful doctor and the good shepherd, both of which apply to Christ himself. It is, of course, quite possible to cure without compassion, but this can be no more than a shortcut. If Benedict points us all the time to Christ, then in the exercise of his ministry of healing we can see an example of true compassion. The deaf hear and the blind see and the lame walk, and I like to take this metaphorically for the healing needed for all those inner wounds.

What I have increasingly appreciated as I have stayed with the Rule is finding how it provides for the whole range of human weakness and inadequacy, yet with a complete absence of cynicism or pessimism. This is what the human condition is, and this is where God's grace is encountered and the paschal mystery happens. St. Paul had insisted on his weakness as a credential, and there are many echoes of Pauline writing in these chapters. Benedict would seem to be saying that weakness and failure are not necessarily a handicap or a disqualification but can, with help, be made the place in which the power of the crucified and risen Christ can be manifested in our lives. Lent and Easter, the forty days in the desert and the forty days of Easter joy, the paradox of the paschal mystery, this is what underlies the message of Benedict's understanding of sin and healing.

CHAPTER TWENTY-EIGHT

[1]If a brother has been reproved frequently for any fault, or if he has even been excommunicated, yet does not amend, let him receive a sharper punishment: that is, let him feel the strokes of the rod. [2]But if even then he does not reform, or perhaps becomes proud and would actually defend his conduct, which God forbid, the abbot should follow the procedure of a wise physician. [3]After he has applied compresses, the ointment of encouragement, the medicine of divine Scripture, and finally the cauterizing iron of excommunication and strokes of the rod, [4]and if he then perceives that his earnest efforts are unavailing, let him apply an even better remedy: he and all the brothers should pray for him [5]so that the Lord, who can do all things, may bring about the health of the sick brother. [6]Yet if even this procedure does not heal him, then finally, the abbot must use the knife and amputate. For the Apostle says: *Banish the evil one from your midst* (1 Cor 5:13); [7]and again, *If the unbeliever departs, let him depart* (1 Cor 7:15), [8]lest one diseased sheep infect the whole flock.

Here Benedict deals with a most serious matter, recidivism, the persistent offender, the person who has fallen back after having been forgiven and reaccepted. This is a call to growth. Benedict is realistic and honest. He believes in progress and that is the way that he himself implements the whole healing process: in a series of stages. But he also realizes that the response may not be forthcoming, and in that case truth demands amputation, the cutting out of the diseased part. The successive steps are gently shown, and the images that they present are striking: compresses to draw out the stinking puss, ointment to soothe a raw place, medicine to reach deep down into the body, the cauterizing iron that purifies, and, if all of these fail, the final resort is the knife that cuts out the bad. For just as one sick part can infect the whole body, so what is true of the individual is equally true of the body corporate.

CHAPTER TWENTY-NINE

¹If a brother, following his own evil ways, leaves the monastery but then wishes to return, he must first promise to make full amends for leaving. ²Let him be received back, but as a test of his humility he should be given the last place. ³If he leaves again, or even a third time, he should be readmitted under the same conditions. After this, however, he must understand that he will be denied all prospect of return.

This chapter, says David Parry, is short and amiable. Here Benedict recognizes indecision and uncertainty and tries to contain it most positively, so that in the end the right way may be discerned. The notion of patience is a very powerful one in the Rule, and we see it being exercised by the abbot as he stands and waits and watches. But neither does he want to make it so easy that there is apparently no price to be paid for this coming and going, so he does impose certain limitations. There must be no more than three attempts, and each of these returns is to be a new beginning, starting all over again. Boundaries enable growth, as any mother knows, and what Benedict says of the questing monk in search of his monastic identity is as true of any of us as we also try to discern our own right way.

CHAPTER THIRTY

¹Every age and level of understanding should receive appropriate treatment. ²Therefore, as often as boys and the young, or those who cannot understand the seriousness of the penalty of excommunication, ³are guilty of misdeeds, they should be subjected to severe fasts or checked with sharp strokes so that they may be healed.

In describing the exercise of the office of abbot in chapter 2, the words that Benedict used were "accommodate" and "adapt"; here is an example of putting them into practice. Each one of us was addressed in the prologue as son or daughter, the unique child of a loving father. That is something that Benedict never loses sight of throughout the Rule, just as we too should hold onto it in all our dealings with others. We should be concerned with what is appropriate. In the context of the world in which he was writing, the severe disciplining of the young would have been considered appropriate. It is for the healing and growth into freedom that this is applied, his concern here, as ever, is with the ends rather than the means. It is because of those ends, healing and growth, freedom, new life, those positive and life-giving qualities, that I have learned so much from this section of the Rule.

CHAPTER THIRTY-ONE

¹As cellarer of the monastery, there should be chosen from the community someone who is wise, mature in conduct, temperate, not an excessive eater, not proud, excitable, offensive, dilatory or wasteful, ²but God-fearing, and like a father to the whole community. ³He will take care of everything, ⁴but will do nothing without an order from the abbot. ⁵Let him keep to his orders.

⁶He should not annoy the brothers. ⁷If any brother happens to make an unreasonable demand of him, he should not reject him with disdain and cause him distress, but reasonably and humbly deny the improper request. ⁸Let him keep watch over his own soul, ever mindful of that saying of the Apostle: *He who serves well secures a good standing for himself* (1 Tim 3:13). ⁹He must show every care and concern for the sick, children, guests and the poor, knowing for certain that he will be held accountable for all of them on the day of judgment. ¹⁰He will regard all utensils and goods of the monastery as sacred vessels of the altar, ¹¹aware that nothing is to be neglected. ¹²He should not be prone to greed, nor be wasteful and extravagant with the goods of the monastery, but should do everything with moderation and according to the abbot's orders.

¹³Above all, let him be humble. If goods are not available to meet a request, he will offer a kind word in reply, ¹⁴for it is written: A kind *word is better than the best gift* (Sir 18:17). ¹⁵He should take care of all that the abbot entrusts to him, and not presume to do what the abbot has forbidden. ¹⁶He will provide the brothers their allotted amount of food without any pride or delay, lest they be led astray. For he must remember what the Scripture says that

117

person deserves *who leads one of the little ones astray* (Matt 18:6).

¹⁷If the community is rather large, he should be given helpers, that with their assistance he may calmly perform the duties of his office. ¹⁸Necessary items are to be requested and given at the proper times, ¹⁹so that no one may be disquieted or distressed in the house of God.

The healing of wounds and fractures so that we can lead a full and fulfilled life does not stop with people. The responsible handling of others, as well as of our own selves, now leads to the handling of the non-human; what we have been shown of gentleness and compassion and stewardship is now applied to the material world. The totality of Benedict's vision is, for me, one of its most significant features.

I was brought up to believe that the spiritual was of infinitely greater worth than the material, led to believe that God was much more interested in souls then in bodies, that the saying of prayers was of far greater concern to him than the handling of the tools of my daily life. In other words, I found myself trapped in that dualism, which has been common for so long in the West and which I feel has done such damage to our Christian understanding, which finds a split between the sacred and the profane, and introduces this terrible divide into our lives. Such a dichotomy is not to be found with Benedict. Indeed it is contrary to the whole tenor of the relation of the human and the divine that is found in the Scriptures, from which, of course, he drew his inspiration. "Everything God created is good, and nothing is to be rejected if it is received with thanksgiving, because it is consecrated by the Word of God and prayer" (1 Tim 4:4). So Benedict moves naturally between the material and the spiritual and sees both as being part of an integrated unity.

In this chapter Benedict looks at the office of the cellarer of the community, whose title comes from the Latin word *cellarium,* meaning storeroom. At once we realize that we are now going to be given the portrait of a man who is concerned with the day-to-day necessities of life, the man in charge of the store in which all the things that members of the community might need are kept. How are all these things to be handled? The key comes in verse 10, one of the most famous aphorisms of the Rule: "He will regard all utensils and goods of the monastery as sacred vessels of the altar." But the chapter puts this into its wider context. Benedict is concerned with the question of how the cellarer is to relate to the people who ask him for these things and how he is to handle his own self. It is the inter-connection of the people and things that is one of the most important aspects of this discussion. Today many concerned for the environment, such as Wendell Berry, are reminding us of something that we have for far too long failed to observe.

> There is an uncanny resemblance between our behavior toward each other and our behavior toward the earth. By some connection we do not recognise, the willingness to exploit one becomes the willingness to exploit the other. . . . It is impossible to care for each other more or differently than we care for the earth.

The chapter opens with a sketch showing what sort of man the cellarer ought to be, for it is much less the job to which he is assigned than the qualities he brings to it that concern Benedict. I find it fascinating to see that it is to the description given for a bishop in 1 Timothy 3:2-4 that Benedict turns for the portrait of the cellarer, for at once the underlying point is implicitly made: the pastoral care of souls and the careful handling of material objects can be paralleled.

There is much here that is in common with the earlier portrait of the abbot in chapter 2, and indeed the cellarer is said to be like *(sicut)* a father to the community. But that word *sicut* is important. He is not to take over the role of the head of the community; he is a man under orders. Benedict knows only too well that for anyone who has to deal with material possessions, there is always the danger of the abuse of power, the temptation to build up a power complex, and he is careful to say, not only in verses 4 and 5 but again in verse 12, that the cellarer is never to forget that he is a man under orders.

The cellarer is to be wise, mature, temperate, not proud or excitable. The key word is moderation. Just as the brothers are to have sufficient, not superfluous goods (a point that is made very clearly indeed in chapter 55 when Benedict comes to deal with clothing), so also the cellarer is to steer a mid-point between being either extravagant or mean (12). It is waste in particular that Benedict warns against. He uses the word "wasteful" in the first verse, and repeats it in verse 12, adding "greed" and "extravagant." In a society with planned obsolescence built into it, a society which is increasingly throw-away with little regard for things per se, Benedict is giving us a statement about values that I need to hear. There is much more to be said about this, and it is a theme which he will develop in the following chapter.

But the discussion here is essentially about human relationships, about the use and abuse of power, about the exercise of authority. To any of us holding positions of authority and responsibility, there is sound, practical, loving wisdom in this portrait from which we can learn much. Am I tempted to diminish or make people feel dependent on me—even by so small a thing as keeping them waiting? Do I needlessly irritate? Do I overlook the small people, the weak, the powerless? These are questions that rise to mind as Benedict shows me how the cellarer exercises his role amongst the brothers, and how he handles situations in which, with complete community of goods and everything being shared, each is at the mercy of the other and the relations between them become of the greatest importance.

Here the man with access to the source of supplies plays the most sensitive role. The verse from Matthew quoted in verse 16 shows us what is at issue here: the concern not to lead the other astray, not to crush the morale of the other, either by causing anger or dejection. In verses 6 and 7 the cellarer is shown as being very sensitive to the feelings of the community. A refusal is made gently and cheerfully (13) so as not to cause undue distress. He responds with gentleness to those who come to him with extreme or difficult demands. He does not return evil for evil (8). He is mindful that everything he does is seen by God. He is indeed a model of non-violence, and the very way in which he handles people demonstrates a profound spiritual truth: people are to be handled with respect and reverence.

But the cellarer is also to handle himself with gentleness. He is to show these same qualities toward himself in the way in which he takes care of his own body and spirit. For anyone in ministry today, the final verses of this chapter remind us of something that we might be tempted to forget or to neglect. The cellarer is not too proud to admit that he may need help. He is prepared to delegate, not seeing himself as indispensable. He knows the importance of drawing lines so that he is not endlessly accessible. He makes himself available at established times; self-protection requires that boundaries are laid down. Many of us are grateful for a book that Henri Nouwen wrote some years ago on how those in ministry should take care of themselves. Elsewhere he has reminded us of the importance of the "ministry of absence." Handling with care applies just as much to my own self as it does to other people and to the material world. It is this profoundly sacramental understanding that is to color what Benedict is to unfold next for us.

And the purpose? So that he remain calm. Peace is fundamental in the Rule. Even though the word itself is not used all that frequently, Benedict has much to say about the peaceable person. Peace is essentially an inner quality of the human heart, and he knows only too well how much we all need to cultivate that internal peace. There are so many entertaining and extremely human glimpses of the restless, quarrelsome, murmuring, self-important, or complaining behavior of the monks with which I can easily identify, and it shows how well Benedict knows the human situation. But here is the cellarer, a man busy and under pressure just like so many of us today, subject to interruptions, demands, expectations, and the final point that Benedict makes in this chapter is that it is vital that the cellarer pays attention to his own equanimity.

This chapter is one of the most profound, original, and beautiful of the Rule. (It is interesting to see that it is longer than chapter 64, which describes the qualities of the abbot.) It is a portrait of humble love. As I read it I am struck by the example of the simple qualities of humility and kindliness that Benedict expects the cellarer to express in his daily work, in the way in which he handles the people, and the things for which he is responsible. I feel that I am being shown something very important, which does not come across as any moralizing statement or ethical demand, but rather as an example from which I should learn—and once again that it is the figure of Christ himself incarnated in the figure of this busy and down-to-earth man that is the model that Benedict is giving me.

CHAPTER THIRTY-TWO

¹The goods of the monastery, that is, its tools, clothing or anything else, should be entrusted to brothers whom the abbot appoints and in whose manner of life he has confidence. ²He will, as he sees fit, issue to them the various articles to be cared for and collected after use. ³The abbot will maintain a list of these, so that when the brothers succeed one another in their assigned tasks, he may be aware of what he hands out and what he receives back.

⁴Whoever fails to keep the things belonging to the monastery clean or treats them carelessly should be reproved. ⁵If he does not amend, let him be subjected to the discipline of the rule.

In the previous chapter, Benedict said that we were to regard "all utensils and goods of the monastery as sacred vessels of the altar," and in those few words he has given us a whole theology in relation to the material world on which this chapter is to build. But there is another earlier reference in the Rule that we can now recall with advantage. At the end of chapter 4, which looked at the tools of good works, we were told that when we have used them without ceasing, day and night (76), and handled them faithfully (78), we hand them over and receive our reward. Now we see how the ordinary tools of daily life are to be handled in the same way. The description of the procedure is very precise. Tools, clothing, any other equipment, are entrusted to the brothers by the abbot, who keeps a list, so that they may be cared for and, after use, may be collected again. The seriousness with which things are to be handled is emphasized: the abbot is aware of what he is handing out and what he will receive back.

For things matter. We are placed in this world, and it is in and through this world, not by the denial of it, that we shall come to God. But I need guidelines on this. I am surrounded by a materialistic culture and I need help in holding a balance between appreciating the material things in my life and finding myself trapped by them. Since the abbot holds the place of Christ for the community, I now translate what that means for my own self, and I then find that I am being given a most practical and immediate example of how to approach this. All the good things in my life are lent to me by Christ. They are to be cared for. Each is important and Christ has kept a list. They are on loan so that I can fulfill the assigned tasks, and they are to be collected at the end, at the end of my life, the day of judgment. The actual word used for collect, *recolligenda,* is a word used later on in chapter 48 for the actual physical work of harvesting, and I find that it carries significant resonances, not least the biblical ones, of the gathering in of something that has reached its full maturity through the careful husbandry of the farmer.

Benedict is here facing me with something so utterly ordinary and daily that I really cannot escape its practical implications. Things are on loan to me. They are good things. I am to look after them properly and use them responsibly because each and everything matters. Christ has kept a list, and at the day of judgment I shall have to answer for the way in which I have used them. The underlying assumption is, of course, that I shall have handled them in such a way that, just as things grow to harvest, they will have come to fruition in my hands. I must not forget the day of judgment; failure carries reproof, punishment.

I am grateful that Benedict insists on how seriously this is to be taken. It is something that I can easily think about, particularly when the whole idea of stewardship is so popular at the moment, and yet I drift along without doing much about it. I think that it would be a good exercise to make a list of all the good things in my life and then ask myself if I really do handle them with the sense of respect and responsibility that Benedict is asking of me. I then ask, do I really remember that they are only on loan? I guess that I might then find that Benedict's way is a real challenge to the way in which I live.

CHAPTER THIRTY-THREE

¹Above all, this evil practice must be uprooted and removed from the monastery. ²We mean that without an order from the abbot, no one may presume to give, receive, ³or retain anything as his own, nothing at all—not a book, writing tablets or stylus—in short, not a single item, ⁴especially since monks may not have the free disposal even of their own bodies and wills. ⁵For their needs, they are to look to the father of the monastery, and are not allowed anything which the abbot has not given or permitted. ⁶*All things should be the common possession* of all, as it is written, *so that no one* presumes to *call anything his own* (Acts 4:32).

⁷But if anyone is caught indulging in this most evil practice, he should be warned a first and a second time. ⁸If he does not amend, let him be subjected to punishment.

We do less than justice to Benedict if we emphasize his moderation and balance to the detriment of the passion that is also there. In this short chapter when he comes to talk about private ownership, he twice uses the word "evil," which shows that he considers this subject of the utmost importance. It is, however, not so much the physical possessions themselves (for after all he has just been telling me to handle my material possessions with a sacramental reverence) but the underlying attitude toward them that is his concern. The word *habere*, which appears in the Latin title of the chapter and again in verse 3, can mean to "consider" rather than to have. His interest is not, therefore, on external behavior, but on the purity of intention, so that once again it is the disposition of the heart that is the real issue. If this is so, it immediately widens its application and makes this chapter extremely relevant to the attitudes and values with which I approach the affluent society in which I live.

It is interesting to see how Benedict has "reworked" (this is Kardong's word; *RB 1980* uses the more modest word "adapted") the verse that he quotes from Acts 4 in order to seriously alter it to suit his purposes. His concern is with the practice of personal dispossession; the concern in Acts is for communal sharing. This all strengthens the thread that has been running throughout this discussion. Avarice is at stake, which is what I now realize that this chapter is about. If we are foolish enough to let avarice into our hearts, it will become an insatiable tyrant. This is, of course, based on 1 Timothy 6:10: "The love of money is a root of all kinds of evil." This is so serious a matter that it must be uprooted, pulled out by its roots *(amputare,* the Latin makes the point of radical amputation). As with certain plants, the smallest part of a root will continue to flourish. This is a malignant growth, and merely to lop off the top growth will not be sufficient to stop it from going on growing and spreading. This is a totally radical demand. Avarice can never have enough; it gives rise to other vices. That is why it must be totally excluded from the monastery.

Why this radical demand? What is it saying to me? Benedict is forcing me to see that it is not so much possessions in themselves that concern him, as the danger that they are, or can become, the vehicles for relations between people. They can lead me to trust and to love, or they can lead me on to more and more acquisitiveness, and thus to greed, envy, resentment, competitiveness, bitterness. Rather than let any of this start to spread in my life, I should cut it out.

CHAPTER THIRTY-FOUR

¹It is written: *Distribution was made to each one as he had need* (Acts 4:35). ²By this we do not imply that there should be favoritism—God forbid—but rather consideration for weaknesses. ³Whoever needs less should thank God and not be distressed, ⁴but whoever needs more should feel humble because of his weakness, not self-important because of the kindness shown him. ⁵In this way all the members will be at peace. ⁶First and foremost, there must be no word or sign of the evil of grumbling, no manifestation of it for any reason at all. ⁷If, however, anyone is caught grumbling, let him undergo more severe discipline.

This chapter now carries the subject of chapter 33 a step further. Its Latin title takes the form of a question: "Should all receive the same necessities of life?" The answer is taken, as it was previously, from Acts 4:35, quoted right at the start. Everyone gets what they need. This may differ from what they want! Benedict is not showing us a consumerist paradise, fueled by the systematic inflation of false wants and desires. It is the abbot, the father, who discerns what are the real needs and cuts through the delusions in order to see what these may be. This distinction between need and want is one that I can apply to myself and use as a yardstick in my own life.

But Benedict's interest is not in the individual: it is with the building up of harmony and peace amongst all the members. So in many ways the real inspiration for this chapter comes from that passage in 1 Corinthians 12:12-30 on the members of the body of Christ, which is caught in verse 5 where Benedict speaks of "all the members." I like to read it as a prayerful reflection on what follows if the practice of avarice and envy and all the consequent evils are rooted out in each of us and so in the group. If I am content (and this very simple word is to come up again later, repeated twice in a lovely small phrase that Benedict uses in 61,2-3) with what I am given, whether it be my talents and gifts or my material possessions, then I can rejoice in what I have received and look with equal rejoicing on what others have been given. This asks a true mutual concern for one another. Neither the strong nor the weak envy the other. Grumbling is the enemy of this. When I think of those greatest grumblers of all, the Pharisees, who are the prototype of the strong and who are jealous of the mercy shown to the weak, I realize that what is being asked of me is a deep, loving openness, which does not judge, which is in fact simply the exercise of that unconditional love that is ultimately what Benedict is hoping for in us all.

If we are all members one of another, that implies that each one of us is a special, unique individual. The worth of each is something that Benedict returns to time and again in the Rule. If some are stronger while others are weaker, this is not to be a cause for either self-congratulation or commiseration. The passage in 1 Corinthians is about each member of the body having its part to play no matter how humble and seemingly unlovely. So it asks of us acceptance, accepting myself as the person I am, the unique son or daughter of a loving, generous Creator father, and accepting each of my brothers and sisters as of the same unique worth.

This chapter is also a study of peace. If the emphasis in the previous chapter was on personal attitudes, in this chapter it is on the corporate, with the goal and aim of peace, the peace which is described in Acts 4:32: "the believers were all of one mind and one heart."

*

Before I move on any further, I want to stay with these two chapters that come at roughly the midpoint of the Rule, for they show me so clearly the two streams that flow into the text of the Rule as into my own life. Benedict addresses both the personal and the corporate, or, in monastic terms, both the anchoritic or eremetical and the cenobitic. In scholarly terms we might say that he has drawn on two divergent literary sources in order to juxtapose two schools of monastic tradition and draw insights from both. The point that he is making is that both are needed, that one depends on the other, that my approach should be inclusive. So I can look on chapters 33 and 34 as some sort of hinge that is holding together the vertical and the horizontal. I have been prepared by much of the earlier material, in particular by the first seven chapters, for self-understanding, for my solitary relationship with God. But this must not be separated from the shared relationship of my life with others. It is this that Benedict will now show me—both in the utterly practical and down-to-earth chapters that follow, but later on, in a piece of lyrical writing in chapter 73, about what mutual love asks and gives.

CHAPTER THIRTY-FIVE

¹The brothers should serve one another. Consequently, no one will be excused from kitchen service unless he is sick or engaged in some important business of the monastery, ²for such service increases reward and fosters love. ³Let those who are not strong have help so that they may serve without distress, ⁴and let everyone receive help as the size of the community or local conditions warrant. ⁵If the community is rather large, the cellarer should be excused from kitchen service, and, as we have said, those should also be excused who are engaged in important business. ⁶Let all the rest serve one another in love.

⁷On Saturday the brother who is completing his work will do the washing. ⁸He is to wash the towels which the brothers use to wipe their hands and feet. ⁹Both the one who is ending his service and the one who is about to begin are to wash the feet of everyone. ¹⁰The utensils required for the kitchen service are to be washed and returned intact to the cellarer, ¹¹who in turn issues them to the one beginning his week. In this way the cellarer will know what he hands out and what he receives back.

¹²An hour before mealtime, the kitchen workers of the week should each receive a drink and some bread over and above the regular portion, ¹³so that at mealtime, they may serve their brothers without grumbling or hardship. ¹⁴On solemn days, however, they should wait until after the dismissal.

¹⁵On Sunday immediately after Lauds, those beginning as well as those completing their week of service should make a profound bow in the oratory before all and ask for their prayers. ¹⁶Let the server completing his week recite this

verse: *Blessed are you, Lord God, who have helped me and comforted me* (Dan 3:52; Ps 85[86]:17). [17]After this verse has been said three times, he receives a blessing. Then the one beginning his service follows and says: *God, come to my assistance; Lord, make haste to help me* (Ps 69[70]:2). [18]And all repeat this verse three times. When he has received a blessing, he begins his service.

"The brothers should serve one another. . . . Such service . . . fosters love" (1-2). Here is one of those aphorisms that Benedict loves so much, and it opens a chapter about work in the kitchen. This service is to foster love. The figure of Christ the Servant is never far away as Benedict writes about the life of the community. Christ came amongst us as one who serves (Luke 22:27). We think of Philemon 2:7 (Christ "taking the form of a servant"), or the quotation in Matthew 12:18 from the Servant Song of Isaiah applied to him: "Behold, my servant whom I have chosen." Since no servant is greater than his master, Christ intended his example to be followed by his disciples: "The Son of man came not to be served but to serve" (Matt 20:28). It is summed up in the injunction: "Serve one another mutually in charity" (Gal 5:13). Life in community, as the following clutch of chapters shows, brings the opportunity to express that love and service in daily contact with one's brothers or sisters.

There are two New Testament scenes that were probably present in Benedict's mind as he was writing this chapter. The original task of the first deacons in Jerusalem was that of "the service of tables," which is specifically, of course, the subject at issue here. But there is also the example of serving one another in love with the feet washing at the Last Supper. In verse 9 that is directly recalled in the rite with which each week opens and closes. The earliest cenobitic founders saw that the reality of living the paschal mystery gave them the example of Christ's own total self-giving as the culmination of a life of service. Living in Christ, living the Gospel, means service in humble love.

Such an approach to meals and the sharing of food brings Eucharistic understanding into daily life. The washing of the feet at the beginning and end of the week takes place around the meal table. The change-over of the weekly officials takes place in the oratory. The words for the start of the week's work in the kitchen ask a blessing in exactly the same words from the psalms as those for the opening of the Offices. As I see the natural flow between refectory and chapel I ask myself: How do I translate what Benedict is showing me into my own life?

Here is the acid test: Can everything that I have been shown in the previous chapters about stewardship, about service and mutual concern, about the sacramental approach to life, become a reality in my daily routine in the preparation and serving of food? Everything matters. Everything, each kitchen utensil, is to be handled with respect and care. I think again of the cellarer issuing the things for the week and keeping a list so that what is given out may be returned. The very activity of washing is an expression of a sense of responsible and loving stewardship.

Once again this attitude of love and care is shown toward people. While no one is excused from this most ordinary of work in the kitchen, unless for very pressing reasons, equally no one is to be over-burdened or distressed. Extra help is to be given where it is needed (3); extra food and drink are to be available an hour before mealtime (12-13).

I find that the way in which Benedict treats this seemingly prosaic subject forces me to ask some uncomfortable questions about the way in which I live my daily life. What he shows me is simply Gospel teaching about things and people, made specific and therefore inescapable in daily life. This chapter also reminds me of something that I often tend to neglect: service begins at home. Care and concern for the disadvantaged, ministry with the underprivileged, a commitment to good causes in distant parts of the world, does not excuse me from the demands of service to those close to me, in my immediate circle. This is the touchstone of the genuineness of the self-giving love embodied in the service to that wider brotherhood or sisterhood.

CHAPTER THIRTY-SIX

¹Care of the sick must rank above and before all else, so that they may truly be served as Christ, ²for he said: *I was sick and you visited me* (Matt 25:36), ³and, *What you did for one of these least brothers you did for me* (Matt 25:40). ⁴Let the sick on their part bear in mind that they are served out of honor for God, and let them not by their excessive demands distress their brothers who serve them. ⁵Still, sick brothers must be patiently borne with, because serving them leads to a greater reward. ⁶Consequently, the abbot should be extremely careful that they suffer no neglect.

⁷Let a separate room be designated for the sick, and let them be served by an attendant who is God-fearing, attentive and concerned. ⁸The sick may take baths whenever it is advisable, but the healthy, and especially the young, should receive permission less readily. ⁹Moreover, to regain their strength, the sick who are very weak may eat meat, but when their health improves, they should all abstain from meat as usual.

¹⁰The abbot must take the greatest care that cellarers and those who serve the sick do not neglect them, for the shortcomings of disciples are his responsibility.

The word "service" runs like a thread through this chapter, which looks at the care of the sick, for it occurs no less than five times in its ten verses. It is the theme of mutual service of one to another that Benedict is again showing us. In this he is pointing us, as he always is, toward the figure of Christ as the exemplar whom we are to follow. As always with Benedict we go right to the source: Christ himself. Christ spent much of his earthly ministry healing the sick, maimed, crippled, lame, deaf, and blind so that they might live life to the fullest. But Christ also tells us that it is him whom we are serving in the sick, the poor, the needy.

This is not the only time that Benedict quotes these verses from Matthew 25, for they also come in 4,15-16 amongst the tools for good works and again at the opening of chapter 53 on the reception of guests. We all have to have present in our mind the day of judgment. This is a perspective that Benedict will not let us forget. Then we shall be asked what we did or what we failed to do, and this chapter is to encourage our commitment to this so that we shall be able to give answer on that day out of experience of compassionate service.

I like to find that anyone who is attendant on the sick needs to be God-fearing, attentive, concerned (7), and, above all, patient (5). This suggests a holistic approach to healing, the raising of the morale of the whole person, not just a careful application of nursing principles. When so much of today's illness probably has mental or emotional roots, I am glad of this approach. But I equally appreciate that Benedict insists that there are obligations on both sides. He always remains the realist, and so he knows that the sick may be very tiresome and difficult to endure. It is wrong to let someone get away with making selfish and excessive demands. Indeed, to do so would not help them toward standing on their own feet and taking responsibility for themselves, which will encourage their real healing.

The point about baths in the monastic tradition (8) goes back to Athanasius' life of Anthony:

> He never bathed his body in water to remove filth, nor did he as much as wash his feet or even allow himself to put them in water without necessity. No one ever saw him undressed, nor did anyone ever look upon his bare body until he died and was buried.

Here the issue at stake is sexual purity. The emphasis is on modesty, not on squalor. It is to be understood in the context of Greek and Roman baths, which were notoriously licentious places, and the desert monks fled the city. I think we should not make too much of this. Benedict is quite laconic, dealing with it in one verse. His approach is strictly common-sense: "advisable" and "permission" seem nicely judged words.

133

CHAPTER THIRTY-SEVEN

[1]Although human nature itself is inclined to be compassionate toward the old and the young, the authority of the rule should also provide for them. [2]Since their lack of strength must always be taken into account, they should certainly not be required to follow the strictness of the rule with regard to food, [3]but should be treated with kindly consideration and allowed to eat before the regular hours.

Benedict's gentle care for human weakness means that he is always saying that exceptions have to be made in particular cases, that strict rules do not apply. He now writes about the elderly and children and about their need for special understanding. He talks, of course, in immediately practical terms: here are two categories where rules about food are to be relaxed. The sacramental quality of food, the careful preparation and serving of meals, has been a strong element in previous chapters. Now we see how food becomes the way in which we show special consideration to the weak, the old, and the young. Compassion asks for the exercise of patience that Benedict included amongst the virtues listed in the previous chapter. When society seems increasingly to say that productivity and usefulness are the qualities by which we judge the worth of the individual, here Benedict is telling us that respect should be shown to those who apparently contribute little or nothing to the community in these terms.

CHAPTER THIRTY-EIGHT

[1]Reading will always accompany the meals of the brothers. The reader should not be the one who just happens to pick up the book, but someone who will read for a whole week, beginning on Sunday. [2]After Mass and Communion, let the incoming reader ask all to pray for him so that God may shield him from the spirit of vanity. [3]Let him begin this verse in the oratory: *Lord, open my lips, and my mouth shall proclaim your praise* (Ps 50[51]:17), and let all say it three times. [4]When he has received a blessing, he will begin his week of reading.

[5]Let there be complete silence. No whispering, no speaking—only the reader's voice should be heard there. [6]The brothers should by turn serve one another's needs as they eat and drink, so that no one need ask for anything. [7]If, however, anything is required, it should be requested by an audible signal of some kind rather than by speech. [8]No one should presume to ask a question about the reading or about anything else, *lest occasion be given* [to the devil] (Eph 4:27; 1 Tim 5:14). [9]The superior, however, may wish to say a few words of instruction.

[10]Because of holy Communion and because the fast may be too hard for him to bear, the brother who is reader for the week is to receive some diluted wine before he begins to read. [11]Afterward he will take his meal with the weekly kitchen servers and the attendants.

[12]Brothers will read and sing, not according to rank, but according to their ability to benefit their hearers.

This chapter describes another service. A reader is to be appointed each week. His week's work starts on Sunday, after Mass, when he is blessed in the oratory. He says the verse of the psalm that recalls the opening of the day Offices and receives a blessing.

He is chosen for his skills in reading aloud, bringing us to the category of those appointed for some specific form of service. Benedict makes the distinction of those who exercise specialized forms of ministry, men such as the cellarer, the prior, and the deans, chosen for their particular skills, while other duties, such as serving at table, are equally shared amongst everyone and take the form of mutual service that is so delicately and beautifully caught in the phrase of verse 6, "The brothers should by turn serve one another's needs as they eat and drink, so that no one need ask for anything." There is always the hazard with the specialist, of which Benedict is only too aware, that he or she will become puffed up with pride. While once again he shows himself sensitive to the demands of the task, so that, for example, the reader is to be given a special allowance of wine, he also warns against the spirit of vanity that would put the emphasis on personal excellence rather than attention to God.

The purpose of reading at meals is a reminder of the whole purpose of the life that Benedict is laying before us: it is so that we should be listening to God at all times. It goes back to the "Listen" as the opening word of the prologue. Silence is for hearing the Word. In this case the corporate situation of a shared meal asks for an awareness not only of God, but of the presence of one's neighbor. There is real sensitivity in the way in which Benedict suggests how important it is for the brothers to be conscious of one another's wants.

The only one to break the silence is the abbot if he should choose to give some commentary or teaching on what is being read. In the balance of the life that Benedict seeks, I have been made aware of the attention paid to the needs of the body, but it is no less vital to think of the needs of the mind. It is important to nourish, feed, and enrich the intellect. Once again a chapter that might seem to be about an outdated subject referring to the monastic life of the sixth century is, on closer study, full of theological and practical insights that have much relevance to me today.

CHAPTER THIRTY-NINE

¹For the daily meals, whether at noon or in midafternoon, it is enough, we believe, to provide all tables with two kinds of cooked food because of individual weaknesses. ²In this way, the person who may not be able to eat one kind of food may partake of the other. ³Two kinds of cooked food, therefore, should suffice for all the brothers, and if fruit or fresh vegetables are available, a third dish may also be added. ⁴A generous pound of bread is enough for a day whether for only one meal or for both dinner and supper. ⁵In the latter case the cellarer will set aside one third of this pound and give it to the brothers at supper.

⁶Should it happen that the work is heavier than usual, the abbot may decide—and he will have the authority—to grant something additional, provided that it is appropriate, ⁷and that above all overindulgence is avoided, lest a monk experience indigestion. ⁸For nothing is so inconsistent with the life of any Christian as overindulgence. ⁹Our Lord says: *Take care that your hearts are not weighed down with overindulgence* (Luke 21:34).

¹⁰Young boys should not receive the same amount as their elders, but less, since in all matters frugality is the rule. ¹¹Let everyone, except the sick who are very weak, abstain entirely from eating the meat of four-footed animals.

In all traditional societies the family or the extended family sitting around the table and sharing a meal together is something that helps to forge the bonds that unite them. It is also a powerful symbolic image of their shared unity. The care that Benedict takes in legislating for meals reminds us of that. Chapter 43, which links punctuality at table and at chapel, shows us again the significance that he attaches to mealtimes. In a society that grabs food, where many families no longer sit down together with any regular pattern of mealtimes, where fast food service is becoming more and more popular, this sense of respect due to food seems far distant from the general experience today. Thus we read this chapter recalling values that seem to be disappearing.

Benedict establishes both flexibility and certainty in the times of meals and the amount of food. Eating, like saying the Office, pays attention to the seasons of the year, as chapter 41 will describe. There is additional food at times when work is particularly demanding. The young, the old, and the sick are all to receive special attention. There is avoidance of rigidity or undue austerity, with the exception of flesh meat, which was then believed to heighten animal desire.

As I read this chapter it seems that Benedict's concern is not simply about having sufficient food, enough but not superfluous, but about the right handling of these good things. That is why there is a choice of dishes, so that all can expect to eat with enjoyment. That is why when there are fruits and fresh vegetables in season, they are to be added to the table. That is why he is not mean with the bread allowance, but says that it should be a generous one. He has been speaking about the respect due to material things, to created things, since they are a reflection of God the Creator. Now he also addresses the most familiar place in which I am faced by material things every day, namely, at the table. It is something over which I have a certain amount of choice. To look forward to a meal because it is carefully chosen and carefully presented gives to every meal something of a sacramental quality.

The one thing that appalls and shocks Benedict is overindulgence. It is a word that he uses no less than three times in verses 7-9. Many people today who know nothing of the monastic life, who have never heard of Benedict, are recognizing the wisdom of this as they pay the price for failing to eat properly, and have to resort to dieting or health resorts to restore the balance. But, of course, once more it is the attitude, the interior disposition, that Benedict is forcing me to think about. Greed, like avarice, makes me the prisoner of needs and desires that must be endlessly satisfied, and so it takes from me the freedom to enjoy the good things of God.

The quotation from Luke that Benedict uses in verse 9 is taken from that discourse just before the Passover on watching and praying and being alert for the coming of the Lord, when the disciples are to be tested and found wanting. The following chapter opens with the entry of Satan into the heart of Judas. The roots of his subsequent betrayal of Christ lay in the greed and avarice from which Benedict would want to protect us.

CHAPTER FORTY

¹Everyone has his own gift from God, one this and another that (1 Cor 7:7). ²It is, therefore, with some uneasiness that we specify the amount of food and drink for others. ³However, with due regard for the infirmities of the sick, we believe that a half bottle of wine a day is sufficient for each. ⁴But those to whom God gives the strength to abstain must know that they will earn their own reward.

⁵The superior will determine when local conditions, work or the summer heat indicates the need for a greater amount. He must, in any case, take great care lest excess or drunkenness creep in. ⁶We read that monks should not drink wine at all, but since the monks of our day cannot be convinced of this, let us at least agree to drink moderately, and not to the point of excess, ⁷for *wine makes even wise men go astray* (Sir 19:2).

⁸However, where local circumstances dictate an amount much less than what is stipulated above, or even none at all, those who live there should bless God and not grumble. ⁹Above all else we admonish them to refrain from grumbling.

The gifts of which Benedict is speaking when he opens this chapter with a quotation from 1 Corinthians are the gifts of self-control, abstinence, and, above all, sexual abstinence. But he refuses to be dogmatic. As he has done before, he first gives us the ideal—in this case, that monks should not drink wine at all, since the proper amount of drink is the subject of this chapter. But then he immediately goes on to qualify it: he confesses that he is uneasy about dictating to others, which gives us a very human and warm glimpse of his own feelings. He wants the initiative to come spontaneously from us. If I do give up drink, but unwillingly, and in my heart nurse negative feelings or resentments, then the action itself is of little value. As before, on a similar subject in chapter 34 where he is writing about sufficiency and moderation, Benedict ends with a fierce denunciation of grumbling.

No one is really sure how much a half bottle, *hermina,* measure really was, but it has allowed a great deal of joking as well as endless serious academic discussion.

CHAPTER FORTY-ONE

¹From holy Easter to Pentecost, the brothers eat at noon and take supper in the evening. ²Beginning with Pentecost and continuing throughout the summer, the monks fast until midafternoon on Wednesday and Friday, unless they are working in the fields or the summer heat is oppressive.

³On the other days they eat dinner at noon. ⁴Indeed, the abbot may decide that they should continue to eat dinner at noon every day if they have work in the fields or if the summer heat remains extreme. ⁵Similarly, he should so regulate and arrange all matters that souls may be saved and the brothers may go about their activities without justifiable grumbling.

⁶From the thirteenth of September to the beginning of Lent, they always take their meal in midafternoon. ⁷Finally, from the beginning of Lent to Easter, they eat towards evening. ⁸Let Vespers be celebrated early enough so that there is no need for a lamp while eating, and that everything can be finished by daylight. ⁹Indeed, at all times let supper or the hour of the fast-day meal be so scheduled that everything can be done by daylight.

Here is what at first sight seems a rather dull chapter about dividing the eating schedules into four categories. The starting point is Easter, the pivot of the year around which all other times and seasons turn. Easter means resurrection, new life, the risen Christ, the end and purpose of our life, as true for each individual as for the community. The other point of reference is light. Today when electricity has destroyed any sense of the coming of light and of dark, it is good to be reminded of the symbolic significance daily given to us in the pattern of each day. Perhaps we are just beginning to recognize the cost of our disassociation from the natural world and its rhythms. This chapter encourages me to reflect on whether or not I pay sufficient attention to the gift of light.

This chapter also encourages me to look again at fasting (2). Fasting is a subject that is not often discussed these days, although hunger strikes and health dieting are now common. But there, of course, the motives are either political power or health and beauty. The very first statement that Christ makes about fasting deals with the question of motive (Matt 6:16-18). The purpose of fasting is simply to center on God. The discipline of fasting will reveal to me more than any other discipline what really controls me. It is no longer possible to cover up my interior dependencies—food, good things, praise, anger, envy. Fasting, therefore, plays its part in the movement of freedom, of dissociation and non-possession, along which Benedict has been leading me so firmly in this section of the Rule.

Yet as always he is relaxed rather than rigorous. He immediately qualifies with exceptions. Fasting does not mean extreme asceticism for its own sake, nor should it be undertaken to the detriment of health and a sensible concern for our bodies. The role of the abbot is a reminder of the importance of a spiritual director or responsible guide to check extreme impulses and impose some sort of balance.

CHAPTER FORTY-TWO

[1]Monks should diligently cultivate silence at all times, but especially at night. [2]Accordingly, this will always be the arrangement whether for fast days or for ordinary days. [3]When there are two meals, all the monks will sit together immediately after rising from supper. Someone should read from the *Conferences* or the *Lives* of the Fathers or at any rate something else that will benefit the hearers, [4]but not the Heptateuch or the Books of Kings, because it will not be good for those of weak understanding to hear these writings at that hour; they should be read at other times.

[5]On fast days there is to be a short interval between Vespers and the reading of the *Conferences,* as we have indicated. [6]Then let four or five pages be read, or as many as time permits. [7]This reading period will allow for all to come together, in case any were engaged in assigned tasks. [8]When all have assembled, they should pray Compline; and on leaving Compline, no one will be permitted to speak further. [9]If anyone is found to transgress this rule of silence, he must be subjected to severe punishment, [10]except on occasions when guests require attention or the abbot wishes to give someone a command, [11]but even this is to be done with the utmost seriousness and proper restraint.

How are our minds to be filled, in particular just before going to sleep? Body, mind, and spirit go together. This is one of the essential planks of the Benedictine way. It is quite natural, therefore, having looked at the way in which food is to be organized, that Benedict should now turn to the feeding of the mind. The intellect too must be nourished. The suggested material to be read aloud is to give food for meditation, drawing on the works of spiritual masters that will be suitably edifying, so anything that might excite the imagination, such as scenes of battle and conflict from Old Testament history, is to be avoided.

There is little here that has not been said already in one form or another. The proper disposition for any true listening is that of silence, and as the day draws toward its close this point has to be emphasized. There does not seem to be any suggestion that the brothers say Compline in the oratory, rather that it follows on naturally in the same place after that shared reading has come to an end. So the whole group moves from table to reading to praying. The three elements of body, mind, and spirit are brought together as the day comes to its end. The whole thing is wrapped up in silence, that deep interior silence that is such a creative part of life, of any life, since it allows us to hear the Word of God in the depths of our hearts and to rest there through the hours of darkness.

CHAPTER FORTY-THREE

[1]On hearing the signal for an hour of the divine office, the monk will immediately set aside what he has in hand and go with utmost speed, [2]yet with gravity and without giving occasion for frivolity. [3]Indeed, nothing is to be preferred to the Work of God.

[4]If at Vigils anyone comes after the "Glory be to the Father" of Psalm 94, which we wish, therefore, to be said quite deliberately and slowly, he is not to stand in his regular place in choir. [5]He must take the last place of all, or one set apart by the abbot for such offenders, that they may be seen by him and by all, [6]until they do penance by public satisfaction at the end of the Work of God. [7]We have decided, therefore, that they ought to stand either in the last place or apart from the others so that the attention they attract will shame them into amending. [8]Should they remain outside the oratory, there may be those who would return to bed and sleep, or, worse yet, settle down outside and engage in idle talk, thereby *giving occasion to the Evil One* (Eph 4:27; 1 Tim 5:14). [9]They should come inside so that they will not lose everything and may amend in the future.

[10]At the day hours the same rule applies to anyone who comes after the opening verse and the "Glory be to the Father" of the first psalm following it: he is to stand in the last place. [11]Until he has made satisfaction, he is not to presume to join the choir of those praying the psalms, unless perhaps the abbot pardons him and grants an exception. [12]Even in this case, the one at fault is still bound to satisfaction.

[13]But, if anyone does not come to table before the verse so that all may say the verse and pray and sit down at table

146

together, [14]and if this failure happens through the individual's own negligence or fault, he should be reproved up to the second time. [15]If he still does not amend, let him not be permitted to share the common table, [16]but take his meals alone, separated from the company of all. His portion of wine should be taken away until there is satisfaction and amendment. [17]Anyone not present for the verse said after meals is to be treated in the same manner.

[18]No one is to presume to eat or drink before or after the time appointed. [19]Moreover, if anyone is offered something by a superior and refuses it, then, if later he wants what he refused or anything else, he should receive nothing at all until he has made appropriate amends.

But the balance of chapter 42 is not the same thing as being middle of the way, mediocre. Benedict wants people who are wholehearted in their commitment, not halfhearted, half alive. He is writing of a love that is fervent, *fervens,* white hot, burning. Do our hearts burn within us? That is the question. The four chapters which come now are about being lukewarm, casual. Drifting is amongst the less spectacular of sins, but it has nevertheless to be firmly dealt with.

To show a carelessness about time will distort the even flow of movement that gives shape to each day and that is based on respect both for time itself and for the life of the community. To be late, whether for chapel or refectory, shows a disregard for the delicate framework of study, work, and worship that Benedict has been setting up so clearly and humanely in the foregoing chapters, and whose purpose is simply and solely that life may center upon the work of God, the *opus Dei.*

Once again, we are given one of those aphorisms that sums everything up so well in one pithy saying: "Nothing is to be preferred to the Work of God" (3). I have a very simple prayer schedule, one that is reasonably flexible for it has to change according to the circumstances of my life. I know how easy it is to let it slip—in the morning to hear my alarm and to switch it off telling myself that it does not really matter, or in the evening to let other things crowd in instead. But it does matter. That is what Benedict is saying here. I have an assignation with God, and I must keep it, for in the end it is simply the most important thing in life.

147

Again there is humanity and humor in the way in which every allowance is made for human weakness. The opening verses of Psalm 94 (95) at Vigils (Matins) are to be said slowly to give the latecomer every opportunity to get to his right place on time (4). That right place is a symbolic statement about right order in general. Each person and each thing has its proper place. To be out of that place, to be standing where one does not belong, is an outward demonstration of a deeper spiritual truth. To make such a dramatic public sign of amendment may seem rather extreme unless I appreciate the point at issue here. To have a place to stand is a basic human need in order that I know where I belong, and it is necessary both in relation to the places and to the people in my life. It means, above all, that I have time and space for listening to the Word of God in all the many ways that God is reaching out to me. That will be totally impossible if I am always running, late, distracted, feeling ajar and torn apart. Benedict is helping me to find my own center.

"No one is to presume to eat or drink before or after the time appointed" (18). This is not some narrow and negative ruling, but something that shows a real grasp of how human beings work best. It is one that I know from my own experience. It was particularly true in the years when I was bringing up small children who needed the sense of security that comes from knowing that things happen at the right times and in the right places. It is also true of a busy life in other circumstances. Respecting boundaries, not letting things drift, means that I am totally present to whatever I am doing, present with awareness, and therefore with energy for whatever that place, that moment may bring me.

CHAPTER FORTY-FOUR

¹Anyone excommunicated for serious faults from the oratory and from the table is to prostrate himself in silence at the oratory entrance at the end of the celebration of the Work of God. ²He should lie face down at the feet of all as they leave the oratory, ³and let him do this until the abbot judges he has made satisfaction. ⁴Next, at the bidding of the abbot, he is to prostrate himself at the abbot's feet, then at the feet of all that they may pray for him. ⁵Only then, if the abbot orders, should he be admitted to the choir in the rank the abbot assigns. ⁶Even so, he should not presume to lead a psalm or a reading or anything else in the oratory without further instructions from the abbot. ⁷In addition, at all the hours, as the Work of God is being completed, he must prostrate himself in the place he occupies. ⁸He will continue this form of satisfaction until the abbot again bids him cease.

⁹Those excommunicated for less serious faults from the table only are to make satisfaction in the oratory for as long as the abbot orders. ¹⁰They do so until he gives his blessing and says: "Enough."

This is a tough chapter that strikes a harsh and alien chord today. It is essentially about the authority of the person in charge of the sinner to see that there is true repentance, a recognition of what sin does to others and to God, as well as to oneself. It is interesting to see that once again the oratory and the table are linked: faults in ordinary daily life are no less serious than faults of a more strictly spiritual nature. To lie prostrate is an act of humiliation, of course, but it is also a symbolic act of touching the ground, being in touch with the ground of my being, the

149

ground of the universe, and it reminds us of all that Benedict was saying in chapter 7. It is not easy today when I am so often encouraged to point the finger at my parents, my upbringing, my environment, my inherited genes, to be told that I have done something wrong, which hurts those around me and not merely my own self, and that this must be admitted publicly and openly.

The abbot is referred to no less than eight times in this chapter in what is shown to be a long, slow process. True repentance and restoration can never be a superficial matter. I find it illuminating to read this chapter in the context of the four-step return of the excommunicated in the early Church: mourn, listen, prostrate, stand. All those elements are here, and if I think about them as steps in a process, I see that in the end it all comes back to the desire of Benedict that I may stand—stand upright before God, stand in my proper place, amongst the people to whom I belong.

CHAPTER FORTY-FIVE

[1]Should anyone make a mistake in a psalm, responsory, refrain or reading, he must make satisfaction there before all. If he does not use this occasion to humble himself, he will be subjected to more severe punishment [2]for failing to correct by humility the wrong committed through negligence. [3]Children, however, are to be whipped for such a fault.

Whatever is done must be done well. The outer and the inner must be in relation. I am reminded of what Benedict said in an earlier chapter on behavior in choir: "Let us stand to sing the psalms in such a way that our minds are in harmony with our voices" (19,7). If I make a mistake, the chances are that I am simply not paying attention, that I am not wholly present to the work of God, that my thoughts are straying, wandering off in other directions. "Negligence" is a nicely chosen word here! Again, the punishment seems excessively severe, but I can see that its underlying purpose is to emphasize the seriousness of the matter. We are brought back once again to the theme of respect and reverence for everything, but, above all, for the work of God.

CHAPTER FORTY-SIX

¹If someone commits a fault while at any work—while working in the kitchen, in the storeroom, in serving, in the bakery, in the garden, in any craft or anywhere else—²either by breaking or losing something or failing in any other way in any other place, ³he must at once come before the abbot and community and of his own accord admit his fault and make satisfaction. ⁴If it is made known through another, he is to be subjected to a more severe correction.

⁵When the cause of the sin lies hidden in his conscience, he is to reveal it only to the abbot or to one of the spiritual elders, ⁶who know how to heal their own wounds as well as those of others, without exposing them and making them public.

There is no division into separate spheres of life. Benedict tells us this time and again, in different circumstances, in different ways, but the message is the same. His is a holistic spirituality in which exterior and interior correspond, where the same attitudes apply at meals as at prayer. And now he spells it out for us, giving us a list of places to remind us in the most down-to-earth way that respect and reverence for the handling of things applies in the bakery, in the storeroom, the garden, the pottery. Each single thing matters. Own up at once if you drop or damage anything. Own up in public, because by damaging the material object you also in some way hurt the community too. There is a sense here of inter-connectedness, inter-relatedness that our highly individualistic world has lost, though it is something that the older world knew (and I think once again of the world of the Celtic peoples, or the Native Americans). If you do damage to material things, or to the earth itself, you also do damage to the people involved.

But as well as the public admission of fault Benedict emphasizes the interior, the inward. It is probably anachronistic to read back the practice of private confession here. More likely verses 5-6 draw on the desert tradition in which the honest confession of sin and shortcomings was seen as the best way to defeat Satan at his own game, and it recalls 7,44-48 in which we also find this same master-disciple tradition. Living together, living with others, does not necessarily mean that everything is to be public. Just as I know that it is important to cultivate the solitary side of my own self so here, in the case of healing, there is a place in which the secret and hidden side is to be respected. What Benedict is describing here would be seen as in another age being professional, observing confidentiality.

Since in the end the purpose of the correction of faults is remedial, is for healing, this section ends in this delicate, gentle, understanding way. Those public prostrations, those corporal punishments, should not be allowed to detract from what lies at the heart of this chapter, the putting away of sin, of secret sin lying in the heart as well as of the more openly and apparently culpable offenses. This comes with the help of God, but also through the help of others who, because they acknowledge their own woundedness and know pain and fractures in themselves, can help to heal their brothers and sisters.

CHAPTER FORTY-SEVEN

¹It is the abbot's care to announce, day and night, the hour for the Work of God. He may do so personally or delegate the responsibility to a conscientious brother, so that everything may be done at the proper time.

²Only those so authorized are to lead psalms and refrains, after the abbot according to their rank. ³No one should presume to read or sing unless he is able to benefit the hearers; ⁴let this be done with humility, seriousness and reverence, and the abbot's bidding.

This short chapter is about imposing a structure and framework on time that will allow attention to be paid to the work of God night and day. Its concern is once again that everything shall be done "at the proper time" (1), one of those small phrases that sum up the whole essence and purpose of the Rule.

In Benedict's day it would not be at all easy to keep to a timetable that had the degree of flexibility that he has been describing with a community lacking any of today's devices for marking time—clocks, alarm bells. One person must be in charge, in this case the abbot, though he may delegate the responsibility to another brother, someone who will handle his duties conscientiously. On him falls the responsibility of maintaining the movement from one activity to another, so that priority is given to the *opus Dei*.

Good order can, however, carry the danger of becoming mindless, automatic routine. To ensure that his monks are more than simply physically present in church, Benedict sees to it that those leading the psalms and refrains are men who will do it well and thus help to give the readings and the psalms their full meaning. He describes what he is looking for in his approach to worship as "humility, seriousness and reverence" (4). In those three words

Benedict is giving me a formula that I can apply in my own life, not only in prayer but equally in reading and in work, as the following chapter will be exploring.

CHAPTER FORTY-EIGHT

[1]Idleness is the enemy of the soul. Therefore, the brothers should have specified periods for manual labor as well as for prayerful reading.

[2]We believe that the times for both may be arranged as follows: [3]From Easter to the first of October, they will spend their mornings after Prime till about the fourth hour at whatever work needs to be done. [4]From the fourth hour until the time of Sext, they will devote themselves to reading. [5]But after Sext and their meal, they may rest on their beds in complete silence; should a brother wish to read privately, let him do so, but without disturbing the others. [6]They should say None a little early, about midway through the eighth hour, and then until Vespers they are to return to whatever work is necessary. [7]They must not become distressed if local conditions or their poverty should force them to do the harvesting themselves. [8]When they live by the labor of their hands, as our fathers and the apostles did, then they are really monks. [9]Yet, all things are to be done with moderation on account of the faint-hearted.

[10]From the first of October to the beginning of Lent, the brothers ought to devote themselves to reading until the end of the second hour. [11]At this time Terce is said and they are to work at their assigned tasks until None. [12]At the first signal for the hour of None, all put aside their work to be ready for the second signal. [13]Then after their meal they will devote themselves to their reading or to the psalms.

[14]During the days of Lent, they should be free in the morning to read until the third hour, after which they will work at their assigned tasks until the end of the tenth hour. [15]During this time of Lent each one is to receive a book from

156

the library, and is to read the whole of it straight through. [16]These books are to be distributed at the beginning of Lent.

[17]Above all, one or two seniors must surely be deputed to make the rounds of the monastery while the brothers are reading. [18]Their duty is to see that no brother is so apathetic as to waste time or engage in idle talk to the neglect of his reading, and so not only harm himself but also distract others. [19]If such a monk is found—God forbid—he should be reproved a first and a second time. [20]If he does not amend, he must be subjected to the punishment of the rule as a warning to others. [21]Further, brothers ought not to associate with one another at inappropriate times.

[22]On Sunday all are to be engaged in reading except those who have been assigned various duties. [23]If anyone is so remiss and indolent that he is unwilling or unable to study or to read, he is to be given some work in order that he may not be idle.

[24]Brothers who are sick or weak should be given a type of work or craft that will keep them busy without overwhelming them or driving them away. [25]The abbot must take their infirmities into account.

Work, prayer, reading—how are we to hold them together? *Ora et labora* is a short phrase always associated with the Benedictine way. It captures the imagination, for it seems to suggest that not only is work good in itself, but it is close to prayer, becomes prayer. This whole question of work is extremely relevant today when many people are experiencing redundancy, unemployment, or early retirement and are asking what place work plays in their lives, what the loss of work does to their self-esteem. The Protestant work ethic has shaped many of our attitudes, and in capitalist theories work plays a central place.

In contrast, in Benedict's world manual labor was left to the slaves, for the Romans looked down on working with one's hands. But once again the Rule is counter-cultural. Benedict himself, as always, draws on the Bible rather than the values of contemporary society, and there, of course, we find men and women playing their part as co-creators with God. The Hebrews were a working people, and Christ himself was a craftsman for the larger part of his life. Paul, to whom the early monastic writers turned for their directions about work, has a great deal to say about the need to work, both for self-support and in order to have something to share with those in need. The Desert Fathers, of course, also provided endless examples of the place of manual work both in their life and in their teachings. Here then are "our fathers and the apostles" (8), the role model for working with the hands.

Benedict's own approach to the subject of work neither idealizes nor denigrates it, neither makes it an exercise in asceticism nor therapy, but simply sees it as a necessary part of earning one's living. What I find fascinating is that right from the very opening of this chapter Benedict speaks of manual labor and prayerful reading in the same breath (which I take as a reminder that my spiritual reading is hard, demanding work that I should take seriously). *Ora et labora* is in fact not a good summary of the monk's life; *ora, labora, lege* (pray, work, read) would be preferable. Monks are given their assigned tasks, the words repeated twice in verses 11 and 14, in order that the day may be well paced. This allows one activity to flow into another, and there will then be a balance of work, reading, and prayer. To pray without ceasing remains the ultimate goal, prayer refreshed by the images and ideas that times of reading bring to it, and the hours of labor giving further opportunity to ensure that prayer remains like some subterranean stream throughout the whole day.

Prayerful reading, *lectio divina,* is linked with work in that opening sentence. It is a prominent part of the daily *horarium.* Ideally, as in Lent, three hours were given to it, though at other times it was less. Prayer without study will become uninformed; study without prayer will become simply an intellectual exercise. Without work both will become removed from reality. So each has to discipline the other, and again we see the inter-connectedness of Benedict's way of life. This is not just time for reading; it is reading of the Word. It is time for the monk to be present to the Scriptures so that he may feed on them and be molded by them. It is also a way of prayer that many others since, and not least lay people such as myself, have come to value greatly.

It is important not to see *lectio divina* as one more technique or method to be grasped or acquired. It is essentially a process, and a gentle one. Yet it does have its rhythm and framework, and it is useful to see this as four steps or rungs.

The first is *lectio* by which we read some short passage from the Bible, particularly from the psalms, reading slowly and carefully, perhaps aloud, really listening, almost as though hearing it anew.

Then comes *meditatio,* which is the seeking, finding a word or phrase that strikes us, touches us. We repeat it, reflect on it, come to grips with what it is saying to us personally. We do this urgently and with full attention because it is important, it is what God wants to say to us *today.* One of the traditional ways of describing this step is to compare it to a cow chewing the cud, digesting it to get its full goodness, though I also like to think of it as a mother rocking her child back and forth, time and again. The vital thing is that it is to and fro, to and fro, time and again, until it becomes like a heartbeat inside of one's own self.

For then the word touches the heart and we reach the third step, *oratio.* Almost without noticing we have moved from the mind into the heart, the feelings, the emotions. This is no longer thoughts or knowledge about God, using the mind or the imagination, for now we go beyond them. The goal of prayer is not thoughts or knowledge about God; it is being open so that God's love grasps us, takes hold of us. It is as though we now allow ourselves to be drawn to him as though with a magnet, and all the false self, with its games and facades, falls away and instead we surrender totally to God.

This brings us to the final step, *contemplatio,* in which we learn a new language, silence. We are content simply to *be,* standing in the presence of God. We let God take us beyond ourselves. We have found God—or rather let ourselves be found by him. As Abbot Marmion puts it: we read *(lectio)* under the eye of God *(meditatio)* until the heart is touched *(oratio)* and leaps into flame *(contemplatio).*

In that long second paragraph, Benedict goes to a lot of trouble to establish a schedule that is typically flexible and realistic in order that both prayerful reading and manual labor occupy periods of time that will change from season to season throughout the year and will fit in with the regular hours for saying the daily Office. It is this movement from one to the other that most strikes me, for I find Benedict's concern to balance out a timetable so constructed that each day moves between work, reading, and prayer, since all are equally important. Discussion of manual work per se, therefore, occupies only a small proportion of this chapter, although traditionally it is always given the title "The Daily Manual Labor." I feel that it is more useful to see it as an exploration of the right and proper use of time, in which manual work plays its necessary role in that holistic way of life that Benedict is drawing up for us throughout the Rule.

Work has to be done, it is a necessity, without it the community can neither live nor eat, nor have spare food or money to give away to others. This emphasis on the need to earn a living, to sustain the individual and the community, has little in common with what I find most of the time in today's work-oriented world where so much work is competitive, individualistic, about success and promotion and acclaim. This means that we tend to judge the worth of the individual in relation to the sort of work they do; we weigh them on a scale of what are commonly regarded as inferior or superior jobs or careers. This would be utterly alien to Benedict, who never saw work as being for personal advancement, for success or profit or making a name for one's self. For him work is anonymous and corporate. The inter-changeability of tasks, which has been clearly set out in the earlier chapters on the kitchen and refectory, established this principle. Skill is certainly appreciated and care is taken, for example, in the choice of the reader who will edify the understanding of the text and do it justice (38,12). The themes of responsibility, reverence, and respect that have run so strongly through most of the immediately preceding chapters have insisted that everything is to be done with due attention and care. The end and purpose, however, of using one's God-given skill is not to become puffed up (57,2-3). The end and purpose is God: *"So that in all things God may be glorified"* (57,9).

It is not, therefore, so much work as the responsible handling of time that concerns Benedict. The waste of time distresses him. Verses 19-20 show how seriously he thinks about this and how severely he castigates it. What is really shocking to him is idleness. It comes into the opening maxim (and it is unusual for him to be so outright, so didactic), and in verse 18 it is spelled out: wasting time, idle talk, apathy. He does not want work under pressure, filling every moment. Indeed the moderation, the gentleness, is most important, caught in that nice small phrase "without overwhelming" (24). There is very real gentleness in making allowances for those who are weak. When we tend so easily to become workaholic and competitive, I am glad to be told that work should never be allowed to become overwhelming and to be reminded of the importance of doing things with moderation.

The work that Benedict envisages by no means consists only of working in the field or garden or kitchen. There are many other tasks to be performed: the care of the sick, the teaching of children, and even the manual work itself would have been immensely varied, ranging from the making of pots to the very demanding work of copying manuscripts (I wonder how long it took Benedict to actually copy out his Rule by hand). That work should carry dignity was a strange and wonderful new development in the centuries that followed the writing of the Rule.

It was both by the book and by the plough that the early Benedictine communities conquered Europe. They brought to the Europe of the Dark Ages the example of work that was civilizing, whether it was in the promotion of learning or in the colonizing of land. In addition, in the very way in which they handled their large estates they made a further extremely significant contribution: they showed themselves as pioneers in land use and management. Cultivation and husbandry often involved the clearing of land, diking and draining where it was needed, and the use of professional farming techniques. They also showed expertise in such matters as hydraulic engineering, designing and building systems of pipes and drains so that they could bring supplies of fresh water to their communities.

Benedict had taught them that work was a shared activity, part of the solidarity with which they lived together. With this in mind they adopted recent inventions and practiced the appropriate use of new technology as an exercise of responsible corporate stewardship. This vision of commitment to the shared common good, not simply in the handling of the land itself but also in the applying of new skills, speaks to me most urgently today. As I look around me I see an age of greed, when balance seems to be neglected and when the work of human hands seems to result in waste, exploitation, pollution, a denial of the covenant that God made with men and women to cherish and to nurture the earth for the good of all God's family.

That is why I am grateful for the statements about stewardship that I find from contemporary Benedictines. In *Of All Good Gifts,* the American Benedictine sisters ask what we can do in a world that lacks any vision of the sacredness of creation or commitment to the dignity of life. They say:

> Our answer is monastic stewardship: that we use what we are and what we have for the transformation of culture because creation

is the Lord's and we are its keepers; we hold it on trust. We must remember that the earth is not so much inherited from our parents as borrowed from our children. We owe a debt to the next generation.

Or the community of St. Mary and St. Louis in St. Louis, founded from Ampleforth Abbey in England, and now an independent abbey:

Benedictines see creation as a gift of God to be loving nurtured so that it fulfils its purpose in serving the human family. . . . They do not grasp. They try not to waste. They believe in having sufficient but not the superfluous. They have the cautious optimism to believe that with the humble effort to understand and cooperate with the Creator's abundant gifts men and women can bring about on this planet a truly human life for all.

CHAPTER FORTY-NINE

¹The life of a monk ought to be a continuous Lent. ²Since few, however, have the strength for this, we urge the entire community during these days of Lent to keep its manner of life most pure ³and to wash away in this holy season the negligences of other times. ⁴This we can do in a fitting manner by refusing to indulge evil habits and by devoting ourselves to prayer with tears, to reading, to compunction of heart and self-denial. ⁵During these days, therefore, we will add to the usual measure of our service something by way of private prayer and abstinence from food or drink, ⁶so that each of us will have something above the assigned measure to offer God of his own will *with the joy of the Holy Spirit* (1 Thess 1:6). ⁷In other words, let each one deny himself some food, drink, sleep, needless talking and idle jesting, and look forward to holy Easter with joy and spiritual longing.

⁸Everyone should, however, make known to the abbot what he intends to do, since it ought to be done with his prayer and approval. ⁹Whatever is undertaken without the permission of the spiritual father will be reckoned as presumption and vainglory, not deserving a reward. ¹⁰Therefore, everything must be done with the abbot's approval.

It certainly will be demanding to live according to this ideal day after day after day. So Benedict follows chapter 48 by telling the monks (it is significant that this chapter is both highly individualistic and yet also one that involves "the entire community") not only that Lent is the model for the whole of life, but that the season of Lent itself brings an annual opportunity for extra effort. The implication is that what happens in Lent also applies in principle throughout the year. The opening verses 2-5 have a definitely exhortatory ring about them. They sound quite like a homily; indeed there is a homily by St. Leo, the fifth-century pope, on Lent, which Benedict must certainly have known. Then, in verse 5 he addresses the individual need for prayer and abstinence. Once again we are shown the delicate balance between the individual and the community.

Since he is emphasizing special personal effort during Lent, Benedict has to guard against any development into undue individualism that wants to draw attention to itself. The abbot, therefore, must be the point of reference. The reward of any Lenten undertaking has nothing to do with outward display but with the reward of the kingdom. The issue is one of motive. If I let it be known how much I fast, or give to charity, it becomes something public, perhaps even competitive. For me, as for the monk, fruitful participation in Lent is not marked by any external observance but by interior transformation; I think of the epistle of Ash Wednesday on rending our hearts and not our garments.

So also our joy must be an interior joy, just as the observances should be interior and not exterior. Lent points toward Easter. There is a strong theology of joy in this chapter, and the word *gaudium* is used here twice, the only place in the Rule. The forty days before Easter are a time of looking forward "with joy and spiritual longing" (7). Verse 6 tells us something very important about true spiritual joy: it is a gift of the Holy Spirit. There is a difference between a true, deep joyousness and the vapid hilarity that passes for joy, the superficial jolly cheerfulness that often covers up an inner hollowness. It is interesting to see that what Benedict is condemning is idle joking and needless conversation, essentially superficial and shallow.

The paradox is that the joy of Lent is necessarily connected with sorrow, that it is a joy that flows from sorrow. Instead of the terrible guilt with which I have so often been inflicted, by my own conscience and by the Church, Benedict is talking of the sorrow that makes for joy, which is expressed in the monastic concept of compunction. Just as Lent and Easter are inseparable, so also are sorrow and joy. Tears and compunction of heart (4) express the experience of being touched or pricked (which is what the word means, *punctio*), as if by a dart of love. Compunction brings a sense of sharp pain, a stinging that I experience as I am touched, overwhelmed by this love, which reaches out to love and forgive and to end all that separates us. As I reflect what I am, my true state before God, and what I might be, what God wants me to be, I am aroused from my torpor, my willingness just to drift along, and I am stung into action. Compunction draws from me a positive response to the love of God flooding my life and drawing me on to fuller and better things.

Compunction is, therefore, a long way from the negative sort of guilt that can encourage soul-searching, obsessive regrets, and a dwelling on the past. This I know only too well can easily become sterile, a deadening inner monologue, which does not bring me the energy to change and to move forward. If compunction points me inward, it is not in order to trap me in yet more self-recrimination and introspection. Rather it awakens in me a poignant sense of how false I have been to my own deepest and truest self, my own likeness to that loving Father in whose image I was created, and how I have disfigured that creation. Compunction is, therefore, as Michael Casey says, a dual sensitivity. It places before us both the reality of our sinful condition and the urgency of our desire to be totally possessed by God. It is precisely the comparison between what we are and what we could be that constitutes the triggering cause of compunction. "It is an intimate sensation which touches us at our deepest level and often results in tears."

Tears and compunction are never to be confined entirely to Lent. But the time of Lent is a "sacrament." It shows us the symbol of the whole of our life on earth, a gift from Christ himself so that we may share in his sufferings and his passion and the joy of the new life of the resurrection.

CHAPTER FIFTY

¹Brothers who work so far away that they cannot return to the oratory at the proper time—²and the abbot determines that is the case—³are to perform the Work of God where they are, and kneel out of reverence for God.

⁴So too, those who have been sent on a journey are not to omit the prescribed hours but to observe them as best they can, not neglecting their measure of service.

We have been shown the ideal, the *opus Dei* as the one important thing in the monastic life, and if necessity should dictate a breaking of the ordered pattern of life, monks are still to observe it faithfully—and yet Benedict adds with his customary gentleness and flexibility "as best they can" (4).

So monks are to carry their routine of prayer wherever they go, and traveling and working at a distance are no excuse for neglecting the work of God. I like Benedict telling them that they are to kneel out of reverence for God (3). This is not to be any hidden or apologetic saying of the Office but a public demonstration of their commitment to a life of prayer. As I move about, doing my ordinary work, I ask myself whether I too (making of course this same allowance, "as best I can") should have this sort of commitment to prayer in my own life.

CHAPTER FIFTY-ONE

¹If a brother is sent on some errand and expects to return to the monastery that same day, he must not presume to eat outside, even if he receives a pressing invitation, ²unless perhaps the abbot has ordered it. ³Should he act otherwise, he will be excommunicated.

Refectory and oratory, the common meal and the shared liturgy, have been yoked together in the life of the community. Meal times carry an almost sacred dimension, they are the act of the family, the sharing of food binds their common life. So the meal table tells us where we belong.

This chapter has a brutal ring about it, and it is not easy to see what the spiritual concern is that underlies Benedict's apparently extremely hard ruling. But if his underlying interest is in the good order, which brings the sense of belonging and having a place to stand, then the sharing of the meal becomes the sacramental seal of that. It is, therefore, something to be taken very seriously, however costly.

CHAPTER FIFTY-TWO

¹The oratory ought to be what it is called, and nothing else is to be done or stored there. ²After the Work of God, all should leave in complete silence and with reverence for God, ³so that a brother who may wish to pray alone will not be disturbed by the insensitivity of another. ⁴Moreover, if at other times someone chooses to pray privately, he may simply go in and pray, not in a loud voice, but with tears and heartfelt devotion. ⁵Accordingly, anyone who does not pray in this manner is not to remain in the oratory after the Work of God, as we have said; then he will not interfere with anyone else.

"Heartfelt devotion" (4) is an unfortunate translation of the lovely Latin phrase *intentione cordis*, which is the key to this chapter. This is the only time that it is used in the Rule, and it builds on the purity of heart of chapter 20 (3) and on compunction in chapter 49. Intention of heart is close in meaning to purity of heart, for both refer to stripping away. But while purity has perhaps rather a negative ring, intention suggests putting the heart in the right direction. *Intentio* is a powerful word: it always signals movement, usually movement in a particular direction. Parry calls it the heart homing in on God. This involves leaving aside everything in order to return to one's center. It is the prayer that emanates from the deepest level of one's being.

The monk who prays with *intentio cordis* allows his heart to move to God by restricting any outside clamor or external activity. This is the purpose of keeping the oratory simple and quiet, stripping away from it all that might clutter and distract (1,2). The prohibition of wordy prayers, verbose praying, is to free the heart from too much verbal clutter. Once again Benedict is making the connection of the interior with the exterior.

This also applies in my own life. What will help more than anything else, if I am to pray in the stillness of my heart, is to have a place set aside, a corner of the house, a simple icon and a candle—it really matters very little what its actual shape may be so long as it is kept as a place into which I can enter and find uncluttered space and silence.

Monastic spirituality is a spirituality of the heart. In this chapter Benedict adds, in a most striking and beautiful way, to what he has been telling me right from the start in the prologue. He understands heart in the scriptural sense as the core of the human being, the deepest and highest center from which I make contact with God. He is reminding me again very forcibly of how vital this "return to the heart" is if my life is to be rooted in what he wants me to recognize must be its source and spring.

CHAPTER FIFTY-THREE

¹All guests who present themselves are to be welcomed as Christ, for he himself will say: *I was a stranger and you welcomed me* (Matt 25:35). ²Proper honor must be shown *to all, especially to those who share our faith* (Gal 6:10) and to pilgrims.

³Once a guest has been announced, the superior and the brothers are to meet him with all the courtesy of love. ⁴First of all, they are to pray together and thus be united in peace, ⁵but prayer must always precede the kiss of peace because of the delusions of the devil.

⁶All humility should be shown in addressing a guest on arrival or departure. ⁷By a bow of the head or by a complete prostration of the body, Christ is to be adored because he is indeed welcomed in them. ⁸After the guests have been received, they should be invited to pray; then the superior or an appointed brother will sit with them. ⁹The divine law is read to the guest for his instruction, and after that every kindness is shown to him. ¹⁰The superior may break his fast for the sake of a guest, unless it is a day of special fast which cannot be broken. ¹¹The brothers, however, observe the usual fast. ¹²The abbot shall pour water on the hands of the guests, ¹³and the abbot with the entire community shall wash their feet. ¹⁴After the washing they will recite this verse: *God, we have received your mercy in the midst of your temple* (Ps 47[48]:10).

¹⁵Great care and concern are to be shown in receiving poor people and pilgrims, because in them more particularly Christ is received; our very awe of the rich guarantees them special respect.

¹⁶The kitchen for the abbot and guests ought to be separate, so that guests—and monasteries are never without

170

them—need not disturb the brothers when they present themselves at unpredictable hours. [17]Each year, two brothers who can do the work competently are to be assigned to this kitchen. [18]Additional help should be available when needed, so that they can perform this service without grumbling. On the other hand, when the work slackens, they are to go wherever other duties are assigned them. [19]This consideration is not for them alone, but applies to all duties in the monastery; [20]the brothers are to be given help when it is needed, and whenever they are free, they work wherever they are assigned.

[21]The guest quarters are to be entrusted to a God-fearing brother. [22]Adequate bedding should be available there. The house of God should be in the care of wise men who will manage it wisely.

[23]No one is to speak or associate with guests unless he is bidden; [24]however, if a brother meets or sees a guest, he is to greet him humbly, as we have said. He asks for a blessing and continues on his way, explaining that he is not allowed to speak with a guest.

It is only because I carry a heart of silence that I can welcome the guest. The chapter on the oratory of the monastery and the oratory of the heart lays the foundation for what Benedict now gives us, discussion of the exercise of hospitality. This is one of his most important chapters, for hospitality is always seen as a peculiarly Benedictine charism. He opens, as he so often does, with a short and beautiful maxim that lays down the foundational theological principle from which all the rest will flow. Whoever comes is to be received as Christ himself. This idea that Christ is to be received, welcomed, adored is stated no less than three times in this chapter (1; 6-7; 15), repeated at intervals in the course of the practical legislation for the care of guests. If this is what Benedictine hospitality means, it is a lot easier to repeat that maxim than to live it out.

What does it mean to receive another as Christ? I find that the story of Benedict at Subiaco, which St. Gregory records in the *Dialogues,* gives me an illuminating glimpse. Benedict has been alone in the cave for three years, in silence and in solitude, when he is visited by a priest—sent specially by God, who wished Benedict to have company at Easter. The scene is charming and really very humorous. Benedict is so deep in prayer and so far away from everything that he has no idea that it is Easter, but to the priest's greeting he replies: "Easter it is indeed since I have the joy of seeing you." In the face of the first person that he sees, Benedict finds the firstfruits of the resurrection and of the new world to which he is called. I think it is possible to find quite a profound theological implication in his response, so I make it a question for myself: Do I also find the risen Christ in the face of the one who comes? Is this what is being asked of me in receiving the other as Christ?

Christ comes as the stranger. This is so time and again in the Bible where the Godhead is entertained by those who are unaware of who he is—whether it is by Abraham at Mamre or by the two disciples on the road to Emmaus. At the end of time, on the day of judgment, this will also be the question to any of us: Did you welcome me in the stranger? If I am to be ready I must remain alert, awake, not stumbling blindly along like those two on the way to Emmaus with eyes that do not really see, ears that do not really hear.

Benedict has, of course, been telling me this ever since the prologue. But then the whole of his teaching has been leading up to this point and is now brought into play. He has prepared me to welcome all, regardless of rank, and to treat each according to need, so that there is no uniformity, but consideration for weakness or infirmity. He has taught me about true humility and that helps me to be open to receive as well as to give. He has shown me that prayer and *lectio* are the essentials of life, and therefore it will be entirely natural to assume that these are as important to share with others as food or sleep.

It could be only too easy for this to remain on some theoretical level. Benedict wants to make it entirely practical. Step by step we are shown how the stranger is to be welcomed and received. His first welcome will have come from the porter, as we shall see in chapter 66, who will give him a greeting and then announce his arrival to the community. The superior and the brothers meet him with "all the courtesy of love" (3), a well-chosen word that carries a sense of delicate love exercised with gentleness and good manners. The first thing they do is to pray together in order that they may be united in peace (4). *Pax* is a Benedictine watchword, but peace is never easy, and to exchange the kiss of peace must never be a facile empty gesture, for then it will be an evasion of the truth and thereby lose its true significance (5).

The balance is nicely kept between the spiritual and the material, and the guests are invited to share in the holistic way of life of the community. After the invitation to pray, the Scriptures are read for their instruction, and every kindness is shown to them, the Latin *"humanitas"* used here often means a meal. This is preceded by the ritual of pouring water on the hands and the washing of the feet. What that reference to humility means in verse 6 now becomes clear, for it is expressed in a ceremony that will recall Christ's own action at the shared meal of the Last Supper when he stripped himself of those outer garments that denote place or rank, and in all simplicity knelt before each of his friends in turn. In verse 14 the monks are given a specific prayer to recite after the washing, *"God we have received your mercy, . . ."* from Psalm 47 (48). By implication the guest is considered "the mercy of God," and in receiving the stranger we receive mercy from God. The gift we give is only what we have received.

There is to be a separate kitchen for guests, with specially assigned brothers working there, and a God-fearing brother is placed in charge of the guest quarters. Here indeed is that "great care and concern'" of verse 15 that sums up this hospitality so well. But it might also seem that this warmth is lost by the apparently sharp change of tone in that final paragraph when Benedict specifically forbids the brothers to mix and talk with guests.

De Vogüé finds a curious contrast here between the opening of the chapter and its end, and some commentaries make much of this. Columba Cary-Elwes, for example, says that Benedict is in two minds about guests. But I see it otherwise. I find that Benedict is telling me to do two things at once, to hold two things in tension, and this is something that I really appreciate. There is this wonderfully full and generous reception, but there is also the withdrawal and standing back. What this final section makes very clear is, for me, one of the most valuable insights of this chapter. Unless the monastery protects its enclosure, symbolized by the cloister, the warmth and the openness of its hospitality, symbolized by the porter at the open gates, becomes impossible.

It is precisely the sense that its own way of life has an integrity that must be respected, that the silence and the fasting is preserved, that ensures that it has something of value to give to the passing guest. I know that the same is true of my own experience. Unless I have time to withdraw, unless I can preserve and protect the innermost space of my own life, I too become so drained and exhausted that I am not fully present to those who come. Benedict is establishing boundaries, just as he did in the case of the cellarer. As any good psychologist would tell us, this is one of the most essential lessons that we all need to learn.

This is true and responsible care for my own self. It is part of Benedict's total approach to life that all the time tells me about the handling of everything, human and non-human, with respect and reverence. This is caught once again when he says so delicately and beautifully toward the end of the chapter (21-22) that "the house of God," where the guests will be housed (the name is in itself significant), is to be in the care of wise men who will manage it wisely even down to the detail of adequate bedding. Everyone and everything matters in the eyes of God.

CHAPTER FIFTY-FOUR

¹In no circumstances is a monk allowed, unless the abbot says he may, to exchange letters, blessed tokens or small gifts of any kind, with his parents or anyone else, or with a fellow monk. ²He must not presume to accept gifts sent him even by his parents without previously telling the abbot. ³If the abbot orders acceptance, he still has the power to give the gift to whom he will; ⁴and the brother for whom it was originally sent must not be distressed, *lest occasion be given to the devil* (Eph 4:27; 1 Tim 5:14). ⁵Whoever presumes to act otherwise will be subjected to the discipline of the rule.

If all guests are to be welcome as Christ himself, then that surely applies as well to all the people in my life, whoever they may be. The irony is that it is often easier to feel warmth and generosity to those passing temporarily through my life, to the underprivileged and wounded and insecure, to those who need me, than it is to those who are close to me, to members of my own family, those with whom I live and work. Here jealousy, competitiveness, comparing and contrasting come in. In order to remove at least some of the externals that make outward distinctions between his monks, Benedict forbids the giving of gifts and favors. Nothing separates one person from another more than the presents they receive, particularly from parents, inevitably reflecting their set of values and therefore showing, more than anything, class distinctions and questions of taste (ask anyone who went to boarding school). Some of his sternest teaching earlier on in the Rule had been about attitudes toward property and possessions in chapter 33, when he had invoked the devil, as he does again here.

In the preceding chapter Benedict has given us the example of Christ washing the disciples' feet as a model. The thought that seems to underlie this chapter is that of the passage from Ephesians from which the short quotation in verse 5 is taken, which opens with Paul's great outpouring about being worthy of the vocation to which we are called "with all lowliness and meekness, with long suffering, forbearing one another in love."

CHAPTER FIFTY-FIVE

[1]The clothing distributed to the brothers should vary according to local conditions and climate, [2]because more is needed in cold regions and less in warmer. [3]This is left to the abbot's discretion. [4]We believe that for each monk a cowl and tunic will suffice in temperate regions; [5]in winter a woolen cowl is necessary, in summer a thinner or worn one; [6]also a scapular for work, and footwear—both sandals and shoes.

[7]Monks must not complain about the color or coarseness of all these articles, but use what is available in the vicinity at a reasonable cost. [8]However, the abbot ought to be concerned about the measurements of these garments that they not be too short but fitted to the wearers.

[9]Whenever new clothing is received, the old should be returned at once and stored in a wardrobe for the poor. [10]To provide for laundering and night wear, every monk will need two cowls and two tunics, [11]but anything more must be taken away as superfluous. [12]When new articles are received, the worn ones—sandals or anything old—must be returned.

[13]Brothers going on a journey should get underclothing from the wardrobe. On their return they are to wash it and give it back. [14]Their cowls and tunics, too, ought to be somewhat better than those they ordinarily wear. Let them get these from the wardrobe before departing, and on returning put them back.

[15]For bedding the monks will need a mat, a woolen blanket and a light covering as well as a pillow.

[16]The beds are to be inspected frequently by the abbot, lest private possessions be found there. [17]A monk discovered with anything not given him by the abbot must be subjected to very severe punishment. [18]In order that this

vice of private ownership may be completely uprooted, the abbot is to provide all things necessary: [19]that is, cowl, tunic, sandals, shoes, belt, knife, stylus, needle, handkerchief and writing tablets. In this way every excuse of lacking some necessity will be taken away.

[20]The abbot, however, must always bear in mind what is said in the Acts of the Apostles: *Distribution was made to each one as he had need* (Acts 4:35). [21]In this way the abbot will take into account the weaknesses of the needy, not the evil will of the envious; [22]yet in all his judgments he must bear in mind God's retribution.

There is a string of words in this chapter that, although it is overtly about clothing and possessions, in fact describes the character of the Benedictine way of life. Since both clothes and possessions make a statement about who we are and the way in which we think about ourselves, this should not really surprise us. Benedict is showing us, above all, a life of moderation and flexibility, never excessive, dramatic, or going to extremes. He uses the word "necessary" twice (5; 18), and "needed" once (2). His concern is with having sufficient rather than superfluous (11). He is not looking for undue hardship, deprivation, or abject poverty. He clearly legislates in order that all in the community may be given what they require, and the inclusion of the stylus and writing tablets in the list shows that he does not understand this narrowly.

Benedict is splendidly precise. Everything matters, down to the last detail. There is such loving and careful respect and care for clothes, in the way in which they are to be washed and stored after use. There is respect for the person, too. Ill-fitting clothes are unworthy and so there is care about size and fit, since (as I remember only too vividly from childhood miseries) having clothes that are too long or too short is extraordinarily bad for the morale. He picks up the theme of stewardship, and handling with a sense of responsibility. If there are special clothes lent out for use on a journey, they are to be returned, and when any become old and outworn they are to be handed on to those who can use them.

The allocation lies with the abbot, and Benedict reiterates what he has said before: there must be no complaining and no grumbling. Once again it is avarice and envy that are the real sins that must be rooted out. If the sentence from Acts that Benedict quotes in verse 20 is put into context of the whole section of Acts from which it is taken, Acts 4:31-37, we see a community empowered by the Holy Spirit, for whom the sharing of all things in common is not the outcome of any imposed discipline but rather the result of the grace and power that was upon them. So it would seem that the underlying purpose of this chapter is that we all may, like the members of the early Church, be of "one heart and one mind," living with acceptance and contentment and escaping the evil of envy.

Benedict is looking for a certain flexibility in the pattern of the life that he is establishing in order that the community may be in touch with the local region and with different climates (1). He expects that the monks will use "what is available in the vicinity at a reasonable cost" (7). This small point is significant. Living in relationship with the actual place in which one finds oneself means being earthed in the immediate reality not only of time and seasons, but of the very ground itself.

CHAPTER FIFTY-SIX

[1]The abbot's table must always be with guests and travelers.
[2]Whenever there are no guests, it is within his right to invite any of the brothers he wishes. [3]However, for the sake of maintaining discipline, one or two seniors must always be left with the brothers.

The previous chapter was about care for the outer since it mirrors the interior. Clothes, material possessions, food, sleep are all to be taken seriously as an important part of life. What applies to the community applies also to those who are visiting. Yet the life of the community must go undisturbed by constant intrusion. How is this to be handled? The head of the community is the representative figure who can act on behalf of the rest, and so it is the abbot who makes himself available and has a separate kitchen and table always accessible. Careful as ever of maintaining the principle of order, Benedict makes sure that if the abbot is absent there are others who will take his place so that the body will never be without its due head.

CHAPTER FIFTY-SEVEN

¹If there are artisans in the monastery, they are to practice their craft with all humility, but only with the abbot's permission. ²If one of them becomes puffed up by his skillfulness in his craft, and feels that he is conferring something on the monastery, ³he is to be removed from practicing his craft and not allowed to resume it unless, after manifesting his humility, he is so ordered by the abbot.

⁴Whenever products of these artisans are sold, those responsible for the sale must not dare to practice any fraud. ⁵Let them always remember Ananias and Sapphira, who incurred bodily death (Acts 5:1-11), ⁶lest they and all who perpetrate fraud in monastery affairs suffer spiritual death.

⁷The evil of avarice must have no part in establishing prices, ⁸which should, therefore, always be a little lower than people outside the monastery are able to set, ⁹*so that in all things God may be glorified* (1 Pet 4:11).

By now Benedict's main message has been expressed clearly and in a number of different settings, but it remains essentially that the whole of life reflects the choice of God and the desire for the kingdom *"so that in all things God may be glorified* (1 Pet 4:11)" (9). There is no question of a spiritual life existing underground, closeted within the consciousness and not incarnated in ordinary daily activity. Now when he comes to talk of the craftsmen and artisans in the monastery, we can see this message particularly clearly.

Benedict's idea seems to be that the monk gives glory to God precisely by not working as others do, for material gain or for popular success. This can easily escalate and become competitive, in a search for more money, a better reputation. There is inevitably a natural eagerness to exercise our talents, to work according to our own wishes and desires, and he wants us to check this by making God the only end in view. Our skills are to be exercised with humility, with reverence, with restraint. In this way we shall show ourselves to be working in an entirely different field, non-competitive and not concerned about either material gain or a personal reputation. The example of Ananias and Sapphira are held up as a terrible warning about the dangers of avarice, selfishness, greed, and he does not mince words about the heinousness of their sin (5-6).

But it is in the context of that passage from 1 Peter 4 from which Benedict has taken that final quotation (9) that I read and reflect on this chapter. For in that passage, verse 7 speaks of prayer, then 8 and 9 of charity and hospitality, then of the gifts given to each, and how we are to be good stewards of these. The theme of stewardship is at its fullest here, the stewardship of my skills and talents, just as much as the stewardship of all the material things in my life. All that Benedict has been teaching me so lovingly and so patiently is gathered up in this prayer. "That in all things God may be glorified through Jesus Christ, to whom be praise and dominion for ever and ever. Amen" (1 Pet 4:11).

CHAPTER FIFTY-EIGHT

¹Do not grant newcomers to the monastic life an easy entry, ²but, as the Apostle says, *Test the spirits to see if they are from God* (1 John 4:1). ³Therefore, if someone comes and keeps knocking at the door, and if at the end of four or five days he has shown himself patient in bearing his harsh treatment and difficulty of entry, and has persisted in his request, ⁴then he should be allowed to enter and stay in the guest quarters for a few days. ⁵After that, he should live in the novitiate, where the novices study, eat and sleep.

⁶A senior chosen for his skill in winning souls should be appointed to look after them with careful attention. ⁷The concern must be whether the novice truly seeks God and whether he shows eagerness for the Work of God, for obedience and for trials. ⁸The novice should be clearly told all the hardships and difficulties that will lead him to God.

⁹If he promises perseverance in his stability, then after two months have elapsed let this rule be read straight through to him, ¹⁰and let him be told: "This is the law under which you are choosing to serve. If you can keep it, come in. If not, feel free to leave." ¹¹If he still stands firm, he is to be taken back to the novitiate, and again thoroughly tested in patience. ¹²After six months have passed, the rule is to be read to him, so that he may know what he is entering. ¹³If once more he stands firm, let four months go by, and then read this rule to him again. ¹⁴If after due reflection he promises to observe everything and to obey every command given him, let him then be received into the community. ¹⁵But he must be well aware that, as the law of the rule establishes, from this day he is no longer free to leave the monastery, ¹⁶nor to shake from his neck the yoke of the

rule which, in the course of so prolonged a period of reflection, he was free either to reject or to accept.

[17]When he is to be received, he comes before the whole community in the oratory and promises stability, fidelity to monastic life, and obedience. [18]This is done in the presence of God and his saints to impress on the novice that if he ever acts otherwise, he will surely be condemned by the one he mocks. [19]He states his promise in a document drawn up in the name of the saints whose relics are there, and of the abbot, who is present. [20]The novice writes out this document himself, or if he is illiterate, then he asks someone else to write it for him, but himself puts his mark to it and with his own hand lays it on the altar. [21]After he has put it there, the novice himself begins the verse: *Receive me,* Lord, *as you have promised, and I shall live; do not disappoint me in my hope* (Ps 118[119]:116). [22]The whole community repeats the verse three times, and adds "Glory be to the Father." [23]Then the novice prostrates himself at the feet of each monk to ask his prayers, and from that very day he is to be counted as one of the community.

[24]If he has any possessions, he should either give them to the poor beforehand, or make a formal donation of them to the monastery, without keeping back a single thing for himself, [25]well aware that from that day he will not have even his own body at his disposal. [26]Then and there in the oratory, he is to be stripped of everything of his own that he is wearing and clothed in what belongs to the monastery. [27]The clothing taken from him is to be put away and kept safely in the wardrobe, [28]so that, should he ever agree to the devil's suggestion and leave the monastery—which God forbid—he can be stripped of the clothing of the monastery before he is cast out. [29]But that document of his which the abbot took from the altar should not be given back to him but kept in the monastery.

With the short phrase *"that in all things God may be glorified"* (57,9), Benedict sums up the whole of his way of life. This is another pivotal moment in the Rule. He has shown us his purpose and aim, and he has said much about the interior attitudes, the disposition of the heart, that he is looking for in those who would like to follow him. This is a serious undertaking. It is not to be entered upon lightly. The intending novice is expected to give it due reflection (14), prolonged reflection (16). There is no automatic entry. This time of waiting is a test of patience (3; 11), of persistence (3), and of perseverance (9). There is no attempt to hide the hardships and difficulties. The beginning already shows what the future will hold. So now the question that follows must be: Is it for you? Are you truly seeking God?

This is the nub of the matter. This is the end and purpose of life. It is nowhere more simply and beautifully expressed than by St. Anselm in chapter 1 of the Proslogion:

> Now, my whole heart says to God,
>   "I seek your face,
> Lord, it is your face I seek"
>
> O Lord my God,
>   teach my heart where and how to seek you,
>   where and how to find you. . . .

It is the question of Psalm 26 (27). It is the basic question; it is simply what this is all about. If we have the desire to seek the face of God, then those words of the psalm go on to say: "Teach me thy way, O Lord, and lead me in a plain path" (Ps 26 [27]:8, 11). This is exactly what follows here: Benedict is laying out before me the path that will lead to God.

If this is so, if there is within me this deep desire for God, if I can truly say, "I desire thee with my whole heart," then Benedict establishes three tests to ascertain the inner state of mind, since, as he makes clear right from the very start of this chapter, the process of discernment is absolutely necessary (2) before the novice goes on to make his or her promises. I read them prayerfully for they are indeed penetrating questions, and they give me a measuring rod with which to face my own heart and discover my own motives and intentions.

The first criterion is whether the novice shows *sollicitudo,* eagerness, zeal, for the *opus Dei* (7). Before going any further I need to stop for a moment with that powerful and colorful word, "zeal," which is one that can only too easily be absent from my life. I think of ardent desire. I imagine a burning and white hot flame, and I am once again made aware that Benedict is a man of passion, that he is writing out of a passionate and burning desire that we should all find God.

185

This zeal does not mean meticulousness about the details of saying the daily Office, but something much more spiritual. As Michael Casey reminds us, the ability to pray the Office well depends on the rest of the day being lived in fidelity to the call of grace. Prayer cannot be separate from life. When the Office degenerates into something less than prayer, the cause is generally found in the quality of life itself. If there is a burning desire, a flame that draws me into my times of prayer so that I am then totally present to God, this will not be some mere outward observance reluctantly undertaken, and the work of God will then flow out and nourish all my daily work. Fruitful participation in the *opus Dei* in order to find prayer in it must be a two-way thing: the sense of the presence of God funnels from daily life into prayer and nourishes it, but then that prayer in turn nourishes daily life. This is, of course, the *opus Dei* prayed in and through the community. For those of us who pray alone, it is important to remember that we too are praying in step with others, with the worldwide Church as it observes the liturgical pattern of the year, or with any specific community to which we may be connected.

The next criterion is obedience. This should hardly be a surprise since it has from the very beginning been one of the most essential elements in the path by which Benedict is helping each of us to go to God. This is the way in which I follow the example of Christ and return to the Father. The bending of my will toward that as the end and aim of my life puts me in the right direction and keeps me on the straight path. This second test, therefore, asks me to look again at my intention and motive, my interior disposition. It is significant that it appears here in this section, whose tenor is the open-eyed, free, deliberate, and long-matured choice that the novice has to make. So obedience, therefore, cannot be blind when the critical faculties are being exercised in this way.

Third comes eagerness for *opprobia,* an awkward word, which is often unfortunately translated as "humiliations," but which essentially carries connotations of negative, dreary, unattractive, or inglorious situations. It reminds me of the words "lowest and most menial" of the sixth step of humility. Yet Benedict has been telling us how important it is that things are well done and that people use their gifts and abilities. So he obviously does not intend life to be dull and limited, does not want daily tasks to be lifeless and dreary. But he knows, as well as I do, that life is inevitably, for much of the time, far from ideal and that we have to live with that reality: a less than wonderful marriage, a house that is far from spacious and beautiful, a job that is not really rewarding or fulfilling. So how do I handle the frustrations? the limitations? the disappointments? Trivial everyday misery can be the most deadening of experiences, and it can more easily than almost anything lead to resentment or bitterness. Here the novice is being told to accept these trials with eagerness, with that acceptance that will make them life-giving rather than life-denying, surely one of the more difficult things simply because it is so undramatic. Yet the ability to maintain patience and contentment under this sort of deadening pressure is one more way in which we follow Christ. If it feels like a crucifying self-denial, an apparent waste, I must remind myself that so, apparently, was much of Christ's own life. Perhaps I must be content to let that remain a mystery.

This triad of demands or tests of intention, which are foundational for the newcomer, have a very striking parallel with the spiritual program that Benedict set out in chapter 7, the Work of God corresponding to the first degree, obedience to degrees 2–4, and *opprobia* to degrees 5–7. I am here presented once again with demands that are penetrating and insightful and that are intended to help me in that process of growth in self-knowledge before God. Just as in chapter 7, this is not undertaken on one's own without support and guidance (7,55). The novice is put under the guardianship of a senior monk chosen not for academic expertise but for his skill in winning souls, the art of trying to attract the newcomer to appropriate spiritual values, which can only be done gradually and gently. As Michael Casey comments, here is another indication of the horizontalism that pervades the Rule. The community offers support to the novice in his struggles with these necessary hardships, giving him help and encouragement as he reshapes and reorients his life. I am grateful to be told that entry to this life is hard, demanding. I feel that it shows respect for my own self, and does not patronize me, as so often seems to happen when Christian discipleship is made too easy, trivialized, and presented in a facile and easy-going way.

The process of entry into the community is a slow one. As Benedict unfolds the pattern of the scheme that he has devised, we see that it is in order that the final decision may be freely and carefully considered. It is taking commitment seriously, in a way that is increasingly absent in today's society in any form of bond or relationships, not least in the undertaking of marriage. I see how careful Benedict is to establish that this commitment is entered into completely voluntarily, that it is deliberately considered over a lengthy period of time, and that it will be total. He proposes a twelve-month period of formation divided into two, six, and four months respectively, and the Rule is read through at the conclusion of each. The fact that the novices sleep and eat in a separate area is probably so that this may be a time of silence and solitude that will make easier the *meditatio* of verse 5. The verb *meditare* was not a purely interior activity, but involved the repetition of a text aloud so that passages were said over and over again until they were known by heart. Once learned, these texts could then be repeated from memory without a book, not least during times of work or other activities. These texts were essentially biblical, and included, above all, the psalms. The goal of this kind of study was, therefore, far from being purely intellectual: it was more the appropriation of the Word so that it could be formative of one's life.

After this searching of motive and intention, and this long period of reflection, comes the final decision, made entirely freely, but with the knowledge that if the commitment is undertaken it is binding. We live in an age in which we shy away from commitment, we like to keep our options open. Henri Nouwen has written about how spending seven months with the Trappists in the Abbey of the Genesee made him aware of how divided his heart had been and still was. He realized that while he wanted to love God he also wanted to make a career. While he wanted to be a saint, he also wanted to enjoy the sensations of the sinner, and he concluded with his usual wry honesty and humor: "No wonder that living becomes a tiring enterprise! The characteristic of a saint is, to borrow Kierkegaard's words, 'to will one thing.' Well, I will more than one thing, am double-hearted, double-minded, and have a very divided loyalty."

This chapter moves on to the paragraph that opens with verse 17 that describes the admission ceremony itself, and how the community will receive the new novice. It is a public commitment made in the oratory before the whole community in the presence of God and his saints. The horizontalism of the Rule was mentioned earlier, and now I see that it includes not only the support and prayers of the brothers and sisters actually physically present, but also of the whole company of saints. The newcomer is part of a great universal invisible body. This solemn sense of continuity and connectedness, of solidarity, of being inserted into a corporate whole that transcends temporal time, is reiterated by the fact that the written document is to remain permanently in the monastery. Even if the individual departs, the document will stay in its place with those who have gone before and those who will come after.

Three-part formulas occur throughout this chapter: how the novices are to study, eat, and sleep (5), there is a triad of tests (7), and there are three readings of the Rule (9; 12; 13), along with a threefold repetition of the *Suscipe* (22), and finally a triple promise. Yet to speak as though there were three separate promises is misleading, for they cohere, and it is impossible to keep one without keeping the other two. They are not like the three evangelical counsels, poverty, chastity, and obedience, which can be symbolized in the three knots of a cord as with the Franciscans, for example. Rather, all three refer to the same commitment under three different but total aspects. Any one of these taken by itself—"obedience," "conversion of life," "stability"—could perfectly well serve as an all-embracing title for the whole enterprise, which is nothing less than a commitment to living a Godward life, seeking God, and being found by God.

If we start with stability, we can look on this as the perspective with which to view everything else. Benedict puts stability first since without it the other two lose much of their meaning. If we are to live our lives according to this commitment, we must be prepared to live it until the end, to death. If I know deeply and interiorly that this is where I stand, then that unleashes great energy and does away with the inner debate and uncertainty, that endless questioning, that so quickly becomes debilitating.

Although it is particularly associated with Benedict, the idea of stability has a long history within the monastic tradition, and it is, of course, deeply rooted in biblical understanding. "Persevere until death," which Benedict quotes in the prologue, is taken from Philemon 2:8. The psalms make central the theme of steadfastness, which is another way of expressing stability: "Renew a steadfast spirit within me." The ideal of stability runs through many of the sayings of the Desert Fathers, notably: "Stay in your cell and your cell will teach you everything." Already there is this firm strand in the tradition that recommends stability as a spiritual help. But it had never before received such firm and clear handling and been given the central place with such strong sanctions as Benedict now assigns to it.

The novice who has read the Rule carefully, thoughtfully, and has meditated upon it, is in a good position to enter fully into what this understanding of stability means. It is essentially not something abstract or philosophical, but thoroughly practical, for Benedict is never a man to leave things in the air, particularly good intentions! He likes to make things concrete, specific. At the end of chapter 4, there is that short phrase that links stability with enclosure and the community: "Now the workshop where we are to toil faithfully at all these tasks is the enclosure of the monastery and stability in the community" (4,78). So a particular group of people, as much as some sacred geographical spot, shapes our stability. Those vivid negative examples given in chapter 1 can help us to read Benedict's mind rather more clearly, for we see his castigation of the gyrovagues who are so deficient in stability that they spend their whole lives wandering, roaming, never stable, given up to their own wills. This physical instability resulted from, and expressed, their spiritual and psychological rootlessness, for far from being rooted in God and in the search for God, they were rooted in their own selfishness and self-seeking.

Ultimately, stability is internal and spiritual, concerned with the interior, inward disposition. So if I want to think about my own stability, I must ask myself where I am rooted. Am I stable and unwavering in my commitment to my search for God? What militates against stability in my life are all my escape routes: my fantasies and my day dreams, my wandering memory and my wandering imagination, the romantic dreams of some better place, the promise of something better elsewhere. This is, of course, simply escapism, which means that I am not truly present to this moment, to the actual job in hand, to the people who surround me now. There are essential questions that cannot be evaded: Who am I and where am I? They are linked, for I cannot really know myself and know who I am unless I also know where I belong, unless I have some firm ground under my feet. Benedict as ever shows an excellent grasp of psychology.

"Where are you?" That was the question that God asked Adam and Eve as he walked in the garden in the cool of the day, and they hid in the bushes, ashamed of their nakedness and disobedience. As long as they chose to hide and evade this question, which is surely also the fundamental question for any for us, they could not meet God, nor have any relationship with God, not least the relationship of being chastized, punished, and then forgiven. It is only when I stop running away, stand still, and look around me that I begin to see where my place is in the world. If I stand still long enough, I might then be able to explore the place where I am, send down a few roots, let something grow, reach maturity, produce fruits from deep inside myself. This kind of fruit, this kind of "producing," will probably no longer be the glittering fruits and sparkling trophies that I dreamed of in my earlier life, but more rich and satisfying and fulfilled fruition. I think of Christ in his farewell discourses telling his disciples to *abide* in the Father's love, and he asks the same of me, that I abide in him so that I may bear fruit.

The image of roots is one that I find immensely helpful. Just as a tree or a grain of wheat does not produce fruit unless it first puts its roots down into the earth, so also I cannot grow and become fruitful unless and until I sink down roots. The twelfth-century Cistercian, the Blessed Guerric of Igny, has four sermons on St. Benedict in which he makes a parallel between living according to the Rule and living as Benedict did: both show us a life rooted in God. Benedict himself "was like a tree planted by the living waters of divine wisdom. He is not only a model to us but has transmitted to us his way of life, so that if we live our lives wisely we live rooted in God." The Rule is to help us to sink our roots in wisdom, and it all begins when we start to settle down and take our time, see that we cannot do everything ourselves (which is humility) or do it at once, and, above all, when we practice the true silence that will help us to sink our roots in God. "What good is a bird sitting on eggs who flies off and leaves her work unfinished? What plant can flower or bear fruit unless it is left in the place where it is planted?" With such simple images Guerric helps me to ask some important questions about the pattern of my life.

These images further help me in as much as they make a clear distinction between true stability, which is fruitful, and staticness, which is negative and unproductive, the wrong sort of standing still. Christ wants us to be alive, fruitful, drinking the living waters. To be standing as still as a dead tree stump is quite wrong. There is the danger of inertia taking over, of getting trapped into the wrong kind of stability—that pseudostability that keeps me staying there when I should be getting out, so that even if I am physically present I am not alive, awake. I think of Christ turning to the disciples in the garden and asking them to stay awake to support him, and one another, during the struggle, to fight sleep and the forces of darkness. They failed him, as so often I fail through laziness, weakness, carelessness, and, perhaps most insidious of all, sheer inertia. If I took the Rule seriously, I should know that right from the start Benedict is asking for people who are open, alert, attentive, fully alive!

The image of fighting, fighting the forces of darkness further enriches the concept of stability. Benedict was a true Roman and the resonance of *stare*, "to stand," would carry military connotations for him, as does that passage in Ephesians 6:13: "Therefore take the whole armor of God, that you may be able to withstand in the evil day, and having done all, to stand, stand therefore. . . ." By standing still I find where the real battle has to be fought, not the least with the forces within. Maturity comes from facing what has to be faced and not running away from all the dark and murky elements that lie in wait to attack us. "It is by warfare in the soul that we make progress," as one of the Desert Fathers puts it. The ancients also knew only too well the dangers of *accidie*, the condition of inner restlessness, inconsistency, and heedlessness. What this asks is the ability to hang on, to endure, even when there does not seem much prospect of the end of the road. It means holding on against the odds, being willing to keep on keeping on. This is a sort of constancy that does not become either discouraged or cynical in the face of anxiety, boredom. Refusing to give up because I am in it for the long haul brings an entirely different perspective. In the end I am brought back, of course, to Christ himself and to his example, the willingness to endure faithfully and with patience, *patientia*, reminding me that this means both waiting and suffering. What makes this possible? The faithfulness of God. God is faithful to the covenant, and I know that I can rely on him. God's love endures forever. What I hold on to, what keeps me going through the bad times, is this certitude in the faithfulness of God. My stability is possible in the end because of the certain, guaranteed, steadfastness of God.

So the faithful father awaits the return home of the prodigal, just as each one of us also longs to come home, to cease wandering, to give up eating empty husks, to be back with the family in the place where we belong. That is something that Benedict touched on in the very first sentence of the Rule. I can now reflect on the many levels of meaning that the concept of being at home carries. He has shown me the importance of being at home in relation to place and to people, but more fundamentally in relation to my own inner self. "What can we gain by sailing to the moon if we are not able to cross the abyss that separates us from ourselves?" Merton asks. I know that if I find God I will find myself; if I find my true self I will find God.

Those familiar words of Augustine, "Late have I loved Thee! And behold, Thou wert within and I was without, I was looking for Thee out there. . . ." read in a modern translation "Behold, You were within me and I was not at home." It is very easy to become a person who has an address but is never at home. But if I am absent from myself, how can I be there to open the door when Christ stands outside and knocks? Henri Nouwen reminds us that Christ is telling us, "You have a home. . . . I am your home. . . . Claim your home. . . . It is right where you are . . . in your innermost being . . . in your heart."

It is because I am at home in myself that I can also journey. Having presented us with the promise to stay still and be rooted Benedict now turns to the second promise, *conversatio morum,* which carries the implication of journeying, moving forward, the quest. It is the one that makes the other possible. This is the paradox. It was something that Thomas Merton experienced in his own life. It was only because he knew that he had come home when he entered the gates of the monastery at Gethsemani that he was able to set out on his journey, both the interior journey and then finally the journey to the East. This was the vow that he chose to talk about in Bangkok on the morning of December 10, 1968, the day that was to end with his unexpected death. He said that it was the most mysterious of all the vows:

> When you stop and think a little about St. Benedict's concept of *conversatio morum,* that most mysterious of our vows, which is actually the most essential, I believe, it can be interpreted as a commitment to total inner transformation of one sort or another—a commitment to become a completely new man. It seems to me that that could be regarded as the end of the monastic life, and that no matter where one attempts to do this, that remains the essential thing.

Toward the end of that lecture Merton spoke of the Christian monastic view of reality, that "if you once penetrate by detachment and purity of heart to the inner secret of the ground of your ordinary experience you attain to a liberty that nobody can touch." Here is a total transformation that will bring inner freedom.

The novice enters wholly, fully, and freely into the whole observance, the total way of life of the community. *Conversatio* was understood by the ancients to mean a definite way of life. In primitive monasticism, as Augustine Roberts reminds us, the first monks were convinced of the need for "concrete practices as instruments or tools, to help to purify the soul, change the corners of one's heart from vice to virtue, and pass from virtue to God" For Benedict the whole life that he outlines and legislates for in the Rule is this *conversatio*, life according to the school of the Lord's service, the chosen way of spiritual growth by which the monk hopes to purify his heart in dependence on Christ and thus "deserve also to share in his kingdom" (Prol., 50).

The promise that the novice is making is fidelity to this way of life. It means embracing the whole life of prayer and asceticism. There are external renunciations, there are ascetical demands, but the exterior observances are not the end in themselves; the end is the interior conversion of heart, growth in the values of love, humility, purity of heart. The exterior conversion brings with it a way of life that facilitates a deeper, more interior conversion. If I think of how this applies to my own situation, it means that I have to ask myself what way of life I freely choose. Am I prepared to make a total commitment and not pick and choose what pleases me? Am I prepared to follow this way to the end?

Benedict presents this way of life as a dynamic movement centered on Christ. He impresses the Rule with a sense of movement that comes across so strongly in those first paragraphs of the prologue: "Set out on the way . . . run there . . . progress in this way of life . . . run in the path," and it will be caught again in the epilogue with the question "Are you hastening toward your heavenly home?" It is a battle as well. "If you are ready to do battle . . . prepare our hearts and bodies for the battle. . . ." Transformation and conversion mean commitment to a daily struggle against all those vices and inclinations that might take me away from Christ, which is, of course, nothing less than the commitment of my baptismal vows. I like the way in which one of the Desert Mothers puts it:

> Amma Syncletica said: "Great endeavors and hard struggles await those who are converted, but afterwards inexpressible joy. If you want to light a fire you are troubled at first by smoke, and your eyes pour water. But in the end you achieve your aim. Now it is written: 'Our God is a consuming fire.' So we must light the divine fire in us with tears and struggle."

This means perseverance until the end. To say that I will journey on whatever the cost and wherever that may lead me is not to say that I believe I can do this through my own strength of will or strong sense of moral purpose. It shows my utter reliance on God. I am sure of the faithfulness of God, and my promise of stability is based on that. I cannot know the shape of events and circumstances that lie ahead, and I am therefore walking forward in darkness and uncertainty, holding the hand of God in trust that he will hold me up, keep me from stumbling. "Forgetting what is behind me, and reaching out for that which lies ahead, I press towards the goal to win the prize which is God's call to the life above, in Christ Jesus" (Phil 3:13-14). Benedict does not let us forget the goal, nor is he is ashamed to remind us of the prize to be attained. There is always this long-range perspective. The tools are handed out, and the harvest will be gathered in at the end of time. Finally, the day of judgment, which Benedict will never let us forget, puts our life into a long-term perspective.

The journey theme is as old as history itself, and there are many differing images. Once again Benedict touches on something that is primal, universal. The odyssey, the search for the holy grail, the quest have always captured the imagination. The call of Abraham is only too familiar, a prototype for many other calls to leave home. The medieval pilgrim sets out, probably with a group of like-minded pilgrims, to reach a shrine or a holy place. The Celtic monks, however, felt the calling to become exiles for Christ, *peregrini,* setting out in coracles without oars, to be carried wherever the spirit might take them, so that they might find "the place of their resurrection"—that lovely phrase that gives me such delight as I say it to myself. Essentially this is the interior journey, a journey inward, and its goal is conversion of heart. When do we arrive? There is no stopping place in this life no matter how far along the road we may have come. If we refuse to journey on until the day of our death we are also refusing to be fully alive. To live with the promise of continual conversion, of *metanioa,* of turning away from all that will not lead us to Christ, is gospel teaching, and Benedict simply makes it a promise that we are to keep until the end of our lives.

The promise of obedience completes this commitment. The full meaning of obedience, therefore, is only found as part of the whole. It is not some ascetical extra, and again it is simply the way of the Gospel. Benedict has already had much to say on the subject, particularly in 5,13, where he gives the key text John 6:38, the opposition between human and divine will, between my own self-will and that of the Father. The second crucial text, Luke 10:16, is used in chapters 5, 6, and 15 to establish obedience to a superior as the means of obedience to the Father. There are two streams of thought here. Benedict shows us that obedience is something mutual, shared, that we *all* go together to the kingdom. So my obedience is mediated through a number of different sources, and at different levels. There is the obedience of the mind by which I am willing to learn from a spiritual director, from a father in God, from the tradition, from reading, from the community or those who share and shape my life. For obedience is not uncritical or blind. The whole purpose of chapter 58 is to ensure that when the novice comes to make this decision, it will be a clearly thought out choice that is taken with open eyes. Therefore there is this balance. I need the insights and the wisdom of others, but I make them my own.

I have to be willing, ready to hear. The word for obedience comes from the Latin *ob-audiens* meaning to listen, to listen intently. It is my openness and readiness to hear "with the ear of the heart" that Benedict wants. It is the disposition, the attitude, that matters. If there is merely outward conformity, then for Benedict obedience is utterly unacceptable, indeed worthless. A free, open, humble, and loving response to the will of God is at the heart of monastic obedience. It is, above all, love that makes this possible. It is something that I may forget, but if I do then the whole perspective gets lost. It is the image of the Father who stands there, waiting, offering unconditional love, acceptance, and forgiveness to the wayward son and daughter that is at once the goal and the end of the journey and at the same time the means by which I shall accomplish that journey.

It is through obedience that we return to the Father from whom we have strayed through disobedience. Benedict clearly tells us this early in the prologue. Once again I find myself in the place of the prodigal who is lost, has strayed, and is now, with Benedict's help, making the journey home. That there may well be a post-baptismal catechical homily underlying the prologue links monastic obedience to baptismal obedience. Do you turn to Christ? Those simple words are also quite terrifying. They are a question that I am asked at intervals throughout life, notably in the liturgy of the Easter Vigil. Once again it is only in the context of the paschal mystery that I can fully appreciate what is implied in my own obedience. If Christ is the model of obedience, he was obedient to his Father even unto death. When I think of the passion, I am left in no doubt at the costliness of following the Father's will, the loneliness, the anguish, the physical pain shown in the sweat and tears in the garden of Gethsemane. It is only in and through the obedience of Christ that I can also live out my own obedience. Christ is the example that I follow. Obedience is a sharing in the passion of Christ by patience, a mystery that I do not fully understand. But then perhaps that is right, for, as Daniel Rees reminds us, obedience is not a discipline, not a means for the smooth running of a well ordered life, it is a mystery at the heart of the redemption and of Christian life.

Moments after making these three promises the novice will be saying *Suscipe me,* "Receive me." This is surrender, handing over. Traditionally the profession takes place at the offertory of a Eucharistic celebration, which makes the point very clearly. These three promises are placed on the altar, thus symbolizing the voluntary act by which the novice offers himself or herself to God whose presence is represented by the altar. Then they recite Psalm 118 (119):116, praying that this gift may be acceptable. These words are a wonderful prayer. They are words that speak to any of us, and that we may find ourselves saying time and time again throughout our lives. "Take me O Lord, accept me, receive me, uphold me. . . ." No one single word carries the full weight of meaning of the original. They are singing words, words like some Eastern koan, whose full meaning reveals itself as we live with them and change and grow ourselves. It is the fullness of my whole humanity, which Benedict has been helping me to acknowledge and to live with in honesty, that I am here offering to God. As I look back over the path along which Benedict has been leading me, I am aware of his concern for the whole person, not the person who hides or who plays games, or the half person, or the person whom the world encourages me to become. In the familiar words of Irenaeus, "The glory of God is the man [and the woman] fully alive." Benedict's concern, right from the start, was that we should all be wholly alive and take up that offer of life, good life. The self now offered on the altar whom I ask God (or Christ, the word *Domine* is open to either) to receive is that true self.

As I stay with that word "receive," it is its uses in Scripture that deepen its meaning. Benedict first used it in chapter 2, quoting from Romans 8 *("You have received the spirit of adoption")* and then in chapter 53 on the reception of guests *("We have received your mercy in the midst of your temple").* So we receive Christ in one another. The action now becomes a corporate one as the community repeats this verse three times in support of its new member. Then just as the novice has asked for God's acceptance (the personal reciprocal giving and receiving between the new member and God or Christ), so in turn he or she asks each single brother or sister for the same acceptance. It is because I know myself accepted by God that I can also accept my brothers and my sisters. There is a profound insight here that I should not lightly pass over, and this is the relationship between the two acts. It is my own acceptance of myself, before God, in all honesty and humility, that makes it possible for me to accept others in the same way.

How total this handing over is to be is shown in the instructions of the final paragraph of this long chapter. Everything is handed over, including the body itself—the phrase of verse 25, obviously taken from 1 Corinthians 7:4, makes an interesting analogy with marriage. Then, in a further symbolic act of dispossession, there is an exchange of clothing, so that clothes that are essentially personal and a mark of individuality are handed over, and the novice puts on clothing that is a mark of the new life. Should things go wrong and he or she leaves the community, then they return to the clothing of their former life.

The vows, the promise made with God, remain with the community. I too have found that those promises, those words, have become deeply important to me in my own path of discipleship. *"Suscipe me,* receive me, accept me O Lord," are words that I pray wherever I am, and whatever happens to me. These promises depend on the promise of God. This is the hope, the certainty. It is the knowledge of the utter and total dependability of God who will not fail in this promise that makes my own promise possible.

In my own life these three promises have become a point of reference, a lifeline, a survival kit. They are basic to my humanity: the need to stay still and not to try to escape from where I find myself; the need to journey on, to be ready for change, not to cling to the past; the need to listen, to hear and to be heard. And they also help me with the making and the maintaining of relationships. They strengthen me when I want to run away, and they tell me about holding on, hanging on however difficult that may be. They remind me that relationships must not fossilize at some point in the past but be ready to change, even if that means a smashing of idols; they help me to listen, to listen totally to another and to find the voice of Christ in and through that person.

But above all they speak to me of Christ,
Stability: Christ the Rock
Conversatio morum: Christ the Way
Obedience: Christ the Word.

CHAPTER FIFTY-NINE

¹If a member of the nobility offers his son to God in the monastery, and the boy himself is too young, the parents draw up the document mentioned above; ²then, at the presentation of the gifts, they wrap the document itself and the boy's hand in the altar cloth. That is how they offer him.

³As to their property, they either make a sworn promise in this document that they will never personally, never through an intermediary, nor in any way at all, nor at any time, give the boy anything or afford him the opportunity to possess anything; ⁴or else, if they are unwilling to do this and still wish to win their reward for making an offering to the monastery, ⁵they make a formal donation of the property that they want to give to the monastery, keeping the revenue for themselves, should they so desire. ⁶This ought to leave no way open for the boy to entertain any expectations that could deceive and ruin him. May God forbid this, but we have learned from experience that it can happen.

⁷Poor people do the same, ⁸but those who have nothing at all simply write the document and, in the presence of witnesses, offer their son with the gifts.

At first reading the historical context jars so much that it is difficult to approach this chapter prayerfully and find its relevance to my own life. The offering of sons by nobles or by the poor, as the traditional heading of this chapter puts it, could hardly seem more completely remote and absurd. Yet the central theme of offering (the word itself occurs three times, in verses 1, 2, and 4), which sets the keynote, picks up one of the important themes of the Rule.

That we possess nothing is an idea that Benedict has been hammering home, time and time again, in different forms and in differing situations throughout the Rule. He now applies it to children. We have the scriptural precedent in the example of Hannah in 1 Samuel who hands over her longed-for child, saying as she does so that he is now for the rest of his life loaned to the Lord. Everything is on loan. That is what Benedict was saying about all the material things, tools and possessions. We were shown the total handing over of the whole self in chapter 58. Neither things, nor people, nor my own body are mine to possess, own, control.

This is easier to talk about, to think about, than to live out. Benedict knows about compromises, about holding back, about having something in reserve in case it all becomes too costly. He also knows that the half-hearted way is no good. So he builds in the safeguards that will ensure a total commitment. It is interesting to see that he says that if there is a way left open, any escape route that would allow an alternative way of life for the child, this will lead to "expectations that could deceive and ruin him" (6), strong words and ones that obviously come from hard-won experience.

CHAPTER SIXTY

¹If any ordained priest asks to be received into the monastery, do not agree too quickly. ²However, if he is fully persistent in his request, he must recognize that he will have to observe the full discipline of the rule ³without any mitigation, knowing that it is written: *Friend, what have you come for* (Matt 26:50)? ⁴He should, however, be allowed to stand next to the abbot, to give blessings and to celebrate Mass, provided that the abbot bids him. ⁵Otherwise, he must recognize that he is subject to the discipline of the rule, and not make any exceptions for himself, but rather give everyone an example of humility. ⁶Whenever there is question of an appointment or of any other business in the monastery, ⁷he takes the place that corresponds to the date of his entry into the community, and not that granted him out of respect for his priesthood.

⁸Any clerics who similarly wish to join the community should be ranked somewhere in the middle, ⁹but only if they, too, promise to keep the rule and observe stability.

The last sentence of the previous chapter shows Benedict once more carefully eliminating distinctions between people. The poor are accepted in the same spirit as the rich. He continues with this train of thought but in the context of the priest and the layperson, a distinction that could easily become a division in the community.

The priest is not to expect any special consideration. He has to follow the full observance without mitigation, subject to the full discipline of the Rule. He should expect no advancement because of his priestly dignity, and he is not afforded entry too quickly. He is forced to demonstrate persistence like anyone else knocking at the door. In other words, there is to be no distinction of rank or status, no room for privilege of any sort. For anyone entering as a priest, it might be difficult to disengage from an earlier experience of the priesthood. There could be the danger of letting the past shape the present or determine the future, and that, of course, might weaken *conversatio*. Obedience, humility, and stability apply just as much to priests as they have done in earlier chapters to any officials of the monastery.

The very specific reference to obedience, subject to the discipline of the Rule (5), says that he is not to presume, not to grasp at power, but to behave and to act as the abbot bids, a clear reminder of the dangers of self-will or self-direction about which Benedict is always very firm. That the priest is to stand in line, metaphorically and literally, standing next to whomever it may be that he has entered with, is a clear outward demonstration of how he is to take his place as an ordinary member of the community (chapter 63 will simply place the priest in line by means of the date of entry). The pattern of the life that Benedict is establishing is monastic and lay, not diocesan or clerical. He does not want to develop institutions, whether parochial or episcopal. He does not want to encourage any system. Rather he wants to build a family, a community, within which each individual may be formed in the heart and mind of Christ and may live out daily the teaching of the Gospel.

It is, of course, the interior intention that really concerns Benedict, and so there is this scrutiny of motive. The question that Benedict asks is, "Friend, what have you come for?" It was the question that Christ asked of Judas in the garden of Gethsemane. The scriptural context is always illuminating about Benedict's mind, and I believe this is particularly true here. The scene in the garden tells us so much about what is expected of discipleship, teaches about obedience, keeping watch, continuing in prayer, and so on. We might recall the question when Christ turns to the one member of his small community who is not wholly committed. That question of his is one that I can well ask myself. How truly committed am I? Am I the faithful follower or the betrayer? Am I here for the good things (the status, the security, the material comforts)? Am I here to play a role (the person with the money bags suggests the attraction of holding a particular niche in the community)? If I take this verse seriously, it could well challenge me to face some uncomfortable questions about the honesty of my motives and intentions.

CHAPTER SIXTY-ONE

[1]A visiting monk from far away will perhaps present himself and wish to stay as a guest in the monastery. [2]Provided that he is content with the life as he finds it, and does not make excessive demands that upset the monastery, [3]but is simply content with what he finds, he should be received for as long a time as he wishes. [4]He may, indeed, with all humility and love make some reasonable criticisms or observations, which the abbot should prudently consider; it is possible that the Lord guided him to the monastery for this very purpose.

[5]If after a while he wishes to remain and bind himself to stability, he should not be refused this wish, especially as there was time enough, while he was a guest, to judge his character. [6]But if during his stay he has been found excessive in his demands or full of faults, he should certainly not be admitted as a member of the community. [7]Instead, he should be politely told to depart, lest his wretched ways contaminate others.

[8]If, however, he has shown that he is not the kind of man who deserves to be dismissed, let him, on his request, be received as a member of the community. [9]He should even be urged to stay, so that others may learn from his example, [10]because wherever we may be, we are in the service of the same Lord and doing battle for the same King. [11]Further, the abbot may set such a man in a somewhat higher place in the community, if he sees that he deserves it. [12]In fact, whether it is a monk or someone in the priestly or clerical orders mentioned above, the abbot has the power to set any of them above the place that corresponds to the date of his entry, if he sees that his life warrants it.

[13]The abbot must, however, take care never to receive into the community a monk from another known monastery, unless the monk's abbot consents and sends a letter of recommendation, [14]since it is written: *Never do to another what you do not want done to yourself* (Tob 4:16).

A visiting monk is in a rather different category from the ordinary visitor to the monastery, for he is at once the same and yet different. As Benedict describes his reception by the community in this chapter, the basic issue that he is dealing with is that of a reciprocal relationship, a balance and openness that is asking something of both sides.

What are the qualities that Benedict is looking for in the visiting monk? Humility and love and stability are mentioned as essential and necessary, all are elements that are familiar. But he also speaks of contentment, something implicit in his whole way of life that he now finds necessary to emphasize. "He is content with the life as he finds it, . . . is simply content with what he finds" (2-3). It is rather unusual for Benedict to repeat himself so clumsily, and it seems that this is something really important for him. The visiting monk is not to make excessive demands. Anyone who criticizes is discontented; anyone who asks for more than he or she finds can contaminate, can spread poisonous feelings. I feel that when Benedict speaks of "wretched ways," *miseria,* which brings contamination (7), he can only be speaking from experience. It reminds me of the other times when he has used vivid language, uprooting and amputation, in order to prevent the spread of what might become a malignant growth, and again I notice that it is always attitudes that are contagious and have to be dealt with severely before they lead on to worse.

But those who receive the visitor are to be open, ready to listen. There is to be receiving as well as giving. There is to be acceptance of people who come from very different places (using this metaphorically as well as literally). There is to be willingness to hear "reasonable criticisms or observations" (4) and to learn from the example of others (9). So we are shown a complementarity of obligation, a balancing act by which a community, as also an individual, is to be open to new and different insights and understanding. In a world that builds barriers, puts up walls, keeps the other out, and is looking for certainty, we turn to the Rule and find a man who insists on balance, mutual respect, reciprocity, openness. Benedict's age was one of uncertainty, both political and religious, yet he refused to live with a closed mind. Once again I find that a strictly practical situation becomes the means by which the Rule teaches me important truths. There is something gentle and unthreateningly prophetic here, a challenge to narrowness and closed minds, by which people build walls and refuse to listen to the other.

Both kinds of monks, the visiting and the resident, share in the service of the same Lord, both do battle for the same King (10). Earlier on in the chapter Benedict has been strongly emphasizing contentment, the refusal to criticize. Yet now when he speaks of life as a battle he seems to be saying something opposite. Once again I am faced by the need to find a balance in which one thing will be a counterpoise to the other. There can be the wrong sort of contentment and acceptance, close to apathy *(accedie)*, by which I become lethargic, dispirited. The balancing of one thing against another brings a tension between opposites and helps me to live with contradictory forces so that they become energizing and life-giving.

The final question comes in the last verse (13) of the chapter: Am I living out the Golden Rule (which Benedict does not give in its more familiar expression in Matthew but quotes the original form in Tobit)? But the issue is the same, it is this ideal of reciprocity, of mutuality, of giving and receiving, of balance and openness. After reading this chapter in which Benedict is giving such a wise criterion for the behavior of both those who give and those who receive, I find that it raises certain issues for me. Am I content? Am I truly content? Am I open to receive as well as give? Do I try to keep balance and reciprocity playing in my life?

CHAPTER SIXTY-TWO

¹Any abbot who asks to have a priest or deacon ordained should choose from his monks one worthy to exercise the priesthood. ²The monk so ordained must be on guard against conceit or pride, ³must not presume to do anything except what the abbot commands him, and must recognize that now he will have to subject himself all the more to the discipline of the rule. ⁴Just because he is a priest, he may not therefore forget the obedience and discipline of the rule, but must make more and more progress toward God.

⁵He will always take the place that corresponds to the date of his entry into the monastery, ⁶except in his duties at the altar, or unless the whole community chooses and the abbot wishes to give him a higher place for the goodness of his life. ⁷Yet, he must know how to keep the rule established for deans and priors; ⁸should he presume to act otherwise, he must be regarded as a rebel, not as a priest. ⁹If after many warnings he does not improve, let the bishop too be brought in as a witness. ¹⁰Should he not amend even then, and his faults become notorious, he is to be dismissed from the monastery, ¹¹but only if he is so arrogant that he will not submit or obey the rule.

When any member of the community is given a special role to play, then at once there are dangers. They are summed up in the word "arrogant," which comes in the final verse, and is spelled out at intervals in the opening paragraph: pride and conceit, lack of obedience, failure to live under discipline. Benedict goes on to speak of "more and more progress toward God" (4), and in that simple phrase sums up the whole aim and purpose of the Christian life. I find again here what has concerned him in chapter 60, that a person who enters the monastery with particular skills or training from the past might find it difficult to disengage, might therefore fail to grow in openness and, in particular, in the receiving and giving shown in the previous chapter.

In this chapter Benedict is concerned to help anyone who holds office, especially an office that carries expectations of particular holiness, to beware of role playing. They must not forget their essential place with the rest. The following chapter will place the priest in the ranks by reason of his date of entry. Much of what Benedict is saying here points me back to what I have learned in his teaching on humility. It is written with priests in mind, but the principles apply to other situations and persons.

Despite the extreme reserve toward monastic priests in chapters 60 and 62, there is no sign of disrespect for the priesthood as such. The priest is allowed to stand next to the abbot, impart blessings, and say Mass (60,4). There is mention of their duties at the altar (6). It is generally agreed that Benedict's monks did not have daily Mass. The sacrament was probably taken before the monastic meal at a Communion service, and this was no doubt so common as not to require comment. Most abbots were not priests, but they would arrange for monks to be ordained as they were needed, ensuring that they remain firmly under internal control rather than that of the local bishop.

CHAPTER SIXTY-THREE

¹The monks keep their rank in the monastery according to the date of their entry, the virtue of their lives, and the decision of the abbot. ²The abbot is not to disturb the flock entrusted to him nor make any unjust arrangements, as though he had the power to do whatever he wished. ³He must constantly reflect that he will have to give God an account of all his decisions and actions. ⁴Therefore, when the monks come for the kiss of peace and for Communion, when they lead psalms or stand in choir, they do so in the order decided by the abbot or already existing among them. ⁵Absolutely nowhere shall age automatically determine rank. ⁶Remember that Samuel and Daniel were still boys when they judged their elders (1 Sam 3; Dan 13:44-62). ⁷Therefore, apart from those mentioned above whom the abbot has for some overriding consideration promoted, or for a specific reason demoted, all the rest should keep to the order of their entry. ⁸For example, someone who came to the monastery at the second hour of the day must recognize that he is junior to someone who came at the first hour, regardless of age or distinction. ⁹Boys, however, are to be disciplined in everything by everyone.

¹⁰The younger monks, then, must respect their seniors, and the seniors must love their juniors. ¹¹When they address one another, no one should be allowed to do so simply by name; ¹²rather, the seniors call the younger monks "brother" and the younger monks call their seniors *nonnus,* which is translated as "venerable father." ¹³But the abbot, because we believe that he holds the place of Christ, is to be called "lord" and "abbot," not for any claim of his own, but out of honor and love for Christ. ¹⁴He, for his part, must re-

209

flect on this, and in his behavior show himself worthy of such honor.

¹⁵Wherever brothers meet, the junior asks his senior for a blessing. ¹⁶When an older monk comes by, the younger rises and offers him a seat, and does not presume to sit down unless the older bids him. ¹⁷In this way, they do what the words of Scripture say: *They should each try to be the first to show respect to the other* (Rom 12:10).

¹⁸In the oratory and at table, small boys and youths are kept in rank and under discipline. ¹⁹Outside or anywhere else, they should be supervised and controlled until they are old enough to be responsible.

Order has always been a basic concern for Benedict. As he looked out from his cave at Subiaco and saw a world in which the last remnants of Roman imperial order were breaking down, he saw the urgent need of helping people to bring order into their lives. He knew only too well that there must be both an inner and an outer order and that the two depend on one another. By this stage of the Rule, he has written about all the differing members of the community, from the abbot through those who hold any kind of office, whether temporary or permanent, to the ordinary members. He knows about unique gifts and talents and how not to level down a group of people into any dull conformity. If now he has to help all these varied people impose some sort of coherent framework on their working relationships, we may be sure that he had plenty of personal experience with the problems it raised. The *Dialogues* give some vivid glimpses of the tensions in the community at Monte Cassino with its range of widely varying backgrounds, experience, position, education, social and racial standing.

In this chapter Benedict is saying that what each member brings in terms of past experience, status, education, wealth, and worldly success now counts for nothing. For it is the moment of entrance that determines place in the community. This is a strong symbolic statement about the new order in which the love of Christ and the values of the Gospel will operate. The moment that counts is that of entry, of acceptance of the call, when in all humility and openness to the future the novice prays *Suscipe me, Domine*.

That each and every person counts is seen in the attention given to the young (which 3,3 has already made clear). This is gospel teaching, where Jesus sets up a small child in the midst of the disciples. Yet the epistles also insist on the observance of certain social arrangements in which wives, children, and slaves are firmly kept in their place. It is interesting to see how Benedict handles this; he manages to keep a balance between the two. Every person has his or her proper place, each is made aware of their worth. The tools in this delicate operation are respect and love (10), both familiar themes of the Rule. Benedict is not interested in any rules or the jurisdictional aspects of rank. At the end of the chapter (17), he refers to Romans 12, and I find it revealing if I read this chapter in the context of that wonderful outpouring of Paul on the building up of the body of Christ. For Paul starts with a verse that could be a description of the the entry of the novice into the community, "present your bodies a sacrifice, holy, acceptable to God," and the succeeding verses speak of the gifts and the virtues of each as the many members become one: the individual giftedness of each separate son or daughter that Benedict has so continuously emphasized.

Recognition of this uniqueness is outwardly expressed in the way in which we greet one another, the most immediate way in which love and respect are lived out in daily life (10-13; 15; 16). There is much practical insight here, for Benedict is both a good sociologist and a good psychologist. But it goes deeper. This is about the figure of Christ himself, present amongst us, symbolized by the abbot as the father who holds the place of Christ but is simultaneously the exemplar for each of us to find the face of Christ in all whom we see.

I take the words in verse 13, "out of honor and love for Christ," as a text for myself. I do not belong to any community, my life seems to consist of a succession of interlocking circles, family, work, interests, and I am also often on my own. But what Benedict is saying can still apply. A competitive, success-oriented, highly individualistic world needs love and respect more than ever. He is giving us a basis for right relationships, the working out of an inter-dependence and complementarity of one with another that can link us all into a mysterious, unseen communion with each other in and through the figure of Christ himself.

CHAPTER SIXTY-FOUR

¹In choosing an abbot, the guiding principle should always be that the man placed in office be the one selected either by the whole community acting unanimously in the fear of God, or by some part of the community, no matter how small, which possesses sounder judgment. ²Goodness of life and wisdom in teaching must be the criteria for choosing the one to be made abbot, even if he is the last in community rank.

³May God forbid that a whole community should conspire to elect a man who goes along with its own evil ways. But if it does, ⁴and if the bishop of the diocese or the abbots or Christians in the area come to know of these evil ways to any extent, ⁵they must block the success of this wicked conspiracy, and set a worthy steward in charge of God's house. ⁶They may be sure that they will receive a generous reward for this, if they do it with pure motives and zeal for God's honor. Conversely, they may be equally sure that to neglect to do so is sinful.

⁷Once in office, the abbot must keep constantly in mind the nature of the burden he has received, and remember to whom he will have *to give an account of his stewardship* (Luke 16:2). ⁸Let him recognize that his goal must be profit for the monks, not preeminence for himself. ⁹He ought, therefore, to be learned in divine law, so that he has a treasury of knowledge from which he can *bring out what is new and what is old* (Matt 13:52). He must be chaste, temperate and merciful. ¹⁰He should always *let mercy triumph over judgment* (Jas 2:13) so that he too may win mercy. ¹¹He must hate faults but love the brothers. ¹²When he must punish them, he should use prudence and avoid extremes;

212

otherwise, by rubbing too hard to remove the rust, he may break the vessel. [13]He is to distrust his own frailty and remember *not to crush the bruised reed* (Isa 42:3). [14]By this we do not mean that he should allow faults to flourish, but rather, as we have already said, he should prune them away with prudence and love as he sees best for each individual. [15]Let him strive to be loved rather than feared.

[16]Excitable, anxious, extreme, obstinate, jealous or over-suspicious he must not be. Such a man is never at rest. [17]Instead, he must show forethought and consideration in his orders, and whether the task he assigns concerns God or the world, he should be discerning and moderate, [18]bearing in mind the discretion of holy Jacob, who said: *If I drive my flocks too hard, they will all die in a single day* (Gen 33:13). [19]Therefore, drawing on this and other examples of discretion, the mother of virtues, he must so arrange everything that the strong have something to yearn for and the weak nothing to run from.

[20]He must, above all, keep this rule in every particular, [21]so that when he has ministered well he will hear from the Lord what that good servant heard who gave his fellow servants grain at the proper time: [22]*I tell you solemnly,* he said, *he sets him over all his possessions* (Matt 24:47).

The body has its head, the community has its leader. Here is a portrait of that head, with an exploration of the qualities needed in any leadership position. The opening sentences, however, about the selection of the abbot are confusing and imprecise, which is unusual for Benedict. This muddled start to the subject has given scholars a splendid opportunity to try to read what might really have been in his mind, what, for example, "sounder judgement" (1) might involve. Behind these laconic statements, it is quite clear that it is to the Holy Spirit that all must look and that all these procedures are simply to be channels for that. What is at issue is that the motivation is pure "zeal for God's honor" (6).

The provisions in verses 4 and 5 that, if things do not go well with the election, then the wider Church of the region is to be called in to help gives us an interesting glimpse of the interaction of the monastic community with the wider Church. It is a reminder that the monastic community is in the Church and for the Church, and that relationship is a two-way thing. Those who live outside, whether they are officially connected with the hierarchical Church of the diocese or are simply the ordinary Christians around, both gain from and contribute to the monastic life. It is important not to forget that the institutional Church and monastic life have continually interacted one with the other. Monasticism began as a charismatic phenomenon outside the hierarchical structure of ecclesiastical authority, and at the time at which Benedict was writing the situation was still pretty fluid, with bishops exercising some control but with no clear-cut and universal pattern emerging.

As soon as he has dealt with the question of choice, Benedict turns to the real subject of this chapter: the qualities demanded by the work of the abbot. Despite the precise nature of the subject, the chapter can still provide anyone in a position of authority, whether parent, teacher, priest, or business executive, with a theological description that is both wise and practical. The tasks that the abbot assigns will concern both "God or the world" (17), a nice summary of that holistic spirituality that Benedict has been giving us that does not separate the material and the spiritual. The abbot is concerned with the whole of life, with sleep and food and drink and discipline and prayer, but not least with personal relationships. So now the question is: What sort of a man is this to be?

The description in verse 5 of "a worthy steward in charge of God's house" catches once again the theme of stewardship that has been so important throughout the Rule and that carries the connotations of respect, reverence, and handling with care. As the portrait builds up, I begin to see what Benedict is looking for: a person who is gentle and compassionate. Mercy is mentioned three times (9; 10), and prudence twice (12; 14). When he comes to deal with faults, it is important to have the perspective that can separate the sin from the sinner (11). But it is equally important when things go wrong to face the truth. When it comes to the need to punish, there is a very nice picture of the abbot being beware not to rub too hard to remove the rust in case the vessel gets broken. This is for me a picture that catches so completely Benedict's emphasis on gentleness, on compassion, on handling with care. But it is also surely more than that. In using that image of the person as a vessel, he is saying something incarnational. Is he not telling us that each person is a Eucharistic vessel?

Compassion does not mean collusion, a failure to deal with faults. These, as we have already seen, call for correction and healing. Faults are to be pruned away with prudence and love (14). The purpose is to promote the unique capabilities of every person in the way that best suits them, a delicate operation that equally well applies to any of us in our relations with others. It is beautifully caught in verse 19, "He must so arrange everything that the strong have something to yearn for and the weak nothing to run from." Benedict chooses the example of Jacob as a man of gentleness who knew that if he drove his flocks too hard they would all die in one day. In the passage from Genesis from which he takes the quotation in verse 18, we read of Jacob's gentle handling of tender children and the flocks that were with young, and how he said, "I will lead on softly," a phrase that gives me peculiar delight.

The long list of negative qualities that comes in verse 16 is a total contrast to the moderation and discernment that he is hoping for. "Excitable, . . . extreme, obstinate, . . . never at rest" (16). This picture of someone who is uncertain, ajar, not at home in themselves, strikes a chord with me. It catches so well what I feel at those times when I am at war with myself. I know that this is serious both for me and for others; so long as I am not at ease with myself and do not love and accept myself, I cannot hope to allow others to feel at ease or to feel loved and accepted. Perhaps this is no more than the exercise of compassion that Benedict understands so well, which recognizes the worth of the individual and loves each one as they need to be loved. We should not miss the significance of the fact that Benedict again uses the suffering servant of Isaiah (13) as the model we are to follow.

It would be quite impossible to live out this ideal of the servant and the steward, able to love and cherish, if we were simply relying on our own inner resources. But Benedict reminds us that there are sources and springs of wisdom on which to draw, not least a treasury of knowledge (9). He quotes from that passage in Matthew's Gospel where Jesus speaks of the householder (a most appropriate image for this chapter) who brings out from his treasure what is old and what is new. We know already the importance that Benedict attached to reading and to prayerful reflection.

In chapter 73, the final chapter of the Rule, he will make it clear that he expects his followers to read further and to take into account the riches of the Fathers and the earlier monastic tradition, but above all to draw on the Bible: "What page, what passage of the inspired books of the Old and New Testaments is not the truest of guides for human life?" (73,3). Being subject to a rule could easily be static. As I read about the relationship of the abbot and the Rule I realize that what he is saying also applies to anyone in a position of authority and their relationship with the appropriate received wisdom of that role, whether that be a manual on good parenting or on personnel mangement. Whatever it may it is essential that it is vitalizing, not static. Everything in Benedict's way speaks of life and growth and progress.

The person and the law are thus manifest in the abbot and the Rule. Both principles of authority are sacred, and both must be held together. They point to the two aspects of Christ himself or otherwise the fullness of Christ is simply not present. For it is, of course, always the presence of Christ himself that Benedict has in mind. Benedict's criteria for choosing the abbot, "goodness of life and wisdom in teaching" (2), gives a nice juxtaposition of living and learning held in balance. Here I find wise advice, which I might very easily miss, about the importance of the balance of heart and head held together.

It is the biblical images and resonances that bring out the real wealth and riches of this chapter and which enable me to read it prayerfully and to return to it again and again for insights to apply to my own life situation. Chapter 2 had the image of the abbot as shepherd, and now in verse 20 the image is that of the servant who gives grain at the proper time to his fellow servants. Each of these words is pregnant with significance, but it is the role of the servant that sets the keynote. The quotation that follows verse 13 about keeping one's own frailty ever before one's eyes (a phrase I have taken from the translation by Luke Dysinger) and not crushing the bruised reed is taken from the suffering servant passage of Isaiah 42:1, which opens, "Behold my servant whom I uphold. . . ." The quotation from Matthew 24 that comes in the final verse (22) is taken from our Lord's discourse on being ready and faithful in watching, for that is what he will be looking for from his faithful and wise servant (Matt 24:45) when he comes to see how he has been taking care of the household. This is the servant who rules his household well and gives to his fellow servants grain, wheat. I like to find here an echo of the earlier Eucharistic implication of each one as a Eucharistic vessel. Finally "the proper time" (21), such a simple and short phrase, yet one that sums up the whole idea of the right ordering of time and space, the stewardship of the material as well as the personal, the holistic spirituality of this important chapter.

216

CHAPTER SIXTY-FIVE

¹Too often in the past, the appointment of a prior has been the source of serious contention in monasteries. ²Some priors, puffed up by the evil spirit of pride and thinking of themselves as second abbots, usurp tyrannical power and foster contention and discord in their communities. ³This occurs especially in monasteries where the same bishop and the same abbots appoint both abbot and prior. ⁴It is easy to see what an absurd arrangement this is, because from the very first moment of his appointment as prior he is given grounds for pride, ⁵as his thoughts suggest to him that he is exempt from his abbot's authority. ⁶"After all, you were made prior by the same men who made the abbot."

⁷This is an open invitation to envy, quarrels, slander, rivalry, factions and disorders of every kind, ⁸with the result that, while abbot and prior pursue conflicting policies, their own souls are inevitably endangered by this discord; ⁹and at the same time the monks under them take sides and so go to their ruin. ¹⁰The responsibility for this evil and dangerous situation rests on the heads of those who initiated such a state of confusion.

¹¹For the preservation of peace and love we have, therefore, judged it best for the abbot to make all decisions in the conduct of his monastery. ¹²If possible, as we have already established, the whole operation of the monastery should be managed through deans under the abbot's direction. ¹³Then, so long as it is entrusted to more than one, no individual will yield to pride. ¹⁴But if local conditions call for it, or the community makes a reasonable and humble request, and the abbot judges it best, ¹⁵then let him, with the advice of God-fearing brothers, choose the man he wants

and himself make him his prior. ¹⁶The prior for his part is to carry out respectfully what his abbot assigns to him, and do nothing contrary to the abbot's wishes or arrangements, ¹⁷because the more he is set above the rest, the more he should be concerned to keep what the rule commands.

¹⁸If this prior is found to have serious faults, or is led astray by conceit and grows proud, or shows open contempt for the holy rule, he is to be warned verbally as many as four times. ¹⁹If he does not amend, he is to be punished as required by the discipline of the rule. ²⁰Then, if he still does not reform, he is to be deposed from the rank of prior and replaced by someone worthy. ²¹If after all that, he is not a peaceful and obedient member of the community, he should even be expelled from the monastery. ²²Yet the abbot should reflect that he must give God an account of all his judgments, lest the flames of jealousy or rivalry sear his soul.

This is the least prayerful chapter in the Rule. It is fairly bristling with tension. Perhaps because of his own personal experience, Benedict is wary of the office of prior, probably because of the problems arising from the appointment by an outside authority and the dangers of a power struggle that it carries. The ideal, of course, is what we have been given in the previous chapter, a community of "peace and love" (11). But Benedict is completely realistic about human nature and its weaknesses and what happens when the spirit of pride enters in.

When he lists the personal sins of the erring prior, it seems significant that he mentions pride three times, in addition to conceit and contempt. When there is this split between the head and one of the responsible members, it leads to a state of confusion in the whole community, becomes an open invitation to faction and disorder of every kind and to the envy, quarrels, slander, and rivalry that he lists in verse 7. He is worried that the abbot may get drawn into this maelstrom of violence and fears how destructive such conflicting aims and goals will become. This is the price that is paid for anyone putting his or her personal ends above the interests of the group. It is a dark warning against exploiting a position of power or authority for self-advancement to the detriment of the whole.

Benedict clearly cannot let such an evil and dangerous situation (10) go unchecked, and he lays down a number of parameters that are to operate. First, he reminds the community that decision-making lies with the abbot (though, of course, with all the safeguards that he has given in chapters 2 and 64). He allows the abbot to have deans to work under his direction, approving of them since a number is a safeguard against pride (13). If things go wrong there is a system of correction, carefully worked out in the final paragraph with the ultimate sanction that, if he still remains "not a peaceful and obedient member of the community" (21), he is to be expelled from it.

A split personality can be as dangerous to the corporate situation as to the individual. It is something that we can all be only too aware of around us. We can see it at work in a marriage where husband and wife are deeply at odds and damage the whole family, in a parish where people split into factions and tear apart the tissue of the congregation, and in a community caught in a power struggle and living off negative energy because it fails to deal with the underlying issues. But if Benedict knows how destructive divergent and centrifugal elements can be, he also knows the importance of accepting the wide range and variety of human nature and human experience. The question is how to hold these elements together and integrate them so that the whole body becomes life-giving rather than life-denying. In the previous chapter Benedict has been showing us the role of the abbot holding the center with loving firmness. So that is what I now ask myself: Can the center hold? Where is the axis on which everything turns? If the abbot points me to Christ, it will be there that I shall find the creative force and power to make my relationships meaningful and life-giving.

CHAPTER SIXTY-SIX

¹At the door of the monastery, place a sensible old man who knows how to take a message and deliver a reply, and whose age keeps him from roaming about. ²This porter will need a room near the entrance so that visitors will always find him there to answer them. ³As soon as anyone knocks, or a poor man calls out, he replies "Thanks be to God" or "Your blessing, please"; ⁴then, with all the gentleness that comes from the fear of God, he provides a prompt answer with the warmth of love. ⁵Let the porter be given one of the younger brothers if he needs help.

⁶The monastery should, if possible, be so constructed that within it all necessities, such as water, mill and garden are contained, and the various crafts are practiced. ⁷Then there will be no need for the monks to roam outside, because this is not at all good for their souls.

⁸We wish this rule to be read often in the community, so that none of the brothers can offer the excuse of ignorance.

This chapter is such an amazing contrast, for here Benedict writes with warmth and love and a gentle sense of humor. He gives a nice and funny picture of a sensible old man, who is competent to take a message and deliver a reply, who answers a knock or a call promptly, who has a room near the entrance, and who, because he is old, will not be tempted to go wandering off (1). (The *Rule of the Master* has an almost equally entertaining description of two decrepit brothers who have a cell near the gate so that they can open and close it, do what manual labor they can, feed the dogs and other animals, and keep a lamp lit near the gate.) But Benedict's concern is not really with any of these externals.

It is not enough simply to be efficient about opening the door. It is how it is done that counts. The porter responds with love. He calls out *Deo gratias,* "Thank God" that you have come. He asks the guest for a blessing, thereby tacitly saying that he also has something to give. Benedict uses two short phrases here: "the gentleness that comes from the fear of God," and "the warmth of love" (4).

This is one of the most delightful of the portraits in the Rule, and just because it is sketched in so slightly and so delicately, we should not miss its profound implications. The porter stands on the edge, based in the enclosure yet greeting the world outside. So in him we are watching the holding together of desert and marketplace, cloister and world. What is his attitude to the stranger at the gates? In their exchange I like to find echoes of that meeting between Benedict and the priest on Easter Day that is recorded in the *Dialogues.* I have already thought about in the chapter on hospitality where Benedict says that we are to receive everyone who comes as Christ.

There are many themes in this chapter that carry implications for the way in which I live and relate to the world. Benedict is at pains to make the point that the old man cannot wander off. So this brings me back to the importance of stability, the necessity of not running around or running away, but instead staying in one place and facing whatever or whoever comes. In verses 6-7 the monastery is described as a virtually separate and self-contained compound, able to feed itself with the essentials of bread and water and garden produce. I like to take this as an image of what the cloister can mean symbolically. The chapter on hospitality had shown the importance of the welcome of the open door upon the inner enclosure. Here I am reminded of the inner cloister, the inner garden, which needs tending throughout the year, the flowing water, the cultivation of various crafts. All these are very good symbols of how I should cultivate my own inner space and how it is from that that I can go out and greet the world.

CHAPTER SIXTY-SEVEN

[1]Brothers sent on a journey will ask the abbot and community to pray for them. [2]All absent brothers should always be remembered at the closing prayer of the Work of God. [3]When they come back from a journey, they should, on the very day of their return, lie face down on the floor of the oratory at the conclusion of each of the customary hours of the Work of God. [4]They ask the prayers of all for their faults, in case they may have been caught off guard on the way by seeing some evil thing or hearing some idle talk.

[5]No one should presume to relate to anyone else what he saw or heard outside the monastery, because that causes the greatest harm. [6]If anyone does so presume, he shall be subjected to the punishment of the rule. [7]So too shall anyone who presumes to leave the enclosure of the monastery, or go anywhere, or do anything at all, however small, without the abbot's order.

Here follows a chapter that discusses the relations of the inner and the outer. Brothers leave the monastery and need help to integrate that outer journey into their normal life of the enclosure. First, they are reminded that the heart and core of the monastic life is the *opus Dei*, and that it will continue in their absence. Prayer is the underlying continuum of life that keeps everything together; whether physically present or not, all are held in that prayer. That is a consoling thought for us too, wandering the face of the earth, but knowing that the *opus Dei* is continuing without ceasing, day and night, year after year, this great stream of praise into which our own faltering and broken prayer is inserted.

But there is also the more specific and immediate prayer that the brothers ask for as they set out on a journey. Journey prayers and blessings are as old as humankind. They are common to all early and primitive peoples. Celtic men and women, for example, would never dream of setting out on a journey, however short, without first asking God's blessing on the ground beneath their foot and his companionship along the way:

> Bless to me, O God
> The earth beneath my foot,
> Bless to me, O God,
> The path whereon I go.
>
> My walk this day with God,
> My walk this day with Christ,
> My walk this day with Spirit,
> The Threefold all-kindly.

The chapter goes on to look at the interface between the monastery and the world outside. The uneasiness that Benedict clearly feels comes through clearly in what he is writing. That God's created order is good, matter is good, has been made abundantly clear. But not everything is good. Discernment is called for. Gossip and idle talk are amongst the most pernicious of sins, for they are a direct attack on the attitude of respect and reverence. Again it is the interior disposition that Benedict is forcing me to think about. Fantasy, daydreams, speculations—these are not the reality of God's world but come from the sick thoughts whirling around in the mind. It is this that Benedict has no use for. He knows not only that they are dangerous for the individual, but also that they can become contagious. Rumors get fired, wild ideas spread abroad, and these must be contained, so there are strict rules about this. It comes back to the sense of our inter-connectedness.

This is a corporate, shared spirituality. The abbot is the head, the center of the body, and evils can swarm through that body if each member goes about wandering off at will. Again the image is that of a journey that is willed, intended, and has a purpose, not going off like the gyrovague to fulfill one's own interests and concerns. We are part of a whole, with a responsibility toward the whole body, and not least to the head, the abbot, Christ. It is the figure of Christ himself whom we are never to forget in our journeying.

CHAPTER SIXTY-EIGHT

¹A brother may be assigned a burdensome task or something he cannot do. If so, he should, with complete gentleness and obedience, accept the order given him. ²Should he see, however, that the weight of the burden is altogether too much for his strength, then he should choose the appropriate moment and explain patiently to his superior the reasons why he cannot perform the task. ³This he ought to do without pride, obstinacy or refusal. ⁴If after the explanation the superior is still determined to hold to his original order, then the junior must recognize that this is best for him. ⁵Trusting in God's help, he must in love obey.

I find it very interesting that at this stage in the Rule Benedict should return to subjects that he has looked at earlier, but with a subtle change of emphasis. We have already been told much about obedience, and not least those verses in 7,35-43, which make it quite clear that the monk is to obey, along with Christ, carrying his cross willingly. Although that absolute obedience must remain the ideal to which all are still committed, there may be times when it might have to be modified in the light of what day-to-day life is actually like. All the tasks and duties that have to be done and the complex network of relationships that are an inevitable part of community living have been looked at in careful detail in the subsequent chapters, and perhaps there may well be a wry note in verse 2 when Benedict speaks of "the weight of the burden."

Again it is a matter of the interior disposition. Obedience calls for acceptance, which grumbling in the heart, the inner murmuring, spoils. If there is a situation in which the monk wants to question this obedience it is the manner in which he does it that is of the greatest importance. Benedict is very clear that it should be at an appropriate moment, with complete gentleness and patience, without pride. If the superior does not, however, countermand the order, then the monk is to obey (out of love) with confidence in the help of God, knowing that this is what is good for him. Benedict implies that it is a sacrifice to be accepted with joy. It is not, therefore, obedience in the wrong sense; it is simply trying to do this task as best he can for the love of God.

CHAPTER SIXTY-NINE

¹Every precaution must be taken that one monk does not presume in any circumstance to defend another in the monastery or to be his champion, ²even if they are related by the closest ties of blood. ³In no way whatsoever shall the monks presume to do this, because it can be a most serious source and occasion of contention. ⁴Anyone who breaks this rule is to be sharply restrained.

The translation of to defend as "take under his wing" helps me to understand better that phrase of the opening sentence that otherwise has an alien ring. Benedict is talking about taking sides in a way that not only does damage to the individual, but also promotes factions within the whole body. There is always a danger that I give or receive the wrong sort of friendship, and, under the guise of supporting another, I am in fact taking away the responsibility that everyone has of standing on their own two feet. I like to see this as chastity in its fullest meaning of drawing back out of respect for the other's deepest and innermost self.

John Howard Griffin, who visited Merton in his hermitage, tells us that Merton used to focus on the people who came to see him just as much as on the material things that he photographed, but that he did so in such a way that allowed them to be themselves. He never tried to impose, to organize, or to control. This is the example that I need. It is often attractive to protect people from their own true selves, under the guise of helping them, and not least in counseling or spiritual direction. There are many ways that I may be subtly employing to make people dependent on me. There is a passage in which Merton warns me about the dangers of invading the other rather than standing back in the face of the mystery that each of us is:

A person is a person insofar as each has a secret and is a solitude of their own that cannot be communicated to anyone else. I will love that which most makes them a person: the secrecy, the hiddenness, the solitude of their own individual being, which God alone can penetrate and understand.

Benedict has a deep belief and respect for each one of us as sons and daughters made in the image of God. It is up to each of us to take due and proper responsibility for the handling of this amazing gift of our sonship or daughterhood. When I fail to face what has to be faced, or to grasp what has to be grasped, but instead try to find people who will support me (probably finding those who will listen to my story and encourage me to think that my cause is right), I have succumbed to a pernicious way of dealing with my problem. It is also one that tends to erode the good of any group, from the family outward, since, while I enjoy pouring out my story to the supporters and champions who will defend me, before long I may well begin to see my world as divided into factions: those who believe my story and those who do not.

CHAPTER SEVENTY

¹In the monastery every occasion for presumption is to be avoided, ²and so we decree that no one has the authority to excommunicate or strike any of his brothers unless he has been given this power by the abbot. ³*Those who sin should be reprimanded in the presence of all, that the rest may fear* (1 Tim 5:20). ⁴Boys up to the age of fifteen should, however, be carefully controlled and supervised by everyone, ⁵provided that this too is done with moderation and common sense.

⁶If a brother, without the abbot's command, assumes any power over those older or, even in regard to boys, flares up and treats them unreasonably, he is to be subjected to the discipline of the rule. ⁷After all, it is written: *Never do to another what you do not want done to yourself* (Tob 4:16).

This rather strange chapter develops the idea of the honor and respect due to each and every one. The quotation from 1 Timothy comes from a chapter that has this as its theme, and that from Tobit, which is used for the third time, has its context in 4:19, "Honor everyone." There must be this deep regard for each person's life in Christ, and it is absolutely wrong for anyone to presume to infringe it by flaring up and treating another unreasonably (6). "All outbreaks of self-assertiveness are to be avoided." This translation by Parry makes the point pretty clear. I must not arrogate to myself powers and authority that do not belong to me. It is only too easy to condemn another, and the open blow or the exclusion has really started with their condemnation in my own heart. That is a judging and a weighing that should lie with God alone. It is presumptuous to assume or to claim that I have the right to deal with another. That right belongs to Christ or those in community, such as the abbot, who are in the place of Christ.

CHAPTER SEVENTY-ONE

¹Obedience is a blessing to be shown by all, not only to the abbot but also to one another as brothers, ²since we know that it is by this way of obedience that we go to God. ³Therefore, although orders of the abbot or of the priors appointed by him take precedence, and no unofficial order may supersede them, ⁴in every other instance younger monks should obey their seniors with all love and concern. ⁵Anyone found objecting to this should be reproved.

⁶If a monk is reproved in any way by his abbot or by one of his seniors, even for some very small matter, ⁷or if he gets the impression that one of his seniors is angry or disturbed with him, however slightly, ⁸he must, then and there without delay, cast himself on the ground at the other's feet to make satisfaction, and lie there until the disturbance is calmed by a blessing. ⁹Anyone who refuses to do this should be subjected to corporal punishment or, if he is stubborn, should be expelled from the monastery.

The opening sentence is a loving statement in which Benedict calls obedience a blessing. There is a depth of meaning in the expression *obedientiae bonum,* which Benedict got from Cassian. It carries the implication that obedience is a gift rather than a matter of duty. It is something that the good monk gives with gracious charity to his brother. The importance of obedience to God, to authority, and to our brothers and sisters is something that has concerned Benedict throughout the Rule. Obedience depends on listening so totally and openly to the other that through them we discern the face, the voice of Christ himself. This is the root of that obedience that we show to one another.

When Benedict says that the young should obey their elders with all love and concern *(caritate et sollicitudine),* he is using very expressive words. Solicitude suggests a deep and lively sensitivity toward the other, a delicate awareness of their needs, in other words, a love built on respect and concern. Giving in to one another and carrying out the will of the other through love is a manifestation of the love that Christ shows to us. Obedience is therefore presented in very positive terms.

The phrase "this way of obedience" (2) reminds us once again that our life is a journey by which we progress to God. This is totally central to the way that Benedict wants to establish for us all. I feel that the reason he issues such stern safeguards is because he has himself so often watched things going wrong in the community. He knows that matters must be put right "then and there, without delay" (8). This is profoundly wise. The prostration on the ground may present an unacceptable picture, but the underlying ideal of total and immediate response is still valid. "Clear and quick gestures of human sorrow and forgiveness," in Joan Chittister's words, are needed to heal the ruptures and the wounds before they mature and fester.

So love and growth are the key words in this chapter, and they lead us on directly to the penultimate chapter of the Rule that is Benedict's great panegyric on the art of loving.

CHAPTER SEVENTY-TWO

[1]Just as there is a wicked zeal of bitterness which separates from God and leads to hell, [2]so there is a good zeal which separates from evil and leads to God and everlasting life. [3]This, then, is the good zeal which monks must foster with fervent love: [4]*They should each try to be the first to show respect to the other* (Rom 12:10), [5]supporting with the greatest patience one another's weaknesses of body or behavior, [6]and earnestly competing in obedience to one another. [7]No one is to pursue what he judges better for himself, but instead, what he judges better for someone else. [8]To their fellow monks they show the pure love of brothers; [9]to God, loving fear; [10]to their abbot, unfeigned and humble love. [11]Let them prefer nothing whatever to Christ, [12]and may he bring us all together to everlasting life.

This chapter puts the rest of the Rule in perspective. Here, as John Eudes Bamberger has said, we find the essence, the deepest dimension, the core of the Rule. Here, just as in the prologue, we come closest to meeting the man himself, the interior Benedict. We have followed the balance, the assurance of the tranquil and clear-sighted abbot who is an experienced legislator drawing up the whole body of material, the timetable, the duties, the officials, and the external goals that will allow his monks to live together in harmony. But now when we see his concern with the inner dynamic of this life, this must tell us about himself, his own attitude and motives. This is the culmination of all that he been saying about the interior disposition of the heart. More important than attention to outward actions is attention to the inner sources of behavior. Benedict knows that it is possible to do good from a wrong motive. It is to the extent that his life is dominated by love that the monk is genuine or not. The real test of his authenticity is his selfless love. Here Benedict is taking us beyond structures.

Having shown us so carefully the regulations and the observances, all of which are certainly necessary and have their place, he now goes beyond them. This life that he wants us to follow is, in Michael Casey's words, "one progressively saturated and transformed by love in all its variegated manifestations."

So what does Benedict understand by zeal? We return to the theme of energy that he introduced in the prologue. He does not want a collection of passive ciphers, but a dynamic and alive people. This primary spiritual energy, which brings light and fire, passion and fervor, and which prevents what might otherwise be simply plodding, he calls a very ardent love. The Latin *ferventissimo amore* suggests a burning, white-hot love.

The inspiration of the chapter is, as we would expect, totally biblical. Benedict refers to Romans 12 in verse 4, and it could well be that he had this in mind as he was writing and that it gave him the outline, for Romans 12:9-11 successively speaks of rejecting evil and embracing good, of mutual affection, of deference to others, and of unflagging zeal and service, all of which come precisely in that order here. The colon between verses 3 and 4 is important, for it leads on to the exploration of how that love is to be expressed and lived out. The chapter ends with a series of maxims that recapitulate the most important themes that he has touched on in the earlier pages, thus drawing the whole thing together.

Verse 4 brings in the word "respect." Reverence and respect and handling with care have been among the most important threads in the tapestry that Benedict has been weaving. Without respect there can be no acceptance of the other and no true love. A fundamental respect for the uniqueness of others, respect for their freedom of thought and action, is something that Benedict has been showing me in different practical situations time and again. As he describes the building up of the life of the community, he makes it clear that this is something absolutely foundational. Genuine love is free from the exploitation or the manipulation of others. Where this is missing, love becomes a delusion, a subterfuge, a means to an end.

The patience and gentleness of verse 5 are again virtues that Benedict admires and that he has been encouraging. This is the opposite of that violence which is not limited to aggressive behavior but may be a reflection of the underlying violence of feeling that is expressed in the tone of voice or the glance. For of course zeal can be two-edged. It can become aggressive. The "wicked zeal of bitterness" (1) must refer to the rivalries and power games that can tear communities apart, the sort of competition that is unsuitable in the Body of Christ. If you must compete, he seems to say, at least compete in love!

Each of these successive maxims sums up, succinctly and neatly, all that I have been learning throughout the whole Rule. If they had come earlier, I would not have had the practical examples of behavior in day-to-day situations that now give flesh to the bones. Each word that I read here carries some immediate resonance and reminds me of the context in which I first read it. I now ask what "respect," "patience," "pure love," and "fear" would mean if they were not shown to me in the context of the whole of the life that Benedict has laid out for me. For example, if the radical altruism of verse 7 (which is no more than Paul's teaching in Philemon 2:4 on preferring the welfare of others) had come earlier in the Rule, I might have read it as some abstract ethical demand and found it threatening. It is only when I have some secure sense of self, my true self, my real self, in which Benedict has been schooling me, and when I am certain of God's love for me, that I can receive this teaching. Without those two safeguards this command would be disastrous, a burying and a denial of my own self that becomes a form of alienation.

To recognize the full riches of the last two verses, I have to read them and remind myself of the echoes that they bring of earlier verses. For example, in 4,21 he told me to prefer nothing to the love of Christ and in 43,3 claimed that nothing is to be preferred to the Divine Office. If I now understand verse 11 as the love of Christ for each one of us, and that seems likely in the context of this chapter that is exploring relationships, then I am being brought very close now to the heart of the Christian mystery.

In these last two verses everything flows together in a tremendous affirmation of the place of Christ. Christ becomes the center of action in the culmination of this chapter that is also the culmination of the Rule. The nature of the community is determined by conformity to Christ's teachings, not to any other external or internal pressures. It is the relationship with Christ on which the strength of the life of the community depends. So now

I have been given the spirit in which to read and re-read the Rule, meditate on it, interpret it, live it out. This daily growth into seeing and responding to the presence of Christ in each one, so that this interaction with one another means that we become the body of Christ, is the keystone of the life that Benedict wants to build up.

Unless this is made real and lived out in my daily life, I have been reading just one more book of spirituality. But the Rule is not in that genre. It is a manual, a day-to-day practical manual to encourage me to make Christ's love the most immediate and practical reality in my life, and thus to live out the Gospel demands in a most ordinary, daily, and therefore inescapable way.

CHAPTER SEVENTY-THREE

¹The reason we have written this rule is that, by observing it in monasteries, we can show that we have some degree of virtue and the beginnings of monastic life. ²But for anyone hastening on to the perfection of monastic life, there are the teachings of the holy Fathers, the observance of which will lead him to the very heights of perfection. ³What page, what passage of the inspired books of the Old and New Testaments is not the truest of guides for human life? ⁴What book of the holy catholic Fathers does not resoundingly summon us along the true way to reach the Creator? ⁵Then, besides the *Conferences* of the Fathers, their *Institutes* and their *Lives,* there is also the rule of our holy father Basil. ⁶For observant and obedient monks, all these are nothing less than tools for the cultivation of virtues; ⁷but as for us, they make us blush for shame at being so slothful, so unobservant, so negligent. ⁸Are you hastening toward your heavenly home? Then with Christ's help, keep this little rule that we have written for beginners. ⁹After that, you can set out for the loftier summits of the teaching and virtues we mentioned above, and under God's protection you will reach them. Amen.

At the end of chapter 66, which may, according to some authorities, have been the original ending of the Rule, Benedict says: "We wish this rule to be read often in the community" (8). That, of course, applies to those living the monastic life, who will hear a short section of the Rule read aloud daily, or to Benedictine oblates who may commit themselves to the daily reading of a passage. But for myself, and others like me who have no such formal obligation, it is also extremely wise. It is only as I stay with the text, pray with it, and read it time and time again that it becomes formative for my life. I need to treat it as I would *lectio,* mulling it over, chewing it, getting the marrow as it were from what otherwise might appear as dry bones.

What strikes me immediately is Benedict's humility. I have followed him along his road to this point. I have seen the skill with which he has opened up the way and led me gently but firmly into the depths of my understanding of myself and of God's love for me. I have appreciated the sure grasp that he has shown in handling my spiritual formation. Yet he makes few claims for his own work and instead points me elsewhere. He points first of all to the Bible itself, to the Old and the New Testaments, to the Word itself as life-giving. What he promised in the prologue when he said that it was the Gospel which was to be our guide has been abundantly fulfilled. The Rule is saturated in the Bible. It echoes biblical passages, and it is shaped by scriptural images and resonances. Also, the "holy catholic fathers" are mentioned twice in verses 2 and 4 on either side of the biblical passages. They equally are guides leading us to God who is called the Creator here, which is unusual for Benedict. Their preaching and their teaching were always biblical, their theology saturated with biblical themes and concepts, and not least their emphasis on the central themes of the Exodus in the Old Testament and the paschal mystery in the New.

The more detailed list that follows is fascinating for the way in which Benedict points to further reading in the Fathers in two different sources and practices. He points in one direction to the desert, eremetical tradition, the monastic way of Egypt, with its emphasis on the solitary, the ascetic life, and withdrawal. But then Basil comes out of the cenobitic tradition, whose emphasis is on the community as the way, the monastic life as that of a family of brothers or sisters gathered around its head.

It might seem that we are being given a polarization of values: the solitary versus the community, the vertical versus the horizontal, the more ascetic versus the more humane. But Benedict himself, as we saw in the chapter on hospitality, is a man of open mind as well as open door and open heart. What Benedict is doing here is a subtle exercise. He is initiating a dialogue, a conversation, telling us to listen to two sources or streams within the monastic tradition, both of which carry validity and both of which speak to any one of us in our own Christian life. He is telling us that both these sets of values are good and that each has its role to play. If I think of this in relation to the makeup of my own inner landscape, I see that he is telling me to let two streams flow in so that I draw from both and let both interact. I need to see within myself the solitary, the ability to live with myself alone before God, just as much as I need to live in communion, in a relationship of connectedness with others. In this way I create a situation of dialectic.

In an age that seems to be increasingly looking for certainties, this idea of being open to differing, even divergent, aspects of the truth is asking for a refusal to be dogmatic, narrow, inflexible. These seemingly technical verses suddenly take on a great prophetic role. They draw us back to some of the most profound themes of the Rule, to listening, to openness to others, to continuing growth. But, above all, they draw us back to the paradox at the heart of the Gospel as at the heart of the Rule.

The very end, just like the prologue, is a lyrical piece of writing. "Are you hastening toward your heavenly home?" (8). What a most wonderful thing to ask! The fullness of that question comes when I read these words in the context of those poetic images from Hebrews (4:11; 11:14-15) of seeking a country, and of that city that God has prepared for us, both images of home that capture the imagination. The need to come home, the desire to be where I belong, is something that touches one of the deepest of chords in all human experience.

Here, at the very end, we return to the journey theme that opened the Rule, the way back to the Father from whom we have strayed. How neatly Benedict now ties the two together, the beginning and the end. Indeed there are such strong echoes of the prologue here that Benedict actually repeats that same phrase "you will reach" (9). For with Benedict I move forward all the time in hope, trusting in the mercy of God. With Benedict I am committed to continual conversion, to growth, to ongoing and neverending transformation. At one level this is unthreatening and reassuring, and I have the support and structure and rhythm of this life to uphold and support me. But at another level it is totally challenging. He is addressing the heart, the heart expanding with love, and that has no neat and tidy boundaries. If the focal point of Benedict's Rule is growth in the law of love, the love of Christ, how can I say in this life that I have ever fully arrived?

*

Founded as it is on the Gospel, the Rule, like the Gospel it-self, never grows old or goes out of fashion. Like the Gospel it is full of both urgency and compassion. As I reach its end, I realize that the text itself can never become an idol, for its purpose is all the time to point me beyond itself to the Gospel and to Christ. Benedict has such a respect for each one of us, created as unique son or daughter, made in the image of Christ, that he shows a very real concern about stifling that God-given freedom and responsibility. This respect for my own self-worth puts a huge responsibility on me. It is up to me to respond or not. The Rule is addressed to the heart, to the disposition of the heart, and that can never become some closed system to be learned or acquired. As Michael Casey says, Benedict is giving us "not a series of prescribed actions but an invitation to remain alert to the challenge of the Word of God." And so the Rule remains something totally open-ended. Perhaps I should think of it presenting me with a series of open doors.

The Rule of Benedict is a way of life, a life-giving way. To encounter the text in all its fullness and complexity is like encountering a source and stream, always the same and yet always different, or like a tapestry where I follow first one thread and then another and in doing so get different glimpses of the whole. I return to it time and time again throughout my life. Benedict and his practical manual of the love of Christ is always there to help me on my journey, the coming home of the prodigal to the loving embrace of the Father.

SELECTED BIBLIOGRAPHY

Fry, Timothy, ed. *RB 1980, The Rule of St. Benedict in Latin and English with Notes.* Collegeville, Minn.: The Liturgical Press, 1981.

There are a number of different translations of the Rule in English.

COMMENTARIES ON THE RULE

Cary-Elwes, Columba. *Work and Prayer: The Rule of St. Benedict for Lay People.* Trans. Catherine Wybourne. London: Burns & Oates, 1992.

Chittister, Joan. *The Rule of Benedict: Insights for the Ages.* New York: Crossroad, 1992.

de Vogüé, Adalbert. *The Rule of St. Benedict: A Doctrinal and Spiritual Commentary.* Kalamazoo: Cistercian Publications, 1983.

Kardong, Terrence. *Asking Benedict: A Study Program on the Rule of St. Benedict for Classes and Private Use, Questions and Resource Manual.* Richardton, N. Dak.: Assumption Abbey Press, 1992.

_____. *Together Unto Life Everlasting: An Introduction to the Rule of Benedict.* Richardton, N. Dak.: Assumption Abbey Press, 1984.

Parry, David. *Households of God: The Rule of St. Benedict with Explanations for Monks and Lay-People Today.* Kalamazoo, Mich.: Cistercian Publications, 1980.

Stead, Julian. *St. Benedict: A Rule for Beginners.* New Rochelle, N.Y.: New City Press, 1993.

Tvedten, Benet. *A Share in the Kingdom: A Commentary on the Rule of St. Benedict for Oblates.* Collegeville, Minn.: The Liturgical Press, 1989.

Vest, Norvene. *Preferring Christ: A Devotional Commentary and Workbook on the Rule of St. Benedict.* Trans. Luke Dysinger. Trabuco Canyon, Calif.: Source Books, 1990.

BOOKS ABOUT THE BENEDICTINE LIFE

Boulding, Maria, ed. *A Touch of God: Eight Monastic Journeys.* Still River, Mass.: St. Bede's Publications, 1982.

Kardong, Terrence. *The Benedictines.* Collegeville, Minn., Michael Glazier: The Liturgical Press, 1988.

Morris, Augustine. *Oblates: Life with St. Benedict.* Elmore Abbey, 1992.

Rees, Daniel, ed. *Consider Your Call: A Theology of Monastic Life Today.* Kalamazoo, Mich.: Cistercian Publications, 1980.

Roberts, Augustine. *Centered on Christ: An Introduction to Monastic Profession.* 2nd ed. Petersham, Mass.: St. Bede's Publications, 1993.

BOOKS THAT SHOW THE APPLICATION OF THE RULE IN EVERYDAY LIFE

Chittister, Joan. *Wisdom Distilled from the Daily: Living the Rule of St. Benedict Today.* San Francisco: Harper & Row, 1990.

de Waal, Esther. *Living with Contradiction, Further Reflections on the Rule of St. Benedict.* London: Fount, Collins, 1988; and San Francisco: Harper & Row, 1989.

_____. *Seeking God: The Way of St. Benedict.* London: Fount, Collins, 1984; and Collegeville, Minn.: The Liturgical Press, 1985.

Taylor, Brian. *Spirituality for Everyday Living: An Adaptation of the Rule of St. Benedict.* Collegeville, Minn.: The Liturgical Press, 1989.

NOTES AND REFERENCES

ABBREVIATIONS

A.B.R.   *American Benedictine Review*

C. S.* or *C.S.Q. *Cistercian Studies,* or *Cistercian Studies Quarterly, Bulletin of Monastic Spirituality*

M. S.   *Monastic Studies*

W & S   *Word and Spirit. A Monastic Review.* St. Bede's Publications, Petersham, Massachusetts.

PREFACE

I am still amazed at the way in which I first discovered the Rule. I was living in Canterbury, in a house that had been, in the Middle Ages, the prior's lodging of the great medieval Benedictine community. All around me were the remains of the buildings that had served their monastic life. I came to know and to love the great monastic Church. This encounter with such a powerful place led me to discover something of the life and the vision of the men who had built it. I had thought that I would pick up the Rule in order to increase my historical understanding. Instead it changed my life.

That monastic Church of Canterbury is the mother Church of the Anglican Communion, and I now came to realize just how great the extent to which its Benedictine roots have shaped Anglican life and worship. I found that the prior and monks became the dean and chapter (which was why, as the wife of the dean, I found myself living a family life in the home of my husband's monastic predecessor). I found (what I already half knew) that the daily saying of the Offices of morning and evening prayer in the cathedral represented the work of Thomas Cranmer, who, during the Reformation, shortened the seven monastic Offices into Matins and Evensong, so that, like the monks, the Anglicans sing the psalms and hear the Word of God daily. I found that the Anglican *via media* was nothing more than the Benedictine ideal of moderation and balance.

That simple little phrase "the reduction of all life to a touch of God" comes from Paschal Baumstein, "Revisiting Anselm," *C.S.Q.* 28, 3/4 (1993) 218.

There has been considerable recent discussion of the lay character of monasticism, notably Todd Ridler, "The Clericalization of Monasticism," *Review for Religious* (March–April 1990) 227–242. See also Kevin W. Irwin, "On Monastic Priesthood," *A.B.R.* 41:3 (September 1990) 225–262 and Eoin de Bhaldraithe, "Daily Eucharist: The Need for an Early Church Paradigm," *A.B.R.* 41:4 (1990) 378–440.

I have recently come across something that Thomas Merton wrote about his priesthood, which I have found most interesting in this context. Always moving forward in his thinking and facing courageously new questions about himself and his vocation, he was, toward the end of his life, minimizing the importance of his priesthood. In a dialogue in October 1968 at the Center for the Study of Democratic Institutions, when describing the monastic life as a lay movement that began in reaction to the integration of Christianity into the Roman Empire by Constantine, he said that a monk should not be a priest—and in looking back seemed to question his own ordination saying that he did not want to be a priest, but that he went along with it since it was "part of the system." I take this as a sign of that openness of mind that makes him such a prophetic spokesman for the twentieth century, just as I feel that Benedict himself is always leading us into openness. This is to be found in Thomas Merton, *Preview of the Asian Journey,* ed. Walter H. Capps (New York: Crossroads, 1989) 49, a point that I owe to an article by Richard E. Getty in *C.S.Q.* 28 3/4 (1993) 291, n. 35. I feel that this is at variance with what he felt at the time, as the reading of the *Sign of Jonas* suggests so vividly, but nevertheless I find this a most fascinating comment by the later Merton.

The letter of Thomas Merton to Fr. Ronald Boloff, O.S.B., was written on September 26, 1962, and is to be found in *School of Charity,* ed. Patrick Hart (New York: Farrar, Stroux, Giroux, 1990) 147.

Michael Casey, whom I mention here is a Cistercian monk of Tarrawarra Abbey in Australia, has written widely on the monastic life, often in the journal *Tjurunga,* which appears in Australia. I have been fortunate enough to have been able to see the study notes on the Rule that he and David Tomlins produced for the Benedictine Union of Australia and New Zealand, *Benedictine Studies,* and references to either of them later on may very well be due to what I have read there and which is not generally available.

I have found that my increasing interest in the Celtic tradition has deepened and enriched my understanding and appreciation of the Rule. Both take us back to the fullness of the Church in the fifth and sixth centuries, behind the divisions and divides of the Enlightenment and the Reformation, the split between mind and feelings, word and image, East and West. The English title of my book *A World Made Whole: Rediscovering the Celtic Tradition* (London: Harper/Collins, 1991) is an expression of this, while in America the publishers have called it *Every Earthly Blessing: Celebrating a Spirituality of Creation* (Ann Arbor, Mich.: Servant Publications, 1991).

NOTE ON THE TEXT

The translation on which this commentary is based is *RB 1980: The Rule of St. Benedict in English,* ed. Timothy Fry, (Collegeville, Minn.: The Liturgical Press, 1981). As well as the short English translation, there is also a fuller edition, in Latin and English with notes and thematic indexes, which gives a most valuable introduction to the background and origins of its monastic context.

I have not gone deeply into the academic background, nor have I attempted to speak of that favorite topic of academic discussion, the relationship between the Rule of St. Benedict and the *Rule of the Master,* where the scholarship of Adalbert de Vogüé, who first established the priority of RM, holds the field. I make no attempt to cover it in this book since, for those who are interested, there is a vast amount of recent scholarly research. My own interests are much more in seeing the Rule as a guide to life and prayer.

Claude Pfeifer, "What does it mean to live 'According to the Rule'?" *M.S.* 5 (1968) 19–45.

PROLOGUE

My understanding of the prologue owes much to *Conferences on the Prologue to the Rule* given by Damasus Winzen to the community of Mount Saviour Monastery, Pine City, New York, in the spring of 1960, and transcribed and edited by them for publication in 1975. What I say, for example, in the second paragraph about the levels of understanding of the word "father," comes from him.

The Venite, Psalm 94 (95), is said daily as part of the Anglican order of Matins precisely for this reason, and it is one more expression of that continuity of the Anglican with the Benedictine tradition. The tragedy is that those responsible for the new service book, either not knowing or forgetting this, have shortened the psalm to omit the idea of the heart, which is so essential to it.

The Rembrandt painting so caught the imagination of Henri Nouwen that it directly inspired his book *The Return of the Prodigal Son* (New York: Doubleday, 1992).

David Parry's translation and commentary first appeared in 1980 under the title *Households of God: The Rule of St. Benedict with Explanations for Monks and Lay-People Today.*

To read further on the many images of Christ in the Rule, see L. Borias, "Christ and the Monk," *M.S.* 10 (1974) 97–129.

The quotation from Daniel Rees is taken from *Consider Your Call: A Theology of the Monastic Life Today* (Kalamazoo: Cistercian Publications, 1980) 102. This book, written by members of the English Benedictine Congregation and edited by the prior of Downside, is one of the fullest and clearest discussions of monastic life and would be of the greatest help to anyone wishing to deepen their understanding of the subject.

Much of what I say in the paragraph which opens "Our idea of Christ is therefore a glorious one . . ." I owe to Damasus Winzen, *Conferences on the Prologue to the Rule,* 9–10.

The comments on verses 14–20 owe much to Augusta Raabe, "Discernment of Spirits in the Prologue to the Rule of St. Benedict," *ABR* 23:4 (1972) 397–432.

The point about dashing the babies against the rock that is Christ is discussed in *RB 1980,* 475. The same verse, with the same interpretation, will come again in 4,50.

The comments on verse 45 and the use of the word *schola* come from an article by Adalbert de Vogüé, "The Fatherhood of Christ," *M.S.* 5 (1968) 53.

ONE

The two recent translations that I refer to toward the end of this chapter are those by Luke Dysinger in Norvene Vest, *Preferring Christ: A Devotional Commentary and Workbook on the Rule of Saint Benedict* (Trabuco Canyon, Calif.: Source Books, 1990) and Catherine Wybourne in Columba Cary-Elwes, *Work and Prayer: The Rule of St. Benedict for Lay People* (London: Burns and Oates, 1992).

TWO

The idea of the fatherhood of Christ (which comes in the third paragraph of this chapter) had been present in the Church since at least the second century. It had been more recently developed as a response to the Arian heresy when it became necessary to emphasize the divinity of Christ. See Adalbert de Vogüé, "The Fatherhood of Christ." *M.S.* 5 (1968) 45–47. There is also a very useful discussion of this in *RB 1980,* 356ff. Appendix 2, 322–377, is devoted to a detailed study of the abbot.

A vivid idea of the tensions and strains of the society of Benedict's day is given by Jean Leclercq, "The Problem of Social Class and Christology," *W & S,* 2 (1981) 33–51.

The story of the monk and the lamp is used by Henry Mayr-Harting, in his useful and illuminating short study *The Venerable Bede, The Rule of St. Benedict, and Social Class* (Jarrow lecture, 1976).

The parallel with Zen is explored in Diana Law, "Zen Master and Benedictine Abbot," *Tjurunga* 19 (1980) 5–12.

Terrence Kardong devotes a chapter to the abbot in *The Benedictines* (Collegeville, Minn.: The Liturgical Press, 1990) 116–137.

The phrases Christ-agent and Christ-life I also owe to Terrence Kardong, and are taken from his *Asking Benedict, Resource Material,* C.1.a. This is a study program on the Rule for classes and private use, published by Assumption Abbey Press, Richardton, North Dakota, in two sections, one *Questions* and the other *Resource Material.*

Rembert Weakland has written on "Growth through Authority," *Tjurunga,* 14 (1977) 75–92; the sentences that I quote come under the heading "Growth in the Love of Christ: Purification of Motives," but the whole article is profoundly wise, simple, and practical.

The reference to the Merton quotation is *No Man Is an Island* (New York: Harcourt, Brace and Co, 1955) 244.

On the question of divine justice see Terrence Kardong, "Justice in the Rule of St. Benedict," *Studia Monastica,* 1982, XXIV, 43–73, especially 72.

THREE

My opening remarks owe much to an article by Rembert Weakland, "Community in the Monastic Tradition," *A.B.R.* 26:3 (1975) 233–250. In his article "Growth through Authority," *Tjurunga* (1977) 14, Weakland quotes on page 85 a recent discussion that he had in Rome with Fr. Arrupe who said that the whole idea of discernment had started with Benedict, and the Jesuits had just picked it up from him. The idea of the monastic dream in relation to the abbot is discussed in Terrence Kardong, "The Abbot as Leader," *A.B.R.* 42:1 (March 1991) 53–71, but especially 64ff.

The quotation with which this chapter ends is again taken from Rembert Weakland, "Growth through Authority," 86.

FOUR

In trying to understand the pattern of this chapter I have been greatly helped by the article by Michael Casey, "Stranger to Worldly Ways,"

Tjurunga, 29 (1985), especially page 45 where he argues for the value of paying attention to the literary structures of a text.

The piece by Joan Greatrex, "On ministering to 'certayne devoute and religiouse women': Bishop Fox and the Benedictine nuns of Winchester on the eve of the Dissolution," is to be found in *Studies in Church History,* 27 (1990) 229ff. I owe to David Parry, *Households of God,* 33, what I have to say about the tools and the tool-box at the end of the third paragraph.

Philip Jebb contributed the chapter "Wonder Is so Sudden a Gift" to the collected essays *A Touch of God: Eight Monastic Journeys,* ed. Maria Boulding (Still River, Mass.: St. Bede's Publications, 1982). What I quote on fasting can be found on pages 21–22.

The comment on verses 14–19 comes from Michael Casey, "Stranger to Worldly Ways," 44. Verse 20 is from p. 43 of that article.

The quotation from St. Gregory's *Dialogues* is taken from Adalbert de Vogüé, "Keep death before your eyes," *M.S.* 16 (1985) 25–38.

For a useful discussion of dashing the Babylonian babies on the rocks see *RB 1980,* 475.

When I say that I feel that Benedict has a sense of humor, I am thinking that he often shows an almost Zen-like sense of taking down the temperature, as at the end of chapter 7, which I feel can only come from a man who is not over serious or pompous. At the end of all those chapters on the organization of the liturgical code in chapter 18 he in effect says: "Well, if you can do better yourself go on and do it." I find his portrait in chapter 66 of the old man who is to serve as porter full of gentle humor.

The twelfth-century poem on tears can be found in G. Murphy, ed., *Early Irish Lyrics, Eighth to Twelfth Century* (Oxford: Oxford University Press, 1956) 63. I included it in *Every Earthly Blessing,* 104.

FIVE

The reference to Henri Nouwen comes from *The Genesee Diary: Report from a Trappist Monastery* (New York: Image Books, 1976) 64.

Leonard Vickers contributed the chapter "On a Human Note" to *A Touch of God.* What I quoted is to be found on pages 134–135.

I have been helped to understand these two scriptural references by what Terrence Kardong says in *Asking Benedict, Resource Manual,* 13.

There is much that is written on the subject of obedience, but I have been particularly grateful for Augustine Roberts, *Centered on Christ* (Petersham, Mass.: St. Bede's, 1993) 88–104. Joan Chittister devotes one chapter of *Wisdom Distilled from the Rule* to it. In Daniel Rees, ed., *Consider Your Call*, there is some extremely illuminating material on pages 189–205.

SIX

Benedict uses two words that specifically mean silence, *silentium* (only four times and always with reference to the actual practice of silence, in a section on discipline and administration) and *taciturnitas* (which has the much deeper meaning of the virtue or the habit of silence). The second, used here, is definitely more positive: a love of keeping silent, having mastered the curbing of one's tongue.

The quotation from Bonhoeffer is from *Life Together* (London: SCM, 1954) 59–60, and I owe it to David Tomlins, "The meaning and value of silence in Christian living," *C.S.* XVII:2 (1982) 173.

The point about the quotation from Proverbs was made by Norvene Vest, *Preferring Christ: A Devotional Commentary and Workbook on the Rule of St. Benedict* (Trabuco Canyon: Source Books, 1991) 51.

SEVEN

The Cistercian abbot to whom I am referring is Fr. Thomas Davis, abbot of the Abbey of New Clairvaux, California.

The quotation "our rebirth . . ." is taken from Daniel Rees, ed., *Consider Your Call,* 166. As also the phrase "process of deliverance . . . ," 101, where the discussion of the ladder of humility is considered under the sub-heading "St. Benedict and the call to freedom."

Joan Chittister, *The Rule of Benedict. Insights for the Ages* (New York: Crossroad, 1992) 67.

There is an interesting scholarly debate over the understanding of quiet as it is used in the opening verse of the fourth step. Is *tacita* an adjective qualifying *conscientia* or an adverb *tacite?* The scholars disagree. There is a useful discussion of this by David Tomlins in his section on patience in *Benedictine Studies*. McCann argues for the adjective, Wathen and de Vogüé for the adverb. But "with a quiet mind holding fast to patience" gives a slightly more inner approach and is certainly consonant with the scriptural reflections that make up this paragraph. It is also in key to the central motivation of love from Romans 8:37.

The quotation in the fifth step about the struggles that we hide is taken from Chittister, *The Rule of Benedict,* 69.

It was David Parry who drew my attention to the significance of Psalm 72 for appreciating the sixth step.

247

Jean Vanier: in step seven I am in particular thinking of how much we all owe to *Community and Growth* (London: Darton, Longman and Todd, 1979) where he writes with such compassion about the building up of community. Since then there have been many other books reflecting his experience of work with the L'Arche communities.

I owe the phrase that I use to describe the coda to Columba Cary-Elwes, *Work and Prayer: The Rule of St. Benedict for Lay People* (London: Burns & Oates, 1992) 57.

EIGHT

The contrast is commonly made between the *ars spiritualis* of chapters 4 to 7 and the rather dry and mundane and technical discussion of chapter 8 as the opening of the liturgical code. This is how Kardong (*Together Unto Life Everlasting: An Introduction to the Rule of Benedict* [Richardton, N.Dak.: Assumption Abbey Press, 1984] 69) speaks of it, but I want to challenge that and show what I believe is the continuity of thought here.

I owe the phrase about idealized blueprint to Michael Casey in *Benedictine Studies*.

The quotation at the end of the second paragraph is from Benedict Tvedten, *A Share in the Kingdom* (Collegeville, Minn.: The Liturgical Press, 1989) 39.

What Merton says about the coming of the day is taken from *Day of a Stranger*. It is reprinted in Thomas McDonnell, ed., *Thomas Merton Reader* (New York: Image, 1974) 435.

NINE

For a very full and clear discussion of the liturgical code see *RB 1980,* Appendix 3, 379–414. On the puzzle that the language presents and for a short summary of de Vogüé's theory of the Divine Office see Kardong, *Together Unto Life Everlasting,* 70–73. There is a most interesting article by Borias, "Benedict's Reverence for the Trinity," *M.S.* 17 (1986) 155ff.

A further note on the variant ways in which the psalms might be said: there were a number of different methods of performing psalmody in these early years. Sometimes they might be said or sung by the whole community, sometimes by one single voice while all the others listened, sometimes alternatively from side to side in choir, antiphonal style, sometimes the verses were interspersed by antiphons, etc.

Henri Nouwen, *The Genesee Diary: Report from a Trappist Monastery* (New York: Doubleday and Co., 1976) 100 (entry under August 2).

"The anguished suffering mind that had created them and had cried out to God in his suffering reflected much of our own condition." Brian Keenan, *An Evil Cradling* (London: Hutchinson, 1992) 187–188.

The Matthew Kelty quotation is from William O. Paulsell, ed., *Sermons in a Monastery, Chapter Talks by Matthew Kelty* (Kalamazoo: Cistercian Publications, 1983) 10–11.

ELEVEN

The quotation here comes from Terrence Kardong, *Together Unto Life Everlasting,* 76.

TWELVE

The Native American quotation is to be found in T. C. McLuhan, *Touch the Earth: A Self-Portrait of Indian Existence* (New York: Promontory Press, 1987) 36.

THIRTEEN

The comments on Psalm 66 (67) and Psalm 50 (51) are by Joan Chittister, *The Rule of Benedict,* 81.

For a useful discussion on the covenant to continual forgiveness see Terrence Kardong, "Repressed Anger in RB," *Tjurunga,* 20 (1980) 5–17.

The reference to the article by Henri Nouwen is "Forgiveness: The Name of Love in a Wounded World," *Weavings,* VII (March/April 1992) 2.

FOURTEEN

The Celtic reference comes from the Welsh poet Waldo Williams, from the one volume that he published *Dail Pren,* Aberystwyth, 1957, 67.

SEVENTEEN

Cassian's *Conferences,* especially Conference ten with Abba Isaac, tell how he and his friend Germanus talked with Abba Isaac about prayer, and, when he felt that they were ready, he revealed to them (in a long discourse) the secret of continuous prayer, which was to repeat at all times *Deus in adjutorium meum intende.* This type of prayer has always been more highly developed in the East until in our own day the Benedictine monk John Main has encouraged the use of the mantra in meditation and his writings, lectures, and tapes, and those of Laurence Freeman, have made this a widely popular form of meditation.

EIGHTEEN

What Henri Nouwen has to say about Compline is from the same day (August 2) that I quoted above.

NINETEEN

Once again I am indebted to what Michael Casey, in his *Benedictine Studies,* has given me here.

TWENTY

I am aware in writing about this chapter that some scholars see it as a treatise on private prayer, but I am following de Vogüé when he says that, for the ancients, the Office was by no means a mere declamation of texts. Silent prayer occupied a considerable place in it. *The Rule of St. Benedict, a Doctrinal and Spiritual Commentary* (Kalamazoo: Cistercian Publications, 1983) 141. See also *RB 1980,* 412–413.

For the way in which these so-called prayer collects developed significantly in the fifth to seventh centuries, see *RB 1980* 412–413, though Benedict makes no direct reference to them and they may not have been as common in monastic circles as they were in the cathedral tradition.

TWENTY-ONE

I owe the point about Jethro to de Vogüé, who points out that the same terms are found there, *sapeins* and *conversationis.* de Vogüé, *The Rule of St. Benedict,* 267–270.

For the Adelbert van der Wielen reference see his article, "On Co-responsibility in RB," *Tjurunga* (1976) 11.

The comments on verse 5 come from what Kardong said on this chapter in the *Resource Manual,* 22–23.

TWENTY-THREE

Appendix 4 in *RB 1980,* pp. 415–436, deals with the disciplinary measures in the Rule.

de Vogüé, *The Rule of St. Benedict,* 435. In addition, there is an interesting article by Julian Stead, "The Penal Code of St. Benedict," *W & S,* 6 (1984) 58–68.

TWENTY-FIVE

For a discussion of Benedict's use of 1 Cor 5:5 see *RB 1980,* 422–423.

TWENTY-SEVEN

This theme of human weakness is most sympathetically explored by Maria Boulding in *Gateway to Hope: An Exploration of Failure* (Petersham, Mass.: St. Bede's Publications, 1987) especially on p. 92.

THIRTY-ONE

The Wendell Berry quotation comes from *The Gift of Good Land* (San Francisco: North Point Press, 1981).

The comment on the verse from Matthew was made by Kardong in *Resource Manual,* 28. His article "Benedict's Peaceable Kingdom," *The Benedictines* (Collegeville, Minn.: The Liturgical Press, 1983) 28–44, is also extremely useful.

The book that I refer to is by Henri Nouwen, *The Wounded Healer: Ministry in Contemporary Society* (Garden City, New York: Doubleday & Co., 1972).

THIRTY-TWO

In all that I say here I must acknowledge a very big debt to Judith Sutera, "Stewardship and the Kingdom in RB 31–33," *ABR* 41:4 (1990) 348–357, an article that I found most illuminating and stimulating.

THIRTY-THREE

Kardong has some interesting things to say on Benedict's use and abuse of Scripture in 33.6 in *Together Unto Life Everlasting,* 94–95.

In studying this chapter I used Kardong's "Poverty in RB 33–34," *C. S.* XX (1985) 3, 185–254. There he tells us how much of what Benedict has to say on avarice is due to what Cassian teaches in *Institutes* VII.

THIRTY-FOUR

The vigorous sentence about the consumerist society is taken from Kardong, "Poverty in RB 33–34," 200, as is also what I say about the Pharisees, 197.

The transition section which follows this chapter is also due to Kardong. He suggests that we look on these two chapters as a hinge, or as he puts it, "a carefully matched pair of diptych leaves." He discusses Benedict's dialectical editorial method, and the inclusive thinking that we meet in these two chapters.

THIRTY-FIVE

The comment of David Tomlins comes from *Benedictine Studies.*

The idea of the two New Testament scenes I owe to de Vogüé, *Doctrinal & Spiritual Commentary,* 1983, 199.

THIRTY-SIX

Kardong, "Patristic Sources for RB 36," *The Benedictines* (Wilmington, Del.: Michael Glazier, 1988) 2.

THIRTY-EIGHT

Much learned discussion continues to take place about the place of the Eucharist in early Benedictine life. Here it seems to me there is a simple statement that Mass and communion occur on Sunday, the start of the week.

FORTY

In classical Rome the *hemina* was about half a pint, but the general concensus seems to be that the Rule's *hemina* may have been larger than the classical one. *RB 1980* has an interesting note on p. 238–239.

FORTY-EIGHT

The point that *ora, labora et lege* is preferable is made by de Vogüé, *The Rule of St. Benedict,* 242.

Of All Good Gifts is published by Benet Press, Erie, Penn.

FORTY-NINE

See Kardong, *Together Unto Life Everlasting,* 114–115.

I owe a great deal in my understanding of compunction to what Michael Casey has written on the subject. The sentence that I quote comes from *Benedictine Studies.*

FIFTY-TWO

The reference to Parry comes in David Parry, *Households of God: The Rule of St. Benedict with Explanations for Monks and Lay-People Today* (Kalamazoo: Cistercian Publications, 1980) 139.

FIFTY-THREE

A note on the kiss of peace. In the context of the Arian controversies of his day, Benedict would not have been able to pray with Arian visitors, and to give a kiss of peace would suggest that all was well when this was not so. Or are we to take this reference to "delusions of the devil" further? What might have been thought of as extreme or absurd a few years ago may not necessarily now be dismissed as so improbable when some people feel that we cannot deny the presence of diabolical and evil forces.

I owe what I say about the recitation of the psalm verse after the washing of feet to Kardong, *Together Unto Life Everlasting,* 122.

FIFTY-SEVEN

I owe to Michael Casey the phrase about the spiritual life not being closeted underground.

FIFTY-EIGHT

The St. Anselm quotation is taken from Benedicta Ward, *The Prayers and Meditations of St. Anselm* (Harmondsworth: Penguin, 1973). The parallel between the triad of tests and the first seven steps of chapter 7 I owe to *RB 1980,* 448–449.

For what I have to say on *meditatio* see *RB 1980,* 446–447.

The Henri Nouwen quotation comes from Henri Nouwen, *The Genesee Diary,* 76–77.

There is a very good passage on stability in Daniel Rees, *Consider Your Call,* 141.

I owe the idea of taking the story of Adam and Eve in the garden to illustrate stability to Charles Cummings, *Monastic Practices* (Kalamazoo: Cistercian Publications, 1987) 167.

For further exploration of that question that Merton asks about crossing the abyss that separates us from ourselves see my book *A Seven Day Journey with Thomas Merton,* especially the chapter on the solitary self, which explores this theme further. Ann Arbor, Mich.: Servant Publications, 1993. Pp. 55–63.

The modern translation of those words of Augustine is by Barry Ulanov, but I have no reference.

Thomas Merton's talk at Bangkok is found in the *Asian Journal* (New York: New Directions, 1973) 337.

What Augustine Roberts has to say on *conversatio* is to be found in *Centered on Christ: An Introduction to Monastic Profession,* 2nd ed. (Petersham, Mass.: St. Bede's Publications, 1993) 9.

The quote from Abbess Syncletica is from Thomas Merton, *The Wisdom of the Desert: Sayings of the Desert Fathers of the Fourth Century* (New York: New Directions, 1970) 55.

The comment on obedience being a mystery at the heart of redemption is by Rees, *Consider Your Call,* 118.

See *RB 1980,* 451, for a most useful discussion of the historical background of monastic formation and profession.

SIXTY

Most commentators insist that Benedict is quoting out of context in verse 4 (see Parry or *RB 1980,* n. 273). I am unconvinced. That surely would be out of character. That is why I have tried to develop its interpretation as central to Benedict's thinking.

SIXTY-TWO

There is considerable scholarly debate on the question of the Eucharist in the early Benedictine communities. The interpretation of 60,4 raises the issue of how to translate *missa,* for, as Kardong points out, *missas tenere* may be translated as "conclude the prayers." Kardong, to whom I owe most of what I have been saying here, makes this point: the power of the bishop/priests is of a sacramental order; that of the abbot is charismatic. The first power comes from the Church; the second comes from the Holy Spirit.

See Kardong, *Together Unto Life Everlasting,* 130-134, and also the section in *Resource Manual,* 42-43.

SIXTY-FOUR

A useful summary of some of the alternative views on the choice and installation of the abbot may be found in *RB 1980,* 370-375.

The full reference to the comment of Gregory the Great reads: "notable for its discernment and its clarity of language." This, says de Vogüé, is the quality that he had recognized particularly in chapter 58, but which he felt characterized the whole Rule. *RB 1980,* 77.

SIXTY-SEVEN

The journey blessings that I quote are taken from the collection that I edited of the Carmina Gadelica, *Celtic Vision, Prayers and Blessings from the Outer Hebrides* (London: Darton, Longman and Todd) 188. In America published by St. Bede's Publications, Petersham, Mass., 1990.

SIXTY-NINE

The translation of the opening sentence is taken from that of Catherine Wybourne, trans., *Work & Prayer: The Rule of St. Benedict for Lay People* by Columba Cary-Elwes.

John Howard Griffin tells us about Merton focusing on people in the introduction to his book *A Hidden Wholeness: The Visual World of Thomas Merton* (Boston: Houghton Mifflin Co., 1979). That book is now unfortunately out of print. It is a theme that I also touched on in my book on Merton, *A Seven Day Journey with Thomas Merton* (Ann Arbor, Mich.: Servant Publications, 1993), in which his photographs play an important part. In the chapter called "The Demands of Love," I give the quotation that I quote more briefly here, taken from *No Man Is an Island* (New York: Harcourt, Brace and Co., 1955) 244–245.

SEVENTY-TWO

The John Eudes Bamberger article is in *Tjurunga* 6 (1974) 3–13.

I also owe the point about bad zeal to Kardong, "Benedict's Peaceable Kingdom," *Benedictines,* 1.

SEVENTY-THREE

Two articles have deepened my appreciation of this chapter. Thomas Keating, "The two streams of coenobetic tradition in the Rule of St. Benedict," *C.S.* XI:4 (1976) 257–268, and Michael Casey, "Ascetic and ecclesial reflections on RB 73.5," *Tjurunga* (1985).